The Critical Response to

WILLIAM STYRON

Recent Titles in
Critical Responses in Arts and Letters

The Critical Response to

WILLIAM STYRON

Edited by DANIEL W. ROSS

Critical Responses in Arts and Letters, Number 22
Cameron Northouse, Series Adviser

GREENWOOD PRESS
Westport, Connecticut • London

Library of Congress Cataloging-in-Publication Data

The critical response to William Styron / edited by Daniel W. Ross.
     p.   cm.—(Critical responses in arts and letters, ISSN
1057-0993 ; no. 22)
   Includes bibliographical references and index.
   ISBN 0-313-28000-2 (alk. paper)
   1. Styron, William, 1925– —Criticism and interpretation.
  2. Southern States—In literature. I. Ross, Daniel William.
  II. Series.
PS3569.T9Z64 1995
813'.54—dc20   95-23564

British Library Cataloguing in Publication Data is available.

Copyright © 1995 by Daniel W. Ross

Library of Congress Catalog Card Number: 95-23564
ISBN: 0-313-28000-2
ISSN: 1057-0993

First published in 1995

Greenwood Press, 88 Post Road West, Westport, CT 06881
An imprint of Greenwood Publishing Group, Inc.

Printed in the United States of America

The paper used in this book complies with the
Permanent Paper Standard issued by the National
Information Standards Organization (Z39.48–1984).

10 9 8 7 6 5 4 3 2

Copyright Acknowledgments

Contents

x   Contents

Series Foreword

<u>Critical Response in Arts and Letters</u> is designed to present a documentary history of highlights in the critical reception to the body of work of writers and artists and to individual works that are generally considered to be of major importance. The focus of each volume in this series is basically historical. The introductions to each volume are themselves brief histories of the critical response an author, artist, or individual work has received. This response is then further illustrated by reprinting a strong representation of the major critical reviews and articles that have collectively produced the author's, artist's, or work's critical reputation.

The scope of <u>Critical Reponse in Arts and Letters</u> knows no chronological or geographical boundaries. Volumes under preparation include studies of individuals from around the world and in both contemporary and historical periods.

Each volume is the work of an individual editor, who surveys the entire body of criticism on a single author, artist, or work. The editor then selects the best material to depict the critical response received by an author or artist over his/her entire career. Documents produced by the author or artist may also be included when the editor finds that they are necessary to a full understanding of the materials at hand. In circumstances where previous, isolated volumes of criticism on a particular individual or work exist, the editor carefully selectes material that better reflects the nature and directions of the critical response over time.

In addition to the introduction and the documentary section, the editor of each volume is free to solicit new essays on areas that may not have been adequately dealt with in previous criticism. Also, for volumes on living writers and artists, new interviews may be included, again at the discretion of the volume's editor. The volumes also provide a supplementary bibliography and are fully indexed.

While each volume in <u>Critical Responses in Arts and Letters</u> is unique, it is also hoped that in combination they form a useful, documentary history of the critical response to the arts, and one that can be easily and profitably employed by students and scholars.

Cameron Northouse

William Styron's Published Writings: A Checklist

1944-46--Stories, sketches, and reviews in the Duke <u>Archive</u>.

1948--"A Moment in Trieste" in <u>American Vanguard</u>.

1950--"The Enormous Window" in <u>American Vanguard</u>.

1951--<u>Lie Down in Darkness</u> (Bobbs-Merrill).

1953--"The Long March" in <u>discovery</u>. "<u>The Paris Review</u>" in <u>Harper's Bazaar</u>, August.

1956--<u>The Long March</u> (Random House).

1959--"Introduction" to <u>Best Short Stories from "The Paris Review</u>."

1960--<u>Set This House on Fire</u> (Random House).

1961--"The Big Love" in <u>Esquire</u> (November).

1962--"The Death-in-Life of Benjamin Reid" in <u>Esquire</u> (February). "Benjamin Reid: Aftermath" in <u>Esquire</u> (November). "As He Lay Dead, a Bitter Grief" in <u>Life</u> (July 20).

1963--"Slave and Citizen" in <u>The New York Review of Books</u> (February). "The Habit" in <u>The New York Review of Books</u> (December 26).

1964--"A Southern Conscience" in <u>The New York Review of Books</u> (April 2). "Candy" in <u>The New York Review of Books</u> (May 14). "MacArthur" in <u>The New York Review of Books</u> (October 8).

1965--"This Quiet Dust" in <u>Harper's</u> (April)

1966--Portions of <u>The Confessions of Nat Turner</u> in <u>Harper's</u> and <u>The Partisan Review</u>.

1967--<u>The Confessions of Nat Turner</u> (Random House).

1968--"'O Lost!' Etc." in <u>Harper's</u> (April). "The Oldest American" in <u>McCall's</u> (July). "Chicago: 1968" in <u>The New York Review of Books</u> (September 26). "An Elegy for F. Scott Fitzgerald" in <u>The New York Review of Books</u> (November 28).

1971--"The Joint" in <u>The New York Review of Books</u> (April 25). "Calley" in <u>The New York Review of Books</u> (September 12).

1972--"The Red Badge of Literature" in <u>Washington Monthly</u> (March). "Arnheiter" in <u>The American Scholar</u> (Summer).

1973--<u>In the Clap Shack</u> (Random House). "Dead!" in <u>Esquire</u> "A Second Flowering" in <u>The New York Review of Books</u> (May 6).

1974--"The Suicide Run" in <u>American Poetry Review</u>. "Auschwitz" in <u>The New York Times</u> (June 25).

1976--Leslie Lapidus episode from <u>Sophie's Choice</u> in <u>Esquire</u>. "Introduction" to "A Death in Canaan" (Dutton).

1977--"James Jones" in <u>New York</u> (June 6). "A Farewell to Arms" in <u>The New York Review of Books</u> (June 23). "William Blackburn" in <u>Duke Encounters</u>.

1978--"Hell Reconsidered" in <u>The New York Review of Books</u> (June 29).

1979--<u>Sophie's Choice</u> (Random House). "Introduction" to <u>Peter Matthiessen, A Bibliography: 1951-1979</u> (Orirana).

1981--"A Leader Who Prefers Writers to Politicians" in The Boston Globe. "In the Southern Camp" in The New York Review of Books (August 13). "Down the Nile" in GEO (September).

1982--"Lie Down in Darkness" in Hartford Courant Magazine (January 3). This Quiet Dust and Other Writings (Random House).

1985--"Love Day" in Esquire (August).

1987--"A Tidewater Morning" in Esquire (August).

1989--"A Voice from the South" in Sewanee Review. "Darkness Visible" in Vanity Fair (December).

1990--Darkness Visible (Random House).

1993--Inheritance of Night: Early Drafts of Lie Down in Darkness (Duke). A Tidewater Morning: Three Tales from Youth (Random House).

Introduction

In 1951 William Styron published his first novel, <u>Lie Down in Darkness</u>. It was one of the most successful debut novels in the history of American literature. To some extent, Styron's literary reputation has been shaped by the grand expectations that followed from his first novel's success. Yet gradually, Styron has become recognized as one of the most accomplished and creative of all post-World War II American novelists. Along the way, however, there have been discernible shifts in the critical response to Styron, many of which are most evident in reactions that immediately follow the publication of his later novels. Though it can be misleading to categorize, I believe that we can, generally speaking, see four periods in the critical response to Styron's work: the first heralds his exceptional potential; the second registers some degree of disappointment in his work; the third is a period of controversy; the fourth recognizes his status as a major artist.

<u>Lie Down in Darkness</u> received attention that is rare for first novels and brought its twenty-six year-old author instant recognition. Styron became quickly regarded as the immediate heir of the Faulknerian tradition of great and tragic Southern fiction. Early reviews often measured the achievement of this young novelist by comparing him to giants of the modern literary tradition. For Lee Grove this "acrid, vivid first novel" contains "overtones of Faulkner, and in the last pages is reminiscent of Joyce's <u>Ulysses</u>." Louis D. Rubin was somewhat more cautious in his praise of Styron, yet he too saw in <u>Lie Down in Darkness</u> similarities to Joyce and to Woolf, while confirming his belief in Styron's originality. Perhaps the review that most shaped expectations of Styron's greatness to come was the one written by Maxwell Geismar, one of the leading critics of his day. Geismar called <u>Lie Down in Darkness</u> "one of the few completely human and mature novels published since the Second World War. Geismar further praised Styron for breaking with fashionable trends

of the times. He was also one of the first critics to recognize Styron's penchant for dark humor.

Despite that glowing early reception, critical attention to this novel has not been particularly intense. Although Lie Down in Darkness has been the subject of a few articles and of some pages of discussion in books on modern Southern literature, it has not received the kind of critical scrutiny given to the early novels of Updike or Bellow. When critics do focus on the novel, they tend to isolate its religious themes, its Faulknerian characteristics, and its pessimistic view of post-war America.

John Lang's essay is the most concentrated discussion of the religious themes and language in Lie Down in Darkness. Styron's attitude towards religion often appears, in this and in later novels, contradictory. Many characters (and, indeed, Styron himself) seem to scoff at traditional religious institutions; few of Styron's ministers are admirable figures. Yet many of Styron's characters are burdened by an intense longing for religious meaning. Many use religious language to describe their needs and even invoke the name of God in their times of crisis. Lang does a fine job of presenting the religious overtones of Peyton Loftis' presuicide monologue. He identifies the wide range of literary and Biblical allusions in Peyton's stream-of-consciousness meditations. For Lang the novel's fundamental concerns are religious, in spite of the unflattering portraits of the Methodist minister Carey Carr and of Daddy Faith, the charlatan who plays upon the religious devotion of the novel's black characters. Lang calls our attention to a pervasive issue in Styron's fiction: no matter how corrupt or weak religious institutions may become, modern men and women cannot escape the need for a personal relationship with their Creator.

Typically, Styron's subject matter has drawn more attention than his style or his artistic merits. William J. Scheick, however, focuses on style in his discussion of the "rainbow aesthetic" of Lie Down in Darkness. Scheick makes us aware of Styron's craftsmanship, of the thorough consistency of Styron's imagery and symbolism. While this essay can heighten appreciation of Styron's aesthetic gifts, it is content to identify and underscore these patterns without questioning their psychological significance. Yet that significance is also an important part of Styron's aesthetic, and of his achievement as a novelist. For instance, Scheick notes the persistent pattern of drowning imagery in the novel. Besides contributing to the "rainbow aesthetic," these images may be the keys to the personal conflicts of both Peyton and Milton, her alcoholic father. Peyton refers repeatedly to a feeling of drowning before her suicide; the importance of that feeling is enhanced when one considers the harsh quarrels that have divided Peyton from her cold and tyrannical mother, Helen. Both Milton and Peyton are in some sense victims of Helen's inability to love: the novel's images of drowning (and other image patterns could be adduced as well) go far beyond creating an aesthetic effect, emphasizing along the way the disastrous consequences that can evolve from a need for maternal support.

I am suggesting that there is something of a vacuum in the criticism of Lie Down in Darkness. Though the novel does have a rich aesthetic and though religious issues are certainly important in it, it is surprising that so little attention has been paid to the complex web of relationships in the novel. Clearly, the Loftises do not represent a healthy or well-adjusted picture of family life. Jeffrey Berman's essay, written especially for this volume, helps fill the vacuum in criticism of this novel. Berman draws careful attention to the most disturbing aspects of the relationships between the characters: to Helen's maniacal self-destructiveness, to Milton's weakness and dependence and, most alarming of all, to the hints of a repressed, incestuous encounter that haunts Peyton to the end of her life. Berman's psychoanalytic perspective offers a different way of seeing Peyton's tragic death; could it be that Peyton's futile attempts late in the novel to invoke God's help represent a turn to a different kind of father? Does she seek to lie down in darkness to find a new father, a new home, principally because her apparently harmless natural father, the one whom she calls "Bunny," has wounded her irrevocably? One thing is certain: Berman's essay demonstrates that the psychological conflicts in this novel are very intense and damaging, and herein lies a potentially fallow field for future critics of the novel.

Berman's essay makes at least one other important contribution to Styron criticism. By connecting Lie Down in Darkness with Darkness Visible, the recently published memoir of Styron's bout with severe depression, Berman highlights the autobiographical underpinnings of Styron's first novel. Darkness Visible reveals much about the psychological conflicts in Styron himself, conflicts which often re-emerge in the novels in various guises. As Berman notes, Styron seems to be one of the many modern writers who uses writing as a form of rescue. This recognition of the therapeutic nature of writing for Styron opens many doors for those who wish to re-evaluate Styron's fiction, especially in regard to the ways they echo conflicts mentioned in Darkness Visible.

More than any other novel by Styron, Lie Down in Darkness shows the heavy hand of Faulkner's influence. Christopher Metress' recent article does more than compare Lie Down in Darkness to The Sound and the Fury. Using Harold Bloom's theory of the anxiety of influence, Metress demonstrates the ways in which Styron seemed fettered by Faulkner's example and ways in which he established his originality. It is perhaps a tribute to Styron's growth as a novelist that a one-to-one connection between a Faulkner novel and Styron's later works is not so easily made. While some signs of Faulkner's influence continue to draw the critics' notice, Styron seems to have avoided the trap Bloom warns about--of continuing, throughout a career's work, to echo his powerful predecessor rather than finding his own voice.

The Long March (1953) offers another example of Styron's tendency to ground his fiction in his own experiences. This novella was written after Styron's second hitch in the Marine Corps (he was called up during the Korean War). The Long March represents Styron's only major attempt (beyond a short story or two) to publish fiction on his war experiences. Yet Styron seems both determined and unable to say more about his war and military experiences. Much of his recent time has been devoted to working on The Way of the Warrior, a massive war novel that Styron seems unable to finish.

To my mind The Long March is most significant for its treatment of a persistent theme in Styron's work--the coming of age of a young man who responds ambivalently to the macho demands the world places on him. As artist, Styron seems to have been sensitive to this issue from the beginning of his career. If we can believe that Stingo's accounts (in Sophie's Choice) of his own bravado when he joined the Marines during World War II paint an accurate picture of Styron's experience, then it would seem clear that age has tempered Styron's enthusiasm for such adventures.

Judith Ruderman has been especially perceptive about the importance of the military in Styron's work. Her book chapter, much of which is reprinted here, groups several of Styron's war texts, including The Long March, a play called In the Clap Shack, and Styron's essay on the infamous Lt. William Calley. War and military life, as Ruderman notes, both attract and repel Styron. That may be because, as she suggests, military life can represent a conflict between individual freedom and the demands associated with being part of a group. Thus, Ruderman is wise to conclude her discussion of Styron's war writings with a brief analysis of the Calley essay. In this essay, written after The Long March and In the Clap Shack, Styron reveals what he might have feared most about the military, portraying Calley as an archetypal military Frankenstein, a monster turned loose by war to indulge his savage appetites.

Richard Pearce recognizes another interesting strain in The Long March. In a manner resembling David Galloway's discussion of the absurd hero in modern fiction, Pearce emphasizes the absurdist dimension of Styron's novella. The authoritarian commands of Col. Templeton, unprotested by others, are intolerable to the story's hero, Mannix, who insists that actions must have a clear, logical meaning. Pearce identifies their confrontation as a modern version of Dostoevsky's "Grand Inquisitor" scene. In the process of doing so, Pearce, like Geismar, recognizes Styron's gift for black humor.

In recent years The Long March has received little attention from critics. Though few would say that the novella is Styron's best work, many aspects of it are interesting. As critics take a broader perspective of Styron's work, some will no doubt see that the relationship between Templeton and Mannix has some of the father-son characteristics that are common in Styron's other works.

Ever since its publication in 1960, <u>Set This House on Fire</u> has drawn a mixed response. Somewhat typical of reviewers' ambivalence is Thomas F. Curley's comment that, while the novel is "very good," he was left disappointed because he had hoped for or expected a different kind of book, perhaps one more like <u>The Long March</u>, which he holds in high esteem. In retrospect, this kind of evaluation often seems unfair; after all, most of us believe that authors should be permitted the opportunity to break new ground, to expand and grow. But the response is also, in many ways, representative. By this time Styron was reaching the point in his career when he felt pressure to meet expectations established by his earlier work. In 1960 Styron began learning how difficult it is to follow up on early success, especially when you tantalize readers by keeping them waiting seven years between publications. That difficulty is further evidenced by Charles Monaghan's review. Monaghan's praise for <u>Lie Down in Darkness</u> is almost fulsome when he calls the book "manna to an American literary world." Monaghan, however, has a clearer idea than Curley does of why he objects to <u>Set This House on Fire</u>. He persuasively shows that Cass's existentialist language, his desire to see his conflict as one between being and nothingness, is forced.

<u>Set This House on Fire</u> has been a problematic book for Styron's readers for a number of reasons. For one, Styron abandoned his comfortable milieu by setting most of the novel in Italy. Granted, two of the major characters (Cass Kinsolving and Peter Leverett) are Southerners, but their Southernness seems to be of minor importance in this novel. What does matter is their humanity, their ability to survive and adapt in a world that can so easily seem meaningless; here again is the Dostoevskian element in Styron's work.

Styron's hard-nosed portrayal of man's struggle to find meaning in his universe, however, has drawn the appreciation of at least some critics. Thus, for instance, David Galloway sees the novel as providing an example of the modern absurdist hero. It should be noted here that this is the kind of quality in Styron's work that has made him popular with French readers. In general, critics tend to regard <u>Set This House on Fire</u> as being not only Dostoevskian, but Kierkegaardian as well. The novel raises powerful questions, as Dostoevsky and Kierkegaard did, about how man, with his limited vision and understanding, can distinguish good from evil. Therefore, what matters most in this novel is not the nature of actions (Cass's killing of Mason is as clearly wrong as Roskolnikov's premeditated murder), but the ability of the perpetrator to redeem himself--to repent and find cathartic relief from sin.

In this context, Samuel Coale's discussion of <u>Set This House on Fire</u>, and of Styron's work in general, makes a valuable contribution to Styron criticism. Styron's best work has the resonance (and other qualities) of tragedy: in his review of <u>Lie Down in Darkness</u>, Geismar called that book a "domestic tragedy." Coale's discussion of the melodramatic quality of this and other novels could well explain the disappointment that readers like Curley sometimes feel. Coale is also perceptive in his recognition of the narcissistic element of Styron's nostalgia, and of the nostalgia of some of his characters. Like John Gardner, in his review of Sophie's Choice reprinted in this book, Coale is inclined to see a heavy influence of the Southern Gothic tradition in Styron's work (hence his comparison of Styron to Carson McCullers). Like some other post-World War II critics, Coale seems anxious to prophesy an end to the Southern literary tradition: "Perhaps this is where the Southern tradition in American fiction ends, grappling with absolute evil outside its borders, serving up horrors as it would serve up childhood fantasies." Perhaps, but one wonders exactly what the borders of Southern fiction are or, indeed, why one must insist on its having such limitations. What Coale seems to miss (especially in his references to Sophie's Choice) is the extent to which Styron uses narcissistic responses to nostalgia in order to satirize them; this seems to be the case often with his characters' nostalgia and his own. As the examples of Geismar and Pearce indicate, Styron's most sympathetic readers are those who never lose sight of his humor, grim though it often is. Still, I feel that Coale is more on target about this novel than about the others he mentions; Set This House on Fire, especially with its absurdly symbolic names like Cass Kinsolving, is overwrought and, hence, more melodramatic than tragic.

These issues of religious affirmation and repentance, of individual action in an apparently random universe, of tone and genre, have dominated the limited critical debate on Set This House on Fire. Clearly, much work remains to be done on this novel--on its structure, its characterization, its point of view. Styron's portrayal of the shallow, jetset culture surrounding Mason Flagg, though somewhat dated, deserves more comment. David Galloway interprets the novel as worthy of Camus--a drama of tragic absurdity. Critics who have been less kind to this novel would do well to consider Galloway's argument that "in Set This House on Fire Styron has perhaps come closer than any other modern author to actualizing [the tragic hero]." Nowhere does Styron receive higher praise.

The publication of The Confessions of Nat Turner brought new controversy to Styron and his work. Never has the reception of a major American novel been so inextricably linked to the timing of its publication. To some extent, that timing was coincidental. Styron had been researching and planning his novel on Nat Turner for years before America's racial conflicts exploded into urban violence. Surely, if the first reviews are an accurate guide, the early response to this novel would have been different if the times had been more tranquil, but we can only guess at the degree of that difference. Yet the volatile debate over The Confessions of Nat Turner has raised many significant questions not only about Styron's novel but about fiction in general: questions about the appropriateness of subject matter, about the legitimate (or illegitimate) uses of history in fiction, and about an author's unconscious intentions.

The earliest reviews of Nat Turner were highly favorable. Philip Rahv was unrestrained in his enthusiasm. Rahv, to my mind, captures one of Styron's principal virtues when he praises him for choosing "a substantial theme central to the national experience." Rahv is one of several reviewers who regarded Nat Turner as one of America's best post-World War II novels. George Steiner's eloquent and laudatory New Yorker review is almost uncanny in its foresight. At the end he asks the critical question: "Would a Negro recognize Nat Turner for one of his own, would he find Mr. Styron's fiction authentic to his own experience?"

The answer to Steiner's question would come the next year. In 1968 a group of writers published one of the most unusual critical anthologies in the annals of American literature, entitled William Styron's Nat Turner: Ten Black Writers Respond. Most critical anthologies, including the one before your eyes now, strive for some balance of perspective. Ten Black Writers Respond, however, was never intended to analyze Styron's novel so much as to vilify it and him. No matter how much one agrees or disagrees with these critics (who do make some good points), their shrill tone marks their work as being far from "critical" in the best sense of the word. Some of the volume's authors invoked the memory of the recently assassinated Dr. Martin Luther King, Jr., implying that Styron's "crime" of appropriating (or misappropriating) Nat for his fictional purposes was in some ways parallel to James Earl Ray's crime of killing the great Civil Rights leader. Charges of racism abound. Vincent Harding's essay, reprinted here, is fairly typical of those in the volume, though more reasoned than some. With the cooler judgment of calmer racial times, we can now recognize the irony of Harding's own appropriation of Nat ("my Nat") at a time when the goals of the Civil Rights Movement were directed towards greater cultural unity and sharing.

Comparing Harding's response to Rahv's shows just how differently two readers can react to a book. Harding, like several of his black colleagues, assumes that Styron had no business trying to enter the skin and mind of a black man; in stark contrast, Rahv assumes that only a white Southerner could have successfully rendered the novel's great theme. Harding is particularly disturbed by Styron's portrayal of Nat's attraction to white women and the "degradation" of Nat's religious mission. Both issues are valid, but one wonders why Harding gives Styron no credit for exposing the colonial nature of the black man's Christianity and its manipulation by slave owners. Surely one of the ironies of the novel is Nat's refusal to accept the widely-taught white man's New Testament Christianity, which urged the slave to denounce this world for the rewards of an afterlife, for the more assertive Old Testament energy of the prophets. More than anything else, Styron demystifies Nat's messianic drive, exposing the understandable motives (desires for revenge and retribution) that undergird it. Ironically, Harding's very partisan complaint resembles that of Coale, whose essay refers to Styron's penchant for "psychological rationalization." There is no disputing the point that Styron's novels (not just Nat Turner) tend to be profoundly psychological, but it is not clear why Styron is to be faulted more than other modern writers for turning to psychological explanations of behavior.

Perhaps the greatest single problem posed by the response of Styron's black critics (at least to this white Southern reader) is their failure to acknowledge a fact Styron stated in his essay "This Quiet Dust"--that white Southerners also need to come to terms with the realities of slavery, to exorcise and understand their own feelings of guilt in relation to slavery. Indeed, one wonders how these critics might have responded to the novel if they had also considered carefully Styron's attacks in "This Quiet Dust" of his fellow Southerners for assuming too glibly that they "know the Negro."

Not surprisingly, much of the later criticism of The Confessions of Nat Turner has been affected by the response of the ten black critics. Several years after Ten Black Writers Respond, Ernest P. Williams, writing in Phylon, a journal of African-American studies, tried to set the record straight. Williams deserves credit for clarifying some of the "facts" about the historical Nat. Williams concluded that Styron was by no means guilty of all the excesses he was accused of, though he did find some errors in Styron's references to the historical record. Furthermore, Williams signals the spirit in which the black critics produced their volume when he says he did not contribute to it because his relatively neutral views of Styron's book "would have invited brutal castigation by a number of [his] fellow blacks."(1) Other historians, among them Eugene D. Genovese and C. Vann Woodward, have also defended Styron. While it seems fair to say that Styron has been vindicated for his use of historical information, the larger question of appropriate uses of history in fiction has proven more complicated. Styron has contributed to that complication. At first he denied that Nat Turner is a "historical novel," referring to it rather vaguely as a "meditation on history." Later, however, after the attacks by the black critics and after Styron had studied the theories of Marxist critic Georg Lukacs, Styron changed his mind and concluded that the novel fit the Lukacs paradigm for historical fiction. Styron's change of heart seemed too convenient to some critics.

Styron's use of history is likely to continue drawing the interest of critics. Two essays in this volume suggest the dimensions this subject has. Floyd C. Watkins has analyzed Styron's use of history without speculating on the novelist's ideological or unconscious motives. Watkins notes that Styron uses a well-chosen group of concrete images and objects to portray the world of slavery realistically. Watkins values Styron's depiction of Nat's humanity, arguing that "fiction cannot be created about perfect eroes. Extremism denies humanity, and humanness is the first principle of art." James M. Mellard has further probed Styron's use of history in a wide-ranging and provocative essay. Mellard sees the novel as being both "psychohistorical" and "meta-historical" (the latter concept derived from the theory of Hayden White). Mellard further regards the story of Nat as "an American case history." Like the work of the great historians, Mellard says, Styron's book deals with one of the great traumatic events of our history which we have tried to repress. He sees the novel as effecting a release of our repressed guilt about Nat, slavery, and racism in general. As such, the novel "might help lead us a little way out of the nightmare of the American neurosis known as slavery," Mellard says. Such a release of repressed material is inevitably painful, but it is also necessary, as Freud suggested, to allow us to continue doing the work of culture.

A dozen years separate the publication of Nat Turner from Styron's last novel, Sophie's Choice (1979). Many readers feel that Sophie has essentially guaranteed Styron's reputation as an important American novelist. Even though some of the early reviews of the novel expressed some hesitation about it (as John Gardner's did), they all reflect an awareness that the book would have great impact. Though this novel has produced its own kind of controversy, its compassion, its humor, its philosophical toughness, its depth of characterization--to mention only a few of its virtues--marked it as a book to be reckoned with. Sophie's Choice provides further evidence that one of Styron's chief assets, as Rahv pointed out in his review of Nat Turner, is his willingness to engage a theme of great significance.

Gardner's review of the novel in The New York Times represents a good example of the combination of ambivalence and admiration that many critics have felt for Sophie's Choice. Like Coale, whom he has influenced, Gardner wonders if Styron feels the pressure of writing at the end of a Southern literary tradition. Both critics have assumed that such a tradition is monolithic, impervious to evolution. Gardner is at times condescending in his disdain for Styron's "Southern Gothic" imagination and for the "hothouse quality" of Styron's style, yet he regards the novel, rather paradoxically, as "a splendidly written, thrilling book, a philosophical novel on the most important subject of the 20th century." Gardner, who somehow fails to detect the novel's humor, goes on to recognize that his ambivalence towards the book probably lies in those qualities of the Southern Gothic "that have always made Yankees squirm." This remark says much about the difficulty of reading Styron. Yankees are not the only ones who squirm when confronting the fiction of this dark, guilt-ridden, but uncompromising author. Sophie's Choice shows, more graphically than Styron's other novels, that there are some aspects of our fate which we cannot deny or put aside, that the forces of history continue to act on us even as we try our best to escape them. In this view of history Styron is indeed a son of Faulkner. More powerfully than Nat Turner, Sophie's Choice forces readers to face the truth that the hatred and evil that produce slavery lurk within us all, that we are all potential victims or potential perpetrators of some ghastly and inhuman enterprise such as Auschwitz.

Having endured the outrage of black critics over <u>Nat Turner,</u> Styron naturally felt some trepidation about the response to <u>Sophie's Choice</u>. Here again Styron, a white, male, Protestant Southerner was treading on territory beyond his sphere of immediate, personal experience. Fortunately for Styron, the response to <u>Sophie's Choice</u> by Jews and women has not been nearly so vituperative as the black response to <u>Nat Turner</u>. Some have attacked Styron, but many have defended him. One very notable response is Richard L. Rubenstein's fine 1984 article in which he chastises the early reviewers of <u>Sophie</u> for failing to understand that the novel enlarges on the theme of <u>Nat Turner,</u> slavery. Rubenstein is impressed that "a son of the South and an heir of the slave tradition" would examine the tragedy of the Holocaust from his unique perspective.(2) For Rubenstein there is no doubt that Styron's portrayal of the Holocaust is appropriate. In a similar vein Carolyn A. Durham, in another 1984 article, has regarded the feminist, black, and Jewish complaints against Styron as misreading. Styron's novels, she says, and <u>Sophie's Choice</u> in particular, are not racist, sexist, or anti-Semitic; rather, they are about racism, sexism and anti-Semitism, and they expose the structures that reinforce such attitudes. One of those structures is language, as Michael Kreyling has recognized: "A series of men appropriate [Sophie] through the imposition of a superior language." Such arguments do not absolve Sophie fully of guilt, but they do signify reasons why readers feel a powerful sympathy for this woman caught in a complex web of domineering and manipulative relationships.

But not all of Styron's critics have been so kind to his last novel. Two common areas of attack are the novel's plot and its style. Morris Dickstein, in a 1981 review essay of <u>Sophie's Choice</u> and three other novels, raised both of these complaints. Perhaps readers of this volume will be better able to sympathize with Dickstein's complaints about plot than I am; I regard them as prescriptive and inflexible. To me Dickstein's remark that "Roth, Styron, Malamud, and Irving are conservative novelists writing less about art than about themselves"(3) is ironically self-reflexive. Is any one of these novelists as conservative as Dickstein himself, who has his own preconceived ideas--ideas which would presumably exclude many great novels of the <u>Bildungsroman</u> tradition--of what novels must be about? And do novelists necessarily write <u>about</u> art, as Dickstein implies?

Dickstein's reservations about Styron's style, however, should not be easily dismissed. As we have seen, Gardner was also disturbed by the style of <u>Sophie's Choice</u>. Two other articles (not reprinted here because of the limitations of space) have registered serious concerns about the style of <u>Sophie</u>: William Heath's 1984 essay "I, Stingo: The Problem of Egotism in <u>Sophie's Choice</u>" in <u>Southern Review</u> and Ralph Tutt's essay, "Stingo's Complaint: Styron and the Politics of Self-Parody," published in a 1988 issue of <u>Modern Fiction Studies</u>. To some degree, I have responded to these complaints in my own article, "A Family Romance: Dreams and the Unified Narrative of Sophie's Choice," published in Mississippi Quarterly in 1989. Heath seems to me as inflexible as Dickstein about what a novel can and cannot be. Yet, there is no disputing the claim of these critics that Styron's style is sometimes narcissistic. Perhaps the more important issue involves intention or genre. I see Styron's narcissistic narrative style not so much as parody (Tutt's classification), but more as satire. In this regard, the style demonstrates Styron's remarkable range as a novelist. Sophie's story is undoubtedly tragic, yet Styron at times relieves his readers of the heavy burden of this tragedy by intertwining the story of his own youthful folly with Sophie's. Stingo's story has its own tragic aspects (especially in regards to his unprocessed grief for his mother's death), but without some of the more comic aspects of his coming of age, and without his survival (after much self-blame and soul-searching) at the end, Sophie's Choice might be unbearably bleak.

I have included in this volume three other essays on Sophie's Choice. One is Michael Kreyling's aforementioned "Speakable and Unspeakable in Styron's Sophie's Choice." Kreyling boldly confronts one of the novel's major issues: should the Holocaust be discussed, or is its horror beyond words and, hence, does discussion only trivialize the horror? Styron himself debates this issue in the novel by working in his reflections on George Steiner's essays from Language and Silence. Kreyling offers the best analysis of the polyvalent uses and abuses of language in the novel for power and domination, not only by the Nazis, but by a variety of characters, most of whom exercise some form of control over Sophie. Also, Kreyling's discussion of Stingo echoes Berman's idea of writing as rescue. Kreyling sees Stingo, and ostensibly Styron as well, as a "redeeming writer-hero," a lover of language who knows that language has failed to hold the human community together and who must therefore help reform language in order to reform man. Kreyling's compelling analysis of Styron's decision to speak the unspeakable represents a fine testimony to Styron's courage. Meanwhile, John Kenny Crane's discussion of the novel, excerpted from his book on Styron, demonstrates the ways in which psychological criticism can illuminate Sophie's Choice. Crane's concept of "transfer" (which has obvious similarities to the psychoanalytic model of transference) offers a good way for readers to consider the role Stingo plays for Sophie and, ultimately, the role we as readers can play for Styron. Finally, there is the recently-published, superb essay by Richard G. Law on the narrative technique of Sophie's Choice. Using many of the strategies of reader-response criticism, Law points out how Styron's novel involves the reader directly in a series of interpretations and reinterpretations, a process which demonstrates how difficult it is to judge correctly and act responsibly. As I mentioned earlier, Styron's narrative technique merits further analysis, and Law's essay is a step in that direction. In addition, Law addresses many of the issues important to other critics in this volume. His opening paragraph, for example, offers a counter position to Dickstein's belief that the narrative technique lacks distance. Law also speaks to the concerns raised by Steiner, Rubenstein, and Kreyling. More openly than most of Styron's critics, he entertains the notion that I hinted at earlier--"that literature can be about anything; no subjects are off limits." Law points out the importance of Stingo's chief discovery about evil: that it exists as palpably in himself as it did in the monstrous cast of Nazis who made Auschwitz a reality. Thus, rather than asserting that Styron's novel does not do what novels should do (or what they previously have done), Law sees Sophie's Choice as imaginatively expanding the boundaries of fiction into new territory. This idea is a far cry from Coale's belief, cited earlier, that Styron's novels represent the borders of Southern fiction.

Darkness Visible, Styron's most recent book, is proof of his long-standing commitment to social consciousness, to a determination to use his position as an artist to effect positive change. I have already made some suggestions about the ways in which Darkness Visible is likely to affect future critical response to his work as a whole. Although this memoir covers only a very brief period of Styron's life, late 1985 through early 1986, it provides insight into Styron's life and mind that can illuminate his fiction significantly. Since Styron himself has concluded that the symptoms of his depression date back to his early years, especially to his mother's death when he was thirteen, critics will surely realize the value of this confessional narrative as a means of interpreting Styron's work. Thornton F. Jordan's essay, written for this volume, never previously published, gives some idea of how critics can use Darkness Visible as a template for reconsidering much of Styron's fiction. As Jordan notes, the "terror of profound isolation" that was a central factor in Styron's break-down is also portrayed repeatedly in his fiction. Jordan's discussion of the role of "reconstruction" in Styron's fiction offers intriguing perspectives on one of the oldest and most mysterious of all literary problems--the role played by the unconscious in the creative process. With such perspectives before us, it seems likely that psychological interpretations might even become more popular than religious ones in Styron criticism. Certainly, the brief autobiographical memoir gives Styron's readers ample cause to reinvestigate the enormous role played by grief in Styron's work. But as the examples of Kierkegaard and Dostoevsky (already recognized as writers similar to Styron) suggest, religious and psychological perspectives can be closely allied. Perhaps some future Styron critics will argue that the religious quest of so many of Styron's characters comes from a desire to fill a void which is both psychological and spiritual, and which Styron himself has felt all too deeply.

The robust style in which Darkness Visible is written gives one confidence that Styron has indeed passed the worst stages of the crisis. Even this briefest of books has generated strong responses to Styron's style. Reviewer Victoria Glendinning praises the writing: "There is some tremendous writing in Darkness Visible. The rhythmic beat of some sentences demands that they be read aloud."(4) Here, as elsewhere, it seems clear that Styron's style does not appeal to everyone but, when it does appeal, it does so strongly.

I have tried to stress not only what the critical response to Styron has been, but to some degree what it has not been and where it could conceivably go in the future. I will close with a few final remarks on the possible future directions. As yet there is no biography of Styron; when one is written, its details will no doubt encourage new perspectives of Styron's work. Styron's many occasional essays can also shed light on his fiction. Mellard's use of "This Quiet Dust" in his discussion of Nat Turner and Ruderman's reference to the essay on Calley when examining Styron's war fiction are two instances of the value of the essays. Styron's three essays on Benjamin Reid, a black prisoner whose death penalty Styron actively and successfully protested, reveal much about the white Southern writer who made Nat Turner the subject of a novel. The essays and the fiction indicate that a relatively constricted body of ideas and themes are very important to Styron. What makes Styron a remarkable writer is, most of all, the courage with which he confronts these powerful ideas. Perhaps he said it best when he adopted as his epigraph for Sophie's Choice the following quotation from Andre Malraux: "I seek that essential region of the soul where absolute evil confronts brotherhood."

Notes

(1) Ernest P. Williams, "William Styron and His Ten Black Critics: A Belated Mediation." Phylon 37 (1976): 189.

(2) Richard L. Rubenstein, "The South Encounters the Holocaust: William Styron's Sophie's Choice." Michigan Quarterly Review 29 (1984): 442.

(3) Morris Dickstein, "The World in a Mirror: Problems of Distance in Recent American Fiction." Sewanee Review 89 (1981): 388.

(4) Victoria Glendinning, "A Howling Tempest in the Brain." The New York Times Book Review, August 19, 1990, p. 25.

LIE DOWN IN DARKNESS

DOMESTIC TRAGEDY IN VIRGINIA*

Maxwell Geismar

. . . Lie Down in Darkness is a remarkable and fascinating novel--the best novel of the year by my standards--and one of the few completely human and mature novels published since the Second World War.

First of all, Lie Down in Darkness has no "thesis." There is nothing in it about a "frame of reference" or the decline of values. It is simply a domestic tragedy--the story of an upper middle-class family in the Tidewater society in Virginia; but a story that becomes completely absorbing and is treated with brilliance and boldness of insight, with great compassion, and with a sense of dreadful and tragic comedy, too.

. . .

The story itself moves on several levels at once, as all good novels do; the characters, like images seen through a prism, are reflected from every side until the distortions of their personality are finally resolved in not their own views of themselves, but the novelist's central and sympathetic view of them. But Mr. Styron is particularly good on the visual level of his craft; we are at all these ghastly parties, ceremonials, and festivals of a middle-class business society that has inherited the trappings of the planter aristocracy. We not only understand and are identified with the main figures in the tragedy, but watch them behave in their worst moments of folly. The writing itself, graceful and delicate, is rigorously controlled as the medium through which the story is revealed--not as a medium for the author's personality.

*From The Saturday Review of Literature, September 15, 1951. Reprinted by permission.

MEMORABLE FIRST NOVEL DEMOLISHES A FAMILY*

Lee Grove

William Stryon, a young Virginian with the skill of an old master, has written an acrid, vivid first novel of the deterioration of a family.

Lie Down in Darkness, it should be noted, for all its mastery is not pleasant reading, for it provides the sensation of being too close to persons whose lives one would fend off for the protection of his own peace of mind. There is an instinct of the healthy not to wish to get too close to the unbalanced, perhaps because the dividing line between health and sickness is so easily crossed over.

Just when Helen Loftis passed over the line, in Styron's novel, is hard to say. She and Milton Loftis had been married during World War I. He was from a decaying, uppermiddle class family, and she from an Army family with wealth.

It would be doubtful if Milton, who knew her best and understood her not at all, could have traced with any degree of certainty the progress of her illness. Member of an easy-going culture in which whisky was considered God's gift to the Virginia Gentleman, Milton had observed Calvinistic tendencies in Helen during courtship.

Lie Down in Darkness is a fully developed novel with overtones of Faulkner, and in the last pages is reminiscent of Joyce's Ulysses.

The grasp of character and development of action in the book would be a credit to a writer of any age, and, considering Styron's youth, they are indications of great talent. That there is a suggestion of moral affirmation, even though it is rather blunted by little horror piled on little horror, is a hopeful sign in the sky.

*From The Washington Post, December 9, 1951. Reprinted by permission.

WHAT TO DO ABOUT CHAOS*

Louis D. Rubin, Jr.

What we have here [in <u>Lie Down in Darkness</u>] is the breakdown of contemporary morals and the collapse of value standards. What the Loftises are, and what they come to, is the fault of a society trying to do without belief and personal responsibility. The Loftises want something, and none of them knows what it is. What they want is a purpose, a reason for being. In the final chapter, Mr. Styron contrasts their aimlessness with the happy faith of their Negro servant, who is untroubled by <u>accedia</u>. The servant believes, and on the foundations of that belief is able to construct a satisfying life. The Loftises do not believe; and they exist in spiritual hunger.

It is not enough to call Mr. Styron's first novel a "promising attempt," because even with certain faults, it is far more than that. It is an excellently conceived, successfully executed novel. I would quarrel with Mr. Styron's differentiation of his characters, however,; it seems to me that only Milton Loftis is developed entirely satisfactorily. Peyton Loftis, despite a fine monologue chapter at the end, appears to be incompletely constructed, and Milton Loftis' wife Helen could do with considerably more handling, to bring her out of the stereotype classification.

Mr. Styron's style, which draws heavily on Joyce and the interior monologue, is most effective in conveying the daze and pain that he wishes to portray, and while there are elements of Joyce and Thomas Wolfe in his approach to words and to description, the final product is undeniably his own.

*From <u>The Hopkins Review</u>, 5 (1951). Reprinted by permission.

"DISCARDED WATERMELON RINDS": THE RAINBOW AESTHETIC OF STYRON'S LIE DOWN IN DARKNESS*

William J. Scheick

. . . Surprisingly, aside from general observations, little has been said about the aesthetics of [Lie Down in Darkness], and yet, as I shall show, Styron's notion of art not only determines the presence of several motifs and accounts for certain stylistic features but also emerges as a prominent thematic concern in the book.

Informing its aesthetic feature is Styron's conception of beauty, which, especially as personified in Peyton, is the perception of a loveliness intrinsic to human suffering. As Styron's numerous references to music(1) and his specific focus on Harry's painting of an old monk or rabbi looking heavenward (p. 374) indicate, art does not inspire hope so much as it simply celebrates the perennial emergence of human aspiration in spite of a reality which seems to deny the possibility of hope and which always frustrates human expectation. Recurrent bird imagery (e.g., pp. 14, 341) objectifies this aspiration; but Styron carefully coalesces this motif with images of people raising their eyes or arms as if to fly, with the result that these images ironically suggest entreaty as well as affirmation (pp. 61-62), supplication for relief from the reality of flightlessness.(2) Harry, who is sympathetically treated in the book,(3) expresses Styron's artistic design behind this pattern when he says: "I want to paint and paint because I think that some agony is upon us . . . I want to crush in my hands all that agony and make beauty come out, because that's all that's left" (p. 377). In the absence of God and, consequently, of any objective meaning, art's reflection of the subjective experience of a delicate, sad loveliness intrinsic to the frustration of human aspiration is all humanity has; art cannot redeem man--the prevalent crucifixion imagery in the novel is ironic--but it does assert his reality. Styron, as it were, "crushes" the agony or thwarted hope of his characters to reveal an inherent beauty, a technique used throughout the novel and, perhaps, best typified in a passage on a kite, the tail of which has been caught in a tree: "the kite hung disconsolately among the topmost limbs, a splash of blue, like a jaybird snared in honey-suckle" (p. 194). The image of "a splash of blue" in the (Edenically or pastorally suggestive) honeysuckle serves as Styron's "painting" or the beauty latent in disaster; and it is no accident that he chooses the word limbs (cf. p. 86, where the limbs of a tree are likened to "frantic women's arms") or the image of a bird in this passage, for images of upraised arms (limbs) and of flightlessness (the entangled jaybird) are, as I noted, suggestive throughout the novel of the beauty inherent in the frustration of hope.

Because his "splashes" of color frequently suggest the spectrum and because he makes several specific allusions to the rainbow, Styron's technique might be referred to as the rainbow aesthetic of Lie Down in Darkness. Underlying the technique is the well-known Judeo-Christian tradition of the rainbow, that fleeting arch of beauty created after the destruction of the world by a deluge and given to Noah as a sign of God's renewed covenant with man. In a sense, it is for just such a sign that the people in Styron's novel look up and raise their arms.(4) Unlike the rainbow of tradition, however, Styron's aesthetic holds forth no promise, only an image of man's enduring existential "belief" in the fact of "his own ascending spirit" (p. 378). An explicit correlation between the rainbow and the function of art, specifically music, occurs very early in the novel: "A rainbow of juke-box color enveloped the restaurant, a lovely spectrum endlessly shifting; a man with a deep, sad voice sang: 'Take me back and try me one more time'" (p. 40). Like the rainbow tradition, Styron's art derives from human suffering and expresses the human desire for promise, renewal, a chance (like Noah's) to start over. For Styron, art is similar to the result of Helen's dream of vengeance on Dolly and Peyton, a "rainbow of decay" (p. 301), a "sick hue of disaster" like that of crumpled Christmas wrapping (p. 155), a sad beauty not signifying the possibility of renewal but simply emanating from and asserting the agony endemic to man's inevitably frustrated aspiration.

Styron's rainbow imagery also suggests a relation between art and religion. When Daddy Faith raises his arms, making "a wide arc with his hand" on which "half a dozen diamond rings spun and glittered" and, as well, made "beautiful flashes above the throng" (p. 103), he is, by means of this arc of refracted light, offering rainbow-like comfort in a colorful sign of promise (discounting Styron's satire[5]), a comfort similar to that given by rainbow-like stained glass windows in a church (p. 290). The colorful theatrical setting of Daddy Faith's performance, moreover, emphasizes this rainbow effect. On his raft is a "sort of stage" with a curtain replete with symbols "in green and red phosphorescent fabrics" and framed by "tall golden rods"; Daddy Faith's robe is "a blue splash against the red shields and green prophetic talismans" (pp. 392, 395). Like art, in Styron's view, religion expresses the spectral beauty crushed from human suffering; indeed religion exists only because human misery is a fact. But unlike art, religion interprets that beauty as a sign of redeeming promise and as warrant for a belief in something beyond man's aspiring spirit. From the perspective of Styron's rainbow aesthetic, Daddy Faith's "blue splash" and upraised arms are in actuality less an expression of assurance in man's eventual aerial ascent and transcendence than a sadly beautiful image of the avian-like aspiration of humanity entangled in the fatal necessity of the natural world, like the jaybird in the honeysuckle.(6)

In the novel alcoholic intoxication provides another means whereby people try to create a rainbow perspective of illusory promise. At one point Loftis, who thinks of drink as his "salvation," draws "desperate arcs in the air with his glass," the same champagne glass through which he has earlier watched Peyton and Harry: "above the remote whine of the strings, and through the sphere of his glass, iridescent as a rainbow . . . he saw their lips touch" (pp. 25, 278, 304). In yet an earlier scene, empty eggnog glasses "sparkle with soapy rainbow hues in the twilight" (p. 157); since the glasses are empty, the drinkers are presumably full of cheer, of a sense of renewal in spite of the twilight reality. Unlike those of Daddy Faith, Loftis' arcs are desperate because the rainbow world of drunkenness provides no faith at all. Like art and religion, alcoholic intoxication conveys a beautiful perspective derived from the human agony which drives one to drink, but it fails to provide any sense of belief, either in God (as does religion) or in man (as does art). Whereas religion creates a presumptuous illusion of promise, drunkenness offers only an evasion of despair; the rainbow aesthetic of Styron's art lies between them, offering no promise yet staving off despair, simply portraying a defiant respect for the sad beauty of man's endlessly frustrated yet ever-assertive aspiration.

The reality to which the artist, the evangelist, and the alcoholic respond is characterized in Styron's novel in unrestrained motion, a "cosmic cataclysm" (p. 103) imaged as a deluge leading to a rainbow aesthetic just as the disaster of Noah's time is said to have resulted in the rainbow.(7) The novel abounds in imagery suggesting that the modern holocaust, manifested in the dispersion of atoms through the explosion of the atomic bomb, is like a modern-day Noah's flood. Peyton, for instance, typically identifies her troubles with this deluge. Throughout her monologue she reiterates an image appearing early in the novel, where she explains in a letter to her father (who also experiences the terror of "the deep" [p. 98]) how her thoughts seem, as it were, to be at sea without "any distinctness or real point of reference" and imbued with a depression which "seeps" into her mind; as she walks "deeper and deeper into some terrible despair," she feels "adrift, as if I were drowning out in dark space somewhere" (p. 38; cf. pp. 349-50). This fear of an "inward" flood threatening to obliterate her selfhood underlies Peyton's attraction to the legend of Saint Christopher (p. 341), for she seeks a father-figure to save her from her encounter with the deluge in her mind. Peyton's mother, whom Carey Carr describes as "a drowned woman" (p. 239), feels at times as if a "crushing wave of agony and remorse [has] swept over her" (p. 70); and, at one point, she perceives that her incomplete plans have "begun to dissolve like sand in water, melted off with all the cruel underneath edges showing" (p. 115).

In this passage, the juxtaposition of flood and fire imagery (dissolving and melting) is characteristic of Styron's ability to include in his flood motif the traditional Christian notion, particularly evident in the American Protestantism emphasized in the novel, that the final apocalypse will be by fire. References to "hot demanding waves," "waves of heat," "a sea of smoke," and "a tidal wave of heat" (pp. 35, 68, 132, 149) catch up the hell and bomb motifs in the book as well as yoke the image of a fiery apocalypse to the image of a contemporary deluge. It is a subtle touch, for according to Judeo-Christian tradition, the rainbow represented God's promise that the world would never again be destroyed by water, and so the logic of Styron's imagery suggests either that there is no God or that He does not keep His promises.

The novel suggests the former notion, implying that the rainbow is nothing more than a rainbow, just as the book's rainbow aesthetic is simply an expression of the beauty inherent in human disaster. In the novel, the current fiery holocaust is indeed another deluge, and even the firmament becomes a sea covering humanity: "the sky seemed to be spread like a bottomless lake above them"; "it was as if all the air had become an ocean" (pp. 258, 387).

Art, religion, and alcoholic intoxication are, then, the three primary responses to this deluge in the novel. The rainbow perspective Loftis achieves through drink transforms surging reality into submarine serenity: "to drink [is] to drown himself utterly as in the sea"; to drink is to be saved, "sheltered from the sky like drowning, only better: the sun within submarine, aqueous" (pp. 306, 339). Loftis relies on alcohol in the same way that Helen relies on sleep to metamorphose the tidal waves of reality into calm "waves on a shore, fathomless upon lost drowned shoals of memory" (pp. 28-29). Religion too allows people to create a rainbow-like escape from man's "fathomless past" (p. 133), or memory, by transforming the encounter with the deluge into a rite of passage to salvation. Through the ritual of baptism the apocalyptic flood becomes "the true waters that will wash and caress . . . and flood away the various sorrows of [one's] mind" (p. 145; cf. p. 400). No doubt Styron intends a scriptural analogy, in this instance, between Noah's flood and baptism: "In that ark a few, that is, eight souls were saved through water. Its counterpart, Baptism, now saves you also" (I Peter 3: 20-21). Like intoxication and religion, art too seemingly transforms the reality of contemporary chaos, not by submergence or by transcendence but through revelation of the sad beauty inherent in human frustration. Art, Styron implies, does not submerge consciousness or transcend memory; it embraces reality so as to reveal beautiful, if painful, insights. Styron's art is like "the merest wisp of music, faintly heard only during unwitting moments when memory wash[es] at . . . minds like breakers against crumbling stones" (p. 267). Similar imagery applies to Harry's painting, which depicts "the ruins of a city, shattered, devastated, crumbled piles of concrete and stone" and which recalls to Peyton Harry's remark about "small blind sea things pitched up wriggling on the rock of life to await the final engulfing wave" (pp. 374, 378).

All three modes of response--religion, intoxication and art --indicate the human desire to slow down, halt, and transcend the catastrophic waves of "time's conscience-obliterating flow" (p. 188). When Loftis drinks, his mind becomes "suspended . . . in a state of palmy beatitude" (p. 55); everything appears drowsy or lazy to him and begins "very slowly a sweet process of transfiguration . . . as in some leisurely seraphic progression toward ultimate truth" or as if taking "on the quality of perfection" (pp. 51-52). Loftis' escape into his alcoholic world, however, never sharpens his conscience and so never actually provides him with such ultimate insight. Nor do the rainbow theatrics of revivalist religion, which actually encourages an evasion of conscience through the assumption of an illusory ark-like security in total dependence upon God and through the semi-mystical sensation of transcendent moments of frozen time; this feature of religion is more mundanely (and satirically) evident in Carey Carr's desire for a "vacant, idle day when [he] would be free from worry" (p. 110). Art, too, suspends time. It conveys an experience everyone has occasionally, a sudden mental focus, when the sealike "seesawing" of moods stops "for one instant," and thought rests "at precise, unhurried equilibrium" (p. 131); as Loftis intuits, "life tends toward a moment" (p. 15).(8) The artist may to some degree be considered intoxicated and to some extent religious, but rather than deny faith or accept an easy faith, he commits himself, simply, to a belief in the actuality of human aspiration and in the sorrowful loveliness intrinsic to the inevitable frustration of that aspiration. In art, as demonstrated by Styron, "time's conscience-obliterating flow" is frozen neither by submerging beneath (as in drunkenness) nor transcending beyond (as in religion) the deluge of reality, but by presenting a sadly beautiful melody or splash of color. The artist is a person of "conscience" (p. 194), and time is suspended in his work (Styron's use of flashback and of a stalled car is relevant) in order to disclose a rainbow of decay. Like the man in Harry's painting, the artist possesses a conscience or inner life despite and because of the chaos and the devastation of "the final engulfing wave" of the deluge reality surrounding him.

By proffering the illusion that time's flow can be halted or transcended, religion and drunkenness promote an empty hope in man's ability to float safely in or on the flood or reality. While drunk, Loftis sees everything as leisurely floating or swimming, and frequently his thoughts become "untethered, and drift . . . buoyantly away on a flood of alcohol" (pp. 53-54, 181). Through ritualistic submergence ensuring transcendence, baptism promises to keep Christians afloat, and it is significant that Daddy Faith's theatrical appearance commences on a raft (p. 392), suggesting the ark-like security of religion. Peyton, who feels adrift or "as if she were walking undersea" (p. 330), finds a similar security in her attachment to the clock she purchases on the last day of her life. Symbolizing her desire for an escape into an earlier, seemingly more rational time (like the eighteenth century [cf. p. 27], which viewed the universe in terms of Newton's clock analogy), the clock becomes for Peyton a womb or ark of security--it is "churchlike" (p. 373)--rescuing her from the "fathomless past" of her guilt, from a world of cataclysmic fluidity. As she explains to Harry, "We could get inside [the clock] and float merrily along" (p. 378); and, I think, Styron intends her emphasis on "the glow of rubies and diamonds" within the clock (p. 356) to recall Daddy Faith's use of the glitter of gems to make a rainbow effect, to make an arc signifying hope. Since Styron depicts the sky as a sea, this desire to float is equivalent in the novel to the human desire to fly (aspire), and both are equally impossible; for sails, looking "like wings," like "suppliant arms" or "as pretty as kites" (pp. 80, 110, 326), are subject to unpredictable winds causing them to collapse "desolately" (p. 80) like a kite caught in a tree or a bluejay entangled in honeysuckle. Peyton suggests the relation between the desire for flight and the illusion of sailing over the waves of the deluge when she sees herself and Harry, inside the floating arklike clock, being conducted "untroubled through some aerial flight across time" (p. 374).

Images of boats, appearing time and again on the horizon, accentuate the desire of Styron's characters to sail away or keep afloat. Ironically, however, these boat images never serve a romantic function finally nor do they engender a sense of security; for, in contrast to Noah's world-saving ark, they most often are life-destroying battleships or other large boats engaged in the war. Frequently in the novel Styron contrasts the solidity of "battleships and freighters . . . anchored far out" to the easily destroyed and sadly beautiful fragility of sailboats, the sails of which look like uplifted arms, wings, kites or "scraps of cloth being blown above the waves by something invisible" (p. 218); "below the scudding clouds it appeared that each stake and boat and scrap of sail had been swallowed up by the waves" (p. 219). In one episode Peyton thinks of Dick's car as "some kind of boat, as an escape to expectant adventures similar to that of the sailing explorers of early America (pp. 219, 225); but her experience with Dick, as with everyone else, proves otherwise, even as it is anti-thetical to the implied Edenic promise of the green stamp, showing a three-masted schooner resting at anchor, which ironically appears on the envelope of the letter in which she complains of feeling adrift, as if she were drowning (pp. 37-38). Throughout the novel boat imagery is presented with a "terrible" beauty, depicted in a manner suggesting that behind all illusion lies a catastrophic warship reality ready to crush people even as it had decimated the landscape in Loftis' dream (p. 188) and in Harry's painting.

Warship imagery reveals the role of technology in the novel; ostensibly the hope of future civilization, in actuality it manifests the imminent apocalypse. As it appears at the opening and the close of the novel, the train symbolizes this false promise of technology. Technology has led to the invention of the atomic bomb, which, in its wave-like dissolving of matter, has frighteningly increased the pervasiveness of the deluge or cataclysmic "fluidity" of the world. In contrast to art, which depicts frozen moments of colorful though painful insight, technology, as pictured in the train, only augments the ever-increasing momentum of time's flow, clouding man's view of himself: *"the white* fog of smoke from the engine ahead swirls and dips against the window like a tattered scarf and obscures the view" (p. 10). Technology derives from human aspiration, as the smoke imagery and as the prominent image of the arched railroad trestle intimate. But technology is even worse than intoxication and religion; whereas they provide a colorful illusory escape, technology presents only a bleak perversion of the expression of human aspiration. The artist, however, can detect intrinsic loveliness even in technology; by depicting human aspiration, in the train passages framing the book, as a "tattered scarf" and as a "spreading plume of steam" (p. 400--recalling the imagery of uplifted arms, like wings or birds appearing "as black as smoke" [p. 108]). Styron reveals the sad beauty "crushed" from humanity by the advance of a war-world technology ironically derived from man's ceaseless desire to rise "upward toward his own ascending spirit" (p. 378).

In the remarkable final scene of the novel a small fiction, occurring beneath the arch of the train trestle, contributes to Styron's rainbow motif and climactically illustrates his aesthetic practice. Overshadowed by the arch of technology, LaRuth suddenly experiences a fleeting insight into the reality disclosed by Peyton's death; in spite of her religious faith, she momentarily doubts whether everything will be all right eventually. Appropriately, at that moment, she lets a watermelon "rind drop from her fingers" (p. 400). Like the crumpled, brightly-colored Christmas wrapping in an earlier scene, the discarded melon rind, with its rainbow-like arc of colors, objectifies the beauty or fleeting loveliness intrinsic to the destruction of aspiration or hope--a fragile sail torn or collapsed by the wind, a kite caught in a tree, a bird entangled and flightless, a frozen moment of insight shattered by the resurgence of reality. While others may seek to submerge themselves under reality *through* drink or try to transcend it *through* religion or escape it in a technology which is inimical to mankind, Styron, the artist, honestly faces the cataclysmic deluge and offers only brief rainbowlike insights allowing for a vague, anguished, existential belief in the sad beauty "crushed" from human suffering, even in the inherent loveliness of alcoholism, religion, and technology.

In this final scene Styron emphasizes LaRuth's small dejected action below the arching train trestle, because while others look <u>up</u> or raise their arms (in an attempt to fly, to float or sail, to draw arcs, to find a rainbow of promise and redemption), Styron, the artist, looks <u>down</u> to the source of man's ascending spirit, to the ground, as it were, where the arches of a rainbow seem to begin and end. Looking down, the artist observes the truth of the Christian paradox (as filtered through Peyton), that "all souls must go down before ascending" (p. 385); the ascent of the rainbow in Noah's time, the transcending rebirth through baptism, the escape through alcohol, the rise of technology, the emergence of Styron's rainbow aesthetic and of the existential belief it asserts, depend on the human suffering "below," on the sorrow resulting from the endless frustration of "hope, ascending eternally . . . through the darkness" (p. 140).

Styron's frozen moments of brightly-colored, sadly beautiful insights are never sustained; they fade quickly, even as the rainbow vanishes, as "the juice of the discarded melon rinds [runs] like blood in the sand" and as faith "evaporates" (pp. 392, 109) before the sort of doubt LaRuth experiences in the final scene. But if the "splash" of colorful insight is fleetingly brief, if it provides no clue as to what man is or why he exists or why everything in creation necessarily moves toward apparently purposeless dissolution, it does impart a <u>felt</u> sense of human reality; the "crushed" sorrowful loveliness of Styron's rainbow aesthetic existentially discloses, for a moment, the actuality of human aspiration and, thereby, allows man to assert belief in his own reality. In structural design, language, and style <u>Lie Down in Darkness</u> conveys, through evanescent frozen moments, a felt sense of the sad beauty "crushed" from the agony of its characters. The novel is a rainbow of decay, crumpled Christmas wrapping, a discarded watermelon rind--a fleeting glimpse of the sadly beautiful ascent of human hope or aspiration in lives discarded, decaying, and crushed by the inevitable deluge that is the increasing dispersion of reality, both in man's mind and in the manifestation of that mind in such technological developments as the atomic bomb.

Notes

(1) <u>Lie Down in Darkness</u> (New York: Bobbs-Merrill, 1951), pp. 10, 15, 24, 99, 106-07, 131, 189, 266, 383-84. Quotations are from this edition, and appropriate page references are included parenthetically in the text.

(2) Key passages depicting this gesture of supplication appear on pp. 103, 109, 141. 182, 222, 228, 347, 394.

(3) Critics have correctly noted that in the novel only Harry possesses genuine tragic self-awareness: see Jonathan Baumbach, "Paradise Lost: The Novels of William Styron," <u>South Atlantic Quarterly</u>, 63 (Spring

1964), 207-17; David D. Galloway, The Absurd Hero in American Fiction (Austin: University of Texas Press, 1970), pp. 60-61; and Marc L. Ratner, William Styron (New York: Twayne, 1972), p. 52.

(4) In the passage remarking how Helen's "lovely skin" curved "tautly over the fragile arch of her cheekbones and drew her lips outward and down so that it always looked as if she were sorrowing a little over something" and so that her mouth looked "lovely and sad" (pp. 106-07), Styron is playing with the motif of the rainbow, which rises in beauty as a result of the sadness below.

(5) Satire has a place in Styron's novel because laughter is one way of conveying the old beauty inherent in the sadness of human aspiration. In the novel "laughter floated across the lawn and up to the sky" just as music "floated innocently out over the terrace and up to the stars" (pp. 60, 89), because, in Styron's view, laughter achieves the same end as art.

(6) The countless similes based on various flora and fauna, often to satiric effect (see note 5), represent Styron's view of man's natural position as his only source of reality.

(7) Among others, Ratner (p. 44) and William J. Swanson ("Notes on Religion," Cimmaron Review, No. 7 [March 1969], pp. 45-52) have remarked biblical influences on the novel. The rainbow, incidentally, is biblically associated with the apocalypse (Matt. 4: 38-39; Rev. 4:3, 10:1). See also my "The Gothic Grace and Rainbow Aesthetic of Patrick White's Fiction," Texas Studies in Literature and Language, forthcoming.

(8) Significantly, when Helen experiences a "brief moment" when "it seemed that time itself had stopped," she thinks in terms of such art objects as carved glass and statuary (p. 118). Elsewhere in the novel Styron refers to figurines "frozen timeless" (p. 27) and to a Turner painting in which "even moving objects seemed to remain suspended, like flies in amber" (p. 32).

*From Modern Fiction Studies 24 (1978): 247-54.

IN QUEST OF REDEMPTION: THE RELIGIOUS BACKGROUND OF PEYTON'S MONOLOGUE IN LIE DOWN IN DARKNESS*

John Lang

William Styron's first novel, Lie Down in Darkness (1951), dissects the moral and spiritual confusion that typifies our "post-Christian" age. By emphasizing his characters' irresolution, their inability to love, and their failure either to seek or grant forgiveness, Styron demonstrates both their need of salvation and their refusal of the means which might effect their redemption. Lie Down in Darkness might best be termed an etiology of the soul's disorder. Yet although metaphors of disease pervade the book, Styron also indicates the possibility of that disease's remission.

. . .

What [recent criticism of Lie Down in Darkness] overlooks . . . is Styron's careful use of literary allusions--particularly his use of Biblical passages from the libretto of Handel's Messiah--to structure the novel's concluding chapter. That chapter, most of which is devoted to Peyton Loftis' monologue, is fundamental to an understanding of Styron's intentions in the book, intentions that are primarily moral and religious. Peyton's suicide not only confirms the contemporary eclipse of the Messiah but also evinces man's need to recover a relationship with the divine.

Peyton's monologue begins with an epigraph taken from Job 19:23-26, a portion of which likewise opens the triumphal third, and concluding, part of The Messiah.(1) The Biblical text is combined with what seem to be Peyton's own reflections.

> Oh that my words were now written oh that they
> were printed in a book. That they were graven with
> an iron pen and lead in the rock forever. For I know
> that my redeemer liveth and that He shall stand at

> the latter day upon the earth and though worms
> destroy this body yet in my flesh shall I
> Shall I
> Oh my flesh!
> (Strong is your hold O mortal flesh, strong is your
> hold O love.)(2)

Whereas Job concludes, "in my flesh shall I <u>see God</u>," Peyton is torn between belief and despair. Yet this passage serves to remind the reader of a redemptive religious tradition and represents the first of several allusions to <u>The Messiah</u> in Peyton's monologue.

Moreover, even before her monologue commences, Styron introduces the figure of Christ, for Chapter 7 opens not with that monologue but with a description of Potter's Field, where Peyton's body is taken immediately after her suicide. Over that desolate area presides a weatherbeaten statue of Christ. Though "it is almost as if this monument were forgotten" (p. 327), its eyes, Styron notes, "still burn like the brightest fires" (p. 327). Upon the statue appears the legend, "<u>He calleth His own by Name</u>" (p. 327), words that ring with irony among the field's "nameless dead," but words that also recall the difference between human and divine perspectives.

The events recorded in Peyton's monologue take the form of a quest. On one level, the monologue depicts her efforts to locate her husband, who has broken with her because of her adultery. But Peyton's search for Harry also becomes a spiritual pilgrimage, a quest for God motivated by her sense of guilt. The monologue's frenetic pace and its tone of almost unbearable anguish powerfully convey the disorder and confusion of Peyton's mind. Yet within her emotional and spiritual inferno, she seeks a means of salvation.

Initially, however, Peyton pursues a spurious redemption, imagining that the jeweled clock she carries will free her from the bondage of time and sin. Like her parents, Milton and Helen, Peyton longs to escape the destructive effects of temporality. In fact, the first words she speaks in her monologue voice this concern: "I don't have enough time" (p. 335). Obsessed with flux, with "the eternal drift" (p. 344), Peyton conceives of the clock as a refuge and envisions herself inside its sanctuary "perfect, complete, perpetual," the timepiece itself "indestructible, shining, <u>my own invention,</u>" (p. 335; my italics). Within the clock she and Harry will be safe from the menace of mortality. "Here all our guilt will disappear," she muses (p. 354).

Yet despite such hopes, Peyton occasionally betrays doubts about the clock's efficacy, worrying about Harry's response to it. Will "he understand <u>the miracle of my invention</u>," she wonders, "the soaring dark <u>soul-closet?</u>' (p. 374; my italics). Indeed, Harry does not understand. He rejects not only the clock but Peyton herself.

Stripped of the salvation she has fabricated, Peyton turns to the possibility of divine redemption. Her spiritual quest thus becomes an extension of the search for a father has shaped her life. Moreover, as she contemplates suicide, she associates her marital infidelity with her abandonment of God.

> And I thought: it was not he [Harry] who rejected me, but I
> him, and I had known all day that that must happen, by that
> rejection making the first part of my wished-for, yearned-for
> death-act. . . . oh my God, why have I forsaken You? Have I
> through some evil inherited in a sad century cut myself
> off from You forever, and thus only by dying must take the
> fatal chance: to walk into a dark closet and lie down there and
> dream away my sins, hoping to wake in another land, in a far,
> fantastic dawn? It shouldn't be this way--to yearn so for
> dying: . . . then too I want to be bursting with love, and not
> with this sorrow, at that moment when my soul glides upward
> toward You from my dust. What a prayer it was I said; I knew
> He wasn't listening, marking the sparrow but not me. So to
> hell. (pp. 382-83)

Despite Peyton's uncertainty and ambivalence in this passage, Styron makes it clear that she possesses more faith than Harry or Milton or Helen or even the minister Carey Carr. Milton has fled the burden of moral responsibility through alcohol, finding in whiskey "a state of palmy beatitude" (p. 55) that displaces any authentic religious consciousness. His will operates almost exclusively, in Eliot's phrase, "among velleities." For Helen Loftis, religion serves as a means of distancing herself from others, of subjecting them to moral judgments while dissociating herself from guilt. Helen uses the concept of sin to bludgeon Milton and Peyton. Carey Carr, though more perceptive than either of Peyton's parents, fails to achieve a vision of the divine. At novel's end, as he witnesses Milton's attempt to strangle Helen, Carr stands impotent, thinking, "my Lord, You shall never reveal Yourself" (p. 388).

Peyton, in contrast, throughout her monologue retains a measure of religious faith. In fact, up until the moment of her suicide, she carries on a mental dialogue between belief and despair. Returning to scraps of conversation she has heard disputing God's existence, she recalls Albert Berger's comment, "there was no God . . . save Him in the spirit of the creatively evolved, in the electrons of a radar screen or in the molecules of DDT" (p. 340). To this creed of scientific pantheism, Harry has replied, with his characteristically amorphous optimism, "God is life-force, love whatever you will, but not death"--whereupon Peyton had silenced both of them by proclaiming, "For now is Christ risen from the dead, the first fruits of them that sleep" (p. 340; I Corinthians 15:20). In this passage Styron has again drawn upon the libretto of Handel's Messiah, for the verse cited appears in the same aria as the lines from Job used in the epigraph to Peyton's monologue. And when Peyton later thinks of her death, she once more considers it in terms employed in <u>The Messiah</u>. "Oh God," she declares, "I must die today, but will I not rise again at another time and stand on the earth clean and incorruptible?" (p. 358). Her words here echo the penultimate aria in Handel's composition, which reads: "'The trumpet shall sound, and the dead shall be raised incorruptible, and we shall be changed. For this corruptible must put on incorruption, and this mortal must put on immortality" (I Corinthians 15: 52,53).(3)

In contrast to Milton and Helen, Peyton actively addresses herself to the problem of personal salvation conceived as a religious quest. The flightless birds that accompany her throughout her monologue symbolize the guilt that thwarts her desire to ascend to God. Altering a line from Dickinson, Peyton remarks, "Guilt is the thing with feathers" (p. 352). Here her substitution of the word "guilt" for Dickinson's "hope" seems initially to move Peyton further into despair. Yet insofar as her recognition of guilt impels her to search for salvation, this consciousness of sin provides renewed grounds for hope. Thus, on more than one occasion, Peyton describes the birds as "peaceful and without menace" (p. 345; cf. pp. 347, 381). By embodying her guilt, they manifest her need of the divine. As Kierkegaard writes, "it is a well-established ceremonial convention that if the finite spirit would see God it must begin by being guilty. In turning towards himself he discovers guilt. The greater the genius, the more profoundly he discovers guilt."(4) Far from being a symptom of psychological disorder, such a sense of guilt is a mark of religious vitality. Peyton's hallucinations indicate the intensity of her spiritual torment. And unlike her parents she accepts responsibility for her guilt and acknowledges its implications.

Linked to the birds that symbolize Peyton's dilemma is her sense of drowning. In part it derives form the tendency toward alcoholism she shares with her father. But Peyton's drinking, like Milton's, is merely a symptom of spiritual malaise and not the disease itself. As she writes her father, "I feel adrift, as if I were drowning out in dark space. . . . Everywhere I turn I seem to walk deeper and deeper into some terrible despair" (p. 38). Pinpointing the source of her problem, she locates it "in my drowning soul" (p. 362).

Peyton's description of her sense of drowning suggests a parallel in the opening verses of Psalms 69:

> Save me, O God!
> For the waters have come up to my neck.
> I sink in deep mire,
>   where there is no foothold;
> I have come into deep waters,
>   and the flood sweeps over me.
> I am weary with my crying;
>   my throat is parched.

My eyes grow dim
With waiting for my God. (Psalm 69: 1-3)
Just as David's throat is parched despite the waters that threaten to engulf
him, so Peyton, "thinking of gallons of water to drink and cool dew
somewhere" (p. 384), craves something to quench her thirst. In words
echoing Marlowe's Faustus, she cries out, "One drop of anything . . .
would save the life of poor damned Peyton" (p. 357). In the case of
Faustus, the drop he desires springs from Christ's blood streaming in the
firmament: "One drop would save my soul, half a drop! Ah, my
Christ!"(5)

This allusion stresses Peyton's own need for redemption. She thinks at
one point of how "a guilt past memory or dreaming, much darker, impels
me on" (p. 386), and she refers to "that part of me over which I have no
authority: my guilt" (p. 380). While at first glance the latter statement may
seem to be simply another denial of responsibility of the sort that Milton
and Peyton frequently offer, in this instance Peyton's words may reflect
not the desire to escape accountability but rather the Christian conception
of the will's bondage. Peyton cannot, by her own efforts, break free from
sin--as the fate of her bejeweled clock also indicates.

Throughout the day described in her monologue, Peyton's thoughts
return to the question, "and will he not come again? and will he not come
again?" (p. 350; Styron's italics). On the literal level, this refrain refers to
Harry, but figuratively it suggests both the redeemer whom Job envisions
standing on the earth and the Christ whom the Apostle's Creed confesses
will come again to judge the quick and the dead. Like King David in
Psalm 69, Peyton's eyes grow dim with waiting for her God. "Would he
never come again, protect me from my sin and guilt?" she wonders (p.
381).

This concern for judgment, forgiveness, and resurrection pervades her
monologue. On five separate occasions Peyton quotes part or all of two
verses from Psalms 89: "How long, Lord, wilt thou hide Thyself forever:
Shall Thy wrath burn like fire? Remember how short my time is" (p. 350).
These verses reiterate both her sense of God's absence and her sense of
entrapment in time.(6) Peyton clearly fears the loss of the divine. Nor is
she ever certain that the resurrection she so pointedly claimed for Christ
will be her inheritance. Indeed, at one point in her monologue Styron
alters a line from The Messiah to suggest her continuing agonizing doubt.
As Peyton attempts to explain her conduct to Harry's friend Lennie, she
thinks to herself, "Lennie, behold, I tell you a misery." Aloud she simply
comments, "today I'm trying to exorcise . . . my guilt" (p. 369). The word
"misery" in the first quotation replaces the term "mystery" in The Messiah,
where the recitative in which the line occurs goes on to affirm the
resurrection of all believers. "Behold, I tell you a mystery: We shall all be
changed in a moment, in the twinkling of an eye at the last trumpet" (I
Corinthians 15: 51, 52).(7)

On the final day of her life, however, Peyton is less assured of the resurrection than she is oppressed by her intolerable burden of guilt. Overwhelmed by that burden, she decides, "undivorced from guilt, I must divorce myself from life, in this setting part of time" (p. 382). Significantly, Styron borrows the phrase, "in this setting part of time," from the same chapter of Sir Thomas Browne's Urn Burial from which he took the epigraph of the novel. The expression thus recalls Browne's vision of death as the necessary transition to eternal life. From Browne's Christian perspective, death is indeed the Lucina of life since man's mortality plays midwife to God's gift of eternal life. The "diuturnity" to which Milton and Helen aspire--and which is aptly symbolized by Peyton's clock--is, as Browne proclaims, "a dream and folly of expectation" (p. 1). But the alternative need not be despair and death, as to many of Styron's critics seem to assume. Styron clearly holds open the possibility that Peyton's death may be redemptive, as both his use of The Messiah and his other musical and literary allusions testify.

Among the most important of those additional allusions is the opening line of Bach's Cantata #53, "Schlage doch, gewunschte Stunde," a line Peyton repeats three times in the course of her monologue (pp. 349, 359, 372). Bach's cantata expresses the same willingness to embrace death that one finds in Browne's work. For Bach, too, death is portrayed as a necessary prelude to a final vision of the divine. Cantata #53 anticipates the entry of the soul into heaven, where it will behold the face of Christ and be at peace. Despite the presence of death, the mood is one of joy, not gloom. As W. Gillies Whitaker remarks of this composition in his authoritative study of Bach's cantatas, "The tempo must not be slow, . . . and it must be sung happily. The sound of the bell is a welcome one, the call to an ideal life."(8)

This realm of the divine is also evoked through Styron's allusions to Vaughan and Dante. Throughout the novel Styron employs the conventional symbol of light to indicate God's presence or potential presence. At Peyton's wedding, for example, the bride and Dr. Holcomb recite, in a kind of litany, the first and last quatrains of Vaughan's poem, "They Are All Gone into the World of Light."(9) Not only does this poem voice Vaughan's desire to join the departed spirits, it also articulates his certainty that death is not man's end but that God intends to save mankind. In a quatrain of the poem not cited by Peyton or Dr Holcomb, Vaughan writes:

> Dear, bounteous death! the jewel of the just,
> Shining nowhere but in the dark;
> What mysteries do lie beyond thy dust,
> Could man outlook that mark!(10)

Clearly, the world of light to which Vaughan directs his reader negates the threat of mortality. By alluding to Vaughan's poem, Styron hints at the continued availability of this world to modern man.

Through similar allusions to The Divine Comedy, Styron returns to this image of light in Peyton's monologue. Peyton recalls that both Milton and Harry address her as "Blessed Beatrice," conjoining their use of this honorific title with citations from The Paradiso. Milton apostrophizes Peyton as "O Light Eternal, self-understanding, shining on thy own" (p. 372), while Harry depicts the effect of her radiance: "man at that light becometh so content that to choose other sight, and this reject, it is impossible that he consent" (p. 356). In both cases, the lines quoted occur in the final, climactic canto of The Paradiso; there they describe not Beatrice but the ineffable splendor of God, whom Dante at last beholds. Merging the themes of divine love and man's longing for eternity through another such allusion, Styron has Harry proclaim to Peyton, "You will never die, you are the love that moves the sun and other stars" (p. 347; my emphasis), a quotation in which the italicized words once again originally referred to God and composed the concluding line of The Divine Comedy.(11) By having Harry apply these words to Peyton, Styron reveals Harry's failure to grasp the distinction between divine and human love. And the same may be said of Milton. Peyton, in contrast, during her final meeting his Harry, begs him not to call her "Blessed Beatrice" (pp. 376, 377), for her consciousness of sin awakens her to the inappropriateness of this epithet.

Against the darkness through which Peyton moves, Styron sets the light as her origin and goal. Peyton remembers how "once in school we had a play and I was the Spirit of Light" (p. 359), and she longs to recover the exhilaration she felt in "the way he [Milton] carried me up and upward--oh Christ!--when I was the spirit of Light" (p. 370). In Peyton's case, as opposed to that of her parents, this longing to recapture the innocence rather than simply the security of childhood justifies a positive valuation of her nostalgia. Here one encounters an appropriate religious form of such nostalgia, for whereas Milton and Helen seek childhood as an escape from responsibility, Peyton seeks the innocence she associates with childhood in order to free herself specifically from guilt. Peyton's monologue does indeed narrate what Maxwell Geismar has called "the end of innocence," but more importantly, it presents Peyton's attempt to deal with that loss. Geismar mistakenly argues that "her search to find . . .'a new father, a new home' is an impossible one," since to his mind "this yearning for the experience of innocence" manifests a dangerous psychological immaturity.(12) From a Christian standpoint, however, as Kierkegaard recognized, "if I cannot recover innocence, then all is lost from the beginning, because the primary fact is simply that I and everyone have lost innocence."(13)

Driven by guilt but not without hope of regaining paradise, Peyton ascends the loft in Greenwich Village from which she will plunge to her death. Whereas earlier she had tried to pray, only to sense "He wasn't listening, marking the sparrow but not me" (p. 383), now as she climbs she wonders: "Did I have a companion? I felt that someone was watching

me, myself perhaps; at least I knew I was not alone" (p. 385). Mounting
the stairs, she considers the apparent contradiction into which her life has
led her. "Only guilt could deliver me into this ultimate paradox: that all
souls must go down before ascending upward; only we most egregious
sinners, to shed our sin in self-destruction, must go upward before the last
descent" (p. 385). This paradox, of course, recalls the one proposed by Sir
Thomas Browne and the novel's title--the requirement that the soul lie
down in darkness in order to enter the world of light.

The words with which Peyton's monologue concludes merit quotation
in full, both as an example of Styron's powerful prose and as a summary
of her soliloquy's major themes and images:

> I can't pause to remember, for a guilt past memory or
> dreaming, much darker, impels me on. I pray but my prayer
> climbs up like a broken wisp of smoke: <u>oh my Lord, I am dying,</u>
> is all I know, and <u>oh my father, oh my darling,</u> longingly,
> lonesomely, I fly into your arms! <u>Peyton, you must be</u>
> <u>proper nice girls don't. Peyton</u>. Me? Myself all shattered,
> this lovely shell? Perhaps I shall rise at another time,
> though I lie down in darkness and have my light in ashes. I
> turn in the room, see them come across the tiles, dimly
> prancing, fluffing up their wings, I think: my poor
> flightless birds, have you suffered without soaring on this
> earth? Come then and fly. And they move on past me through
> the darkening sands, awkward and gentle, rustling their
> feathers: come then and fly. And so it happens: treading past
> to touch my boiling skin--one whisper of feathers is all--
> and so I see them go--oh my Christ!--one by one ascending
> my flightless birds through the suffocating night, toward
> paradise. I am dying. Bunny, dying. <u>But you must be proper</u>.
> I say, oh pooh.
> Oh pooh. Must be proper. Oh most proper. Powerful.
> Oh most powerful.
> Oh must (p. 386; Styron's italics)

The penultimate phrase in this passage sounds an invocation to God, while
the final phrase registers both Peyton's compulsive mental state and her
sense of the overwhelming necessity for her act. Having found all other
approaches to redemption closed to her, Peyton risks this radical solution
to her spiritual predicament. While Peyton lacks the assurance voiced by
the prophet Micah: "when I fall, I shall rise; when I sit in darkness, the
Lord shall be a light to me" (Micah 7:8)--she is not entirely devoid of
hope that she will rise again. Thus, even in the face of her suicide, Styron
leaves open the possibility that she not only flees <u>from</u> sin but also flees
<u>toward</u> salvation. Peyton herself remarks, "something has always been
close to dying in my soul, and I've sinned only in order to lie down in

darkness and find, somewhere in the net of my dreams, a new father, a new home" (p. 379).

Thrust into a world in which men have lost the capacity to love and in which redemption in time appears all but impossible, Peyton kills herself. Yet she retains hope. Here Styron follows the prescription given by Melville some hundred years earlier: "Our souls are like those orphans whose unwedded mothers die in bearing them: the secret of our paternity lies in their grave, and we must there to learn it."(14)

Were Styron to end his novel with Peyton's leap to her death, however, one might be justified in assuming that her quest for transcendence is futile. After all, the need for redemption, however intense, is no guarantee that redemption is attainable. But Styron presents two final scenes in Chapter 7 that are meant to inform our response to Peyton's suicide. The first is the violent confrontation occurring at the cemetery that culminates in Milton's attempt to strangle Helen. This incident demonstrates the Loftises' utter inability to aid Peyton in her spiritual crisis. Her final words, "Oh must," resonate all the more convincingly when the reader hears both Milton and Helen confess the nullity of their lives: "With nothing left! Nothing! Nothing!" (p. 388).

The second scene, the one on which the novel concludes, depicts a Negro revival meeting reminiscent of the Easter Sunday service in the closing section of The Sound and the Fury. Through this revival Styron further clarifies Peyton's situation. For although Daddy Faith, the black preacher who leads the revival, is a charlatan, the spiritual impulse that motivates the Negroes parallels Peyton's quest for redemption. Daddy Faith's name again invokes the search for a father, and it imbues that quest with added religious significance. Yet Daddy Faith distorts, though he does not totally pervert, the Christian faith he pretends to serve, and Styron measures both the extent of that distortion and the nature of that faith by once again citing from the libretto of Handel's Messiah.

Immediately prior to Daddy Faith's appearance at the baptismal immersion of the black community, his chief assistant proclaims, "Lift up your heads, O . . . ye . . . gates. And be ye lifted up, ye everlasting doors! . . . And de King of Glory shall come in" (pp. 394-95). In The Messiah these lines anticipate the appearance of God, "the Lord strong and mighty."(15) But the Negroes identify Daddy Faith himself as the King of Glory (p. 395) and so displace the figure of Christ. Yet despite Daddy Faith's blatant commercialism and self-deification, he still preaches an ethic of salvation. The first words he speaks are also the opening words of The Messiah, with their promise of Israel's redeemer: "'Comfort ye . . . Comfort ye, my people!'" (p. 396). Citing the Psalms and the prophets, Daddy Faith delivers a message of judgment and redemption that echoes the central concerns of Peyton's monologue.

> "De hand of de Lawd is against de sinful and de unjust, and de candle of de wicked is put out . . . de eyes of de people shall

see His destruction and dey shall drink of de wrath of
d'Almighty . . . Dey gonna holler . . . 'How long, Lawd, wilt
thou be angry fo'ever, shall Thy jealousy burn like fire?'"
Daddy Faith put out his tiny black hands, a motion of compassion
and tenderness. "Comfort ye," he said softly, "comfort ye, my
people. Do you now know dat I will sprinkle clean water upon
you, and ye shall be clean, and a new heart also will I give you
and a new spirit will I put widin you? . . . Be not afraid, my
people. De voice said, Cry! And he said, what shall I cry? All
flesh is grass, and all de goodliness thereof is de flower of de
field. De grass withereth and de flower fadeth, because de sperit
of de Lawd bloweth upon it . . . Sho'ly de people is grass . . .
De grass withereth, de flower fadeth," he said, but de word of
your God shall stand forever." (pp. 398-99)

Daddy Faith delivers this sermon from a raft that represents an
alternative to Peyton's experience of drowning. It surmounts the waves she
dreads. Similarly, the baptismal rite the Blacks undergo transforms the
murderous flood into a redemptive sacrament. During the revival Ella
Swan, Styron's version of Faulkner's Dilsey, experiences the grace of the
God whom Daddy Faith imperfectly attests so. After her immersion she
knows the power of baptism's "sin-destroying seas" (p. 400), what another
character in the novel called the "redeeming waters" (p. 229). Moreover,
unlike Carey Carr, the representative of official Christianity, Ella obtains
a vision of God. "I seen Him," she exclaims enthusiastically (p. 400).

While Styron does not offer the Blacks' superstitious religiosity and
their blindness to Daddy Faith's charlatanism as a solution to the spiritual
anguish of modern man, he nevertheless suggests that genuine faith may
exist even under such debased forms. Against the tyranny of time and
guilt, Daddy Faith's sermon--or rather, the Biblical promises on which it
rests--poses a sustaining belief in the diurnity of God's salvation. Styron's
Messiah is largely in eclipse. Yet the religious quest that underlies both
Peyton's suicide and the Negroes' baptismal rite points to the need for
some principle of redemption. Styron makes this need the central focus of
his novel's concluding chapter, and he structures that chapter around
Christianity's response to the need. That his portraits of individual
Christians and of institutional Christianity are often unflattering does not
negate the novel's fundamental religious concerns. As Styron once
remarked in an interview, "I've always been partially intent on contrasting
the spiritual impulse as it is defined by Christianity with the hypocritical
ritual and hypocritical shallowness and thought that surround much of its
manifestations in life."(16)

Peyton's quest represents, I believe, this authentic "spiritual impulse."
Even in her suicide she chooses the possibility of redemption, and Styron's
imagery and allusions remind the reader of the religious tradition

informing the book. Yet the very desperation of Peyton's act helps map the twentieth-century's spiritual wasteland.(17)

Notes

(1) The aria that opens Part III of The Messiah reads as follows: "I know that my Redeemer liveth, and that he shall stand at the latter day upon the earth. And tho' worms destroy this body, yet in my flesh shall I see God. For now is Christ risen from the dead, the first fruits of them that sleep." George Frederick Handel, The Messiah, Kalmus Miniature Orchestra Scores #159 (Scarsdale, New York: Edwin F. Kalmus, n.d.), pp. 184-89.

(2) William Styron, Lie Down in Darkness (Indianapolis: Bobbs-Merrill, 1951), p. 335; Styron's italics. All further references to this novel will be found in parentheses.

(3) The Messiah, pp. 195-97.

(4) The Concept of Dread (Princeton: Princeton University Press, 1969), p. 96.

(5) Doctor Faustus, V, ii, 144; The Complete Plays of Christopher Marlowe, Ed. Irving Ribner (New York: Odyssey, 1963), p. 409.

(6) These verses also represent the only occasion in Peyton's monologue when she quotes a Biblical passage not found in The Messiah.

(7) The Messiah, p. 194.

(8) The Cantatas of Johann Sebastian Bach: Sacred and Secular, I (London: Oxford University Press, 1959), p. 367.

(9) I am indebted to Cooper Mackin's William Styron, Southern Writers Series, No. 7 (Austin, Texas: Stock-Vaughn, 1969), p. 11, for identifying the lines as Vaughn's.

(10) The Complete Poetry of Henry Vaughan, ed. French Fogle (New York: New York University Press, 1965), p. 271.

(11) Styron has used Laurence Binyon's translation of The Divine Comedy, most readily accessible in The Portable Dante, ed. Paolo Milano (New York: Viking, 1947).

(12) American Moderns (New York: Hill and Wang, 1958), pp. 245, 246.

(13) Soren Kierkegaard's Journals and Papers, trans. and ed. Howard V. Hong and Edna H. Hong (Bloomington: Indiana University Press, 1967), I, p. 424. Plato's theory of spiritual insight as grounded in recollection provides another positive context for nostalgia like Peyton's. In the Phaedrus, Plato speaks of the true philosopher as a man whose mind/soul has wings by virtue of its "clinging in recollection to those things in which God abides, and in beholding which He is what He is." Styron's use of flightless birds to symbolize Peyton's spiritual plight may owe something to Plato's description of the soul in the same dialogue. "The soul . . . when perfect and fully winged . . . soars upward and is the ruler of the

universe; while the imperfect soul loses her feathers and drooping in flight at last settles on the solid ground. . . . The wing is intended to soar aloft and carry that which gravitates downwards into the upper region, which is the dwelling of the gods; and this is that element of the body which is most akin to the divine." See the Phaedrus in The Works of Plato, trans. Benjamin Jowett (New York: Tudor, n.d.), pp. 408 and 404.

(14) Moby-Dick (New York: Signet, 1964), p. 464.

(15) The Messiah, pp. 127-28.

(16) Robert K. Morris, "An Interview with William Styron," in The Achievement of William Styron, ed. Robert K. Morris and Irving Malin (Athens: University of Georgia Press, 1975), p. 33.

(17) This essay was written with the assistance of a grant from the National Endowment for the Humanities through the Endowment's summer seminar program.

*From Southern Humanities Review 17 (1983): 121-31.

"a new father, a new home": STYRON, FAULKNER, AND SOUTHERN REVISIONISM*

Christopher Metress

I

> The presence alone of Faulkner in our midst makes
> a great difference in what the writer can and cannot
> permit himself to do. Nobody wants his mule and
> wagon stalled on the same track the Dixie Limited
> is roaring down.(1) (Flannery O'Connor)

> I think we all ought to get down on our hands and
> knees every night and thank God for Faulkner.(2)
> (Peter Taylor)

> What one misses in the fiction of this period
> [fiction of "The Recent South 1951-82"] is the
> all-pervasive presence of William Faulkner.(3)
> (Thomas Daniel Young)

In the opening pages of his controversial study The Anxiety of Influence, Harold Bloom asserts that "the death of poetry will not be hastened by any reader's broodings, yet it seems just to assume that poetry in any tradition, when it dies, will be self-slain, murdered by its own past strength."(4) Regardless of the many biases and contradictions of Bloom's revisionism, this speculation on the insalubrious influence of past achievement upon future aspirations rings strikingly true not only for Western poetry but Western literature as well. Much of what Bloom claims to be true of poetic influence can also be said to be true of literary influence in general. Do not great novelists, like the great poets, also bequeath to their successors the challenges of their achievement, the anxiety of their influence? Bloom's assertion that "poetry . . . when it dies, will be self-slain, murdered by its own past strength" suggests several curious possibilities when "poetry" is replaced by "literature," or, more specifically, "Southern literature."

Of all the sub-genres of American literature, Southern literature, appropriately enough, is the literature most haunted by its past achievements. If any literature is self-slain it is Southern literature; the post-1950 Southern novelist is constantly measured against the achievements of his or her precursors from the literary renascence of the 1930s and 1940s. Thus, we often see the achievements of contemporary Southern novelists undermined, not by any shortcomings in their own work, but by their failure to survive comparison with the achievements of earlier Southern novelists. Not only must today's Southern novelist write a work that will stand on its own, he or she must also write a work that will bear the weight of tradition, the burden of the past. Because of the monumental presence of William Faulkner, . . . every Southern writer since him has at least been <u>asked</u> about felt presences of the giant in Oxford. Dealing with that influence is a peculiarly modern--and revealing--Southern literary trait.

Of all contemporary Southern novelists, perhaps William Styron most tellingly enacts this revealing struggle with the influence of Faulkner and the Southern literary tradition. With the publication of <u>Lie Down in Darkness</u> in 1951, Styron was hailed as Faulkner's heir-apparent. Immediately, reviewers noticed Styron's Faulknerian style and rhetoric, as well as his Faulknerian concerns with time, tradition, and the endurance of the human spirit. Justified parallels were drawn between Styron and Faulkner, parallels that led to an inevitable comparison between <u>Lie Down in Darkness</u> and its apparent model, <u>The Sound and the Fury</u>. Representative of the initial reviewers, Robert Gorham Davis noted that "Peyton combines the fates of Quentin and Caddy Compson in Faulkner's <u>The Sound and the Fury</u> . . . Styron takes over from Faulkner not only his lost lovely heroine, but also some specific symbolism, such as that of the clock, and the idea of ending the novel at a Negro revival."(5) In his favorable review "The Faulkner Pattern," Malcolm Cowley asserted more boldly the Styron-Faulkner connection, for if "one examines the novel more closely . . . [one] finds that it is as full of reminiscences as if it had dealt with Yoknapatawpha County instead of Tidewater Virginia."(6) Possibly because of such obvious parallels between <u>Lie Down in Darkness</u> and <u>The Sound and the Fury</u>, very few critics have pushed beyond the surface similarities of both novels to truly understand the implications of their kinship and the nature of the Faulknerian influence Southern writers acknowledge but then swiftly go beyond.(7)

A critical comparison of <u>Lie Down in Darkness</u> and <u>The Sound and the Fury</u> certainly needs to be more than what we have had in the past, what one reader has skillfully called "a sort of 'condemned playground' for critics too fond of influence hunting."(8) Styron's first novel is not simply a cataloguing of Faulknerian images, symbols, and themes. Nor can we suggest, as one critic has, that Styron's confrontation with Faulkner remains merely a "pastiche."(9) Lie Down in Darkness is, I propose, better understood as a revisionary novel, attempting not to borrow but to rewrite, wishing not to pay homage but to usurp, The Sound and the Fury and the influence of Faulkner. Lying as it does at the very beginning of what the editors of The History of Southern Literature felt compelled to label "The Recent South, 1951-1982," Lie Down in Darkness proves, contrary to the pronouncement of T.D. Young, that the "all-pervasive, dominating presence of William Faulkner" is, for better or for worse, still a thing too much with us.

II

All of us have learned from Faulkner. You've read Faulkner and seen the South as he saw it. And you've seen some of it like that. I don't think that anyone writing can be without the influence of Faulkner.(10)   (Peter Taylor)

All Southern writers who have written in the past twenty years have had to bear the burden of being called Faulknerian. But the truth, if anyone is interested, is this, certainly and simply: they write about the South, which is their home as well as Faulkner's . . . I can say, quite accurately, that Faulkner has been no influence, technical or otherwise, on my work. I admire the work of Faulkner that I know--by no means all--but with a cold, distant admiration for a genius whom I know to be grand but who has proved irrelevant to my own obsessions, my own ambitions.(11)   (Reynolds Price)

In Deceit, Desire, and the Novel, Rene Girard proposes a "Triangular" desire consisting of subject (the Self), object (the Thing), and mediator (the Other or Rival). According to Girard, desire is neither subject-oriented nor object-oriented but always mediator-oriented. Desire finds its impetus and origin not in the wants of the subject or in intrinsic desirability of any object but in an inextricable and necessarily competitive relationship with the Other. The complex posture of the Other is paradoxically antagonistic: "Everything that originates with this mediator is systematically belittled although still secretly desired."(12) Contemporary Southern fiction, as new and as fresh and as "present" as it may be, is always imprisoned in this tri-angular relationship; in being forever measured against the achievements of an earlier time, Southern fiction finds its subjects (its writers) and its objects (its fictions) forever bound to its mediators. Undoubtedly, William

Faulkner, his Yoknapatawpha myth regularized by Cowley's "Portable" and his critical reputation forged by the post-war rapproachment of Southern critics and New York intellectuals, looms as the great mediator of Southern Literature, the greatest precursor who is "systematically belittled although secretly desired." Thus, despite their great differences, writers as diverse as Reynolds Price, Flannery O'Connor, Walker Percy, and Harry Crews have all found themselves and their works labelled and judged according to the presence of the mediating rival, Faulkner. The Faulknerian label covers all Southern writers and threatens to undermine individual achievement and originality. Though Cleanth Brooks can recently assert, and rightly so, that Faulkner "is an original" and that there "is no one else quite like him in American literature," the contemporary Southern writer rarely finds such welcoming pronouncements of his or her own originality.(13)

In a 1982 reminiscence on the publication of Lie Down in Darkness, Styron voiced this anxious relationship between Faulkner and his progeny, a relationship which forces the Southern writer to achieve originality in defiance of Faulkner's colossal, mediating shadow:

> Lie Down in Darkness also owes an enormous debt to William
> Faulkner, who is of course the god and the demon of all
> Southern writers who have followed him. Writers as disparate
> as Flannery O'Connor and Walker Percy have expressed their
> despair at laboring in the shadow of such a colossus, and I felt
> a similar measliness. Yet, although even at the outset I doubted
> that I could rid myself wholly of Faulkner's influence, I knew
> that the book could not possibly have real merit, could not
> accrue unto itself the lasting power and beauty I wanted it to
> have, unless the voice I developed in telling this story became
> singular, striking, something uniquely my own.(14)

To break from Faulkner, to reshape the oppressive geometry of the triangular desire which imprisons originality, the Southern writer often finds himself or herself in an act of creative revisionism, an act, if you will, of carving out one's own postage stamp which is markedly different from the rival Yoknapatawpha. In a 1951 interview, Styron admitted to finding himself in the posture of a creative revisionist, despairing his heritage while seeking the singular, the striking, the unique:

> I wanted to write a novel that had more than regional
> implications. I wanted to avoid the ancestral theme, too--the
> peculiar, inbred and perverse types that Faulkner, Caldwell and
> other Southern writers have dealt in. At the same time I didn't
> want to exploit the old ideas of wreckage and defeat as a
> peculiarly Southern phenomenon. Elements of this are in the
> book, but they're part of the people rather than the place. I
> like to think that my story could have happened in Massachusetts
> just as well as in Virginia.(15)

This assertive pronouncement of creative difference reveals that from the outset Styron intended <u>Lie Down in Darkness</u> to swerve dramatically from the received content of Faulkner and Southern literature, to resist, as it were, not only the ancestral themes but also the ancestors themselves.(16)

But the great ancestor remained, for later in the same 1951 interview Styron admitted that of all influences on his writing "Faulkner was the hardest to shake off. The early parts of my novel were so imbued with his style that I had to go back and rewrite them completely."(17) More than thirty years later Styron recalled this difficult shaking off of Faulkner: "after I had completed the first forty pages . . . there began a wrestling match between myself and my own demon--which is to say, that part of my literary consciousness which too often has let me be indolent and imitative, false to my true vision of reality, responsive to facile echoes rather than the inner voice."(18) In these two quotations, Styron confesses only part of the truth, but enough of it to manifest his struggle with the influence of Faulkner as a mediating presence, Styron not only had to re- write his own text to rid it of his precursor's influence, but, I propose, he also had to rewrite the precursor's text itself--again as a means of ridding himself of, and dividing himself from, the imposed rival. The demon of Styron's wrestling match is, of course, none other than the "facile" echo of Faulkner himself (whom, we recall, Styron called "the god and demon of all Southern writers") and the text he must rewrite is not so much his own draft of <u>Lie Down in Darkness</u> but Faulkner's completed <u>The Sound and the Fury</u>.

In his repeated wishes to be considered more than a Southern novelist, Styron embraces the anxiety suggested in Flannery O'Connor's proclama- tion that the "woods are full of regional writers, and it is the great horror of every serious Southern writer that he will become one of them."(19) Accordingly, in his first novel Styron takes on the very presence that blocks his way out of the woodsy regionalism of Southern literature; he imitates and then deviates from Faulkner's great text so as to deny the achievement that swallows all Southern writers in a "grayness of uniformity."(20) Thus, the differences between <u>Lie Down in Darkness</u> and <u>The Sound and the Fury</u> become as important, if not more so, than the similarities, and our perception of the two novels' interrelationship changes. Styron's text becomes a necessary confrontation with <u>The Sound and the Fury</u>, necessary in that Styron, echoing the expressed and repressed desires of a whole generation of Southern writers, seeks an imaginative space for himself, a space where he, and not Faulkner, lays claim as the "original."

A most illuminating example of how Styron begins to reformulate his own original space in reaction to <u>The Sound and the Fury</u> is what we can refer to as the Hiroshima backdrop. Styron's novel of the decline of a Southern family is set against the decline of the world family. There is a contemporary backdrop in <u>Lie Down in Darkness</u> that is absent in <u>The</u>

Sound and the Fury. Excluding the dates that head each chapter, and a reference to the performance of the New York Yankees in Jason's section, very little in Faulkner's novel places it in a certain time period. On the other hand, Styron constantly reminds us of the world outside of his Virginia tragedy, refusing to isolate his story from the background of world affairs and, by doing so, attempting to avoid the regionalized stereotype. Thus, whereas Faulkner's tragedy exists almost entirely within a timeless Southern cosmos, Styron's tragedy is empowered by a larger, more completed, history.

For example, in the opening pages of Lie Down in Darkness, Helen Loftis sits in her bedroom moments after learning of Peyton's suicide:

I have brought two children into life and I was a mother for
twenty-three years. This is the first day that I have awakened
knowing that I am a mother no longer and that I shall never be a
mother again. So odd of me. . . . She began to read the
newspaper. The Bomb again, a truce in the offing with the
Japanese; a picture below showed a film actress, known for her
legs, and an eminent cafe owner with a face like a mouse, wed
yesterday in Las Vegas, Nevada. Married. Unable to concentrate,
she laid the paper down. A huge emptiness began to creep over
her, so familiar a thing, this easy, physical sense of languor
and infirmity--as if everything had suddenly drained forth from
her flesh, leaving her as limp as some pale jelly that floats in
the sea.(21)

In this passage, Styron links the personal tragedy and the contemporary tragedy; he refuses to let his characters suffer in isolation, to suffer as merely Southerners in a Southern world. The Compsons suffer because of the past; the Loftises suffer as part of the present. Thus, by interjecting a contemporary backdrop, Styron completes Faulkner's "merely Southern" tragedy.

It is not surprising then to hear Styron insist on the incompleteness of the completely Southern:

the modern South is such powerful material that the author runs
the danger of capturing the local color and feeling that's enough.
He gets so bemused by decaying mansions that he forgets to
populate them with people. I'm beginning to feel that it's a
good idea for writers who come from the South, at least some
of them, to break away a little from all them magnolias.(22)

In these words we hear a desire for a more complete literature to arise out of the South. That completeness, for instance, relies on breaking away from the confines of the South. The Hiroshima backdrop achieves this. Repeatedly seen in light of a larger, more extensive tragedy, the Loftis tragedy is not merely another myth of decay among "all them magnolias." When a critic responds to Lie Down in Darkness by noting how "the social and personal are related when we remember that Peyton commits suicide the same day the U.S. bombs Japan with the atomic bomb,"(23) then Styron has achieved his purpose.

Styron seems to be "completing" his rival in yet another way. Bloom notes that anxious writers often "persuade" themselves (and us) "that the precursor's Word would be worn out if not redeemed as a newly fulfilled and enlarged Word"(24) of the next generation. In a moment of drunken philosophizing, Milton Loftis insists: "We lost our lovewords. Not the South or North, or any of those old things. 'S the U.S.A. We've gone to pot. It's a stupid war but the next one'll be stupider, and then we'll like my father said stand on the last reef of time and look up into the night and breathe the stench of the awful enfolding sound."(25) Here, through Loftis, Styron redeems Faulkner by enlarging his Word. It is not the South, "or any of those old things," which now teeters at the brink of destruction; it is the whole country. Styron is completing his precursor's Word the same way he completed his precursor's text: he is bringing Faulkner out of the magnolias and into the contemporary world, newly fulfilling Faulkner's worn out message. Styron is trying to persuade us, in more than this passage alone, that Faulkner's world and Word must be enlarged to encompass more than the South, must be rewritten to embrace more than decaying mansions. In this respect Lie Down in Darkness rewrites what it judges to be the incompleteness of The Sound and the Fury, and in doing so it attempts to diminish the oppressive power of Faulkner and his text.

Styron's confrontation with Faulkner and The Sound and the Fury is, however, more complex than merely this impulse to complete Faulkner, to fill in the imaginative spaces which Faulkner left empty or untouched. Faulkner's achievement and influence is so large, his imaginative spaces so vast, that Styron must eventually find himself confronting Faulkner on Faulkner's turf. Having completed Faulkner's text by suggesting a larger, a more contemporarily relevant backdrop in his own text, Styron still found himself, regardless of his larger intentions, writing about the South and from a Southerner's point of view. It was inevitable that Styron would discover that "the central problem for the latecomer necessarily is repetition."(26) All Southern novelists face this central problem. How does one write of the South and its people without reverting, or at least being seen as reverting, to established Faulknerian images, symbols, themes, and style? How does one avoid being trapped by such stifling prejudgments as the one Louis D. Rubin, Jr. confesses to in recalling his own first reading of Lie Down in Darkness: had "I and various other critics," Rubin asks, "reviewed William Styron's novel, or had we in effect reviewed a new novel by William Faulkner?"(27)

. . .

This necessity of repetition now explains what most critics have heretofore judged as Styron's borrowings. When Styron crafted his immediate parallels between the Compsons and the Loftises, he was not merely choosing to "borrow." He was making a movement towards repetition so that he might affirm <u>The Sound and the Fury</u>. After this affirmation, Styron then shifted his allegiance away from that text and tried to disassociate himself from Faulkner's influence. Styron's "stance <u>appears</u> to be that of his precursor . . . but the meaning of the stance is undone; the stance is <u>emptied</u> of its priority."(28)

This is exactly what <u>Lie Down in Darkness</u> tries to achieve in relation to <u>The Sound and the Fury</u>. But then the repetitions give way to discontinuities and the stance of <u>The Sound and the Fury</u> is undone. Eventually the discontinuities envelop the repetitions and <u>The Sound and the Fury</u> is emptied of its priority, its originality. Thus the "borrowings" become more important than previously acknowledged. In repeating specifics of <u>The Sound and the Fury</u>, and then twisting those repetitions into discontinuities, Styron attempts, by intimate and daring juxtaposition, to free himself of Faulkner's mediation and lay claim to his own originality.

For instance, one of the great priorities of <u>The Sound and Fury</u> is Benjy's opening narration. It is a priority in that it is a Faulkner original, a property of the precursor. As part of his poetic misprision, his sin against continuity, Styron must both repeat and discontinue this priority. Thus, we have Maudie Loftis. In many obvious ways she is a repetition of Benjy. She is the idiot child, and the youngest child, in a decaying family. Her name is akin to Benjy's original name, Maury. Her innocent love for the juggler in the woods is a repetition of Benjy's innocent love for Caddy. Only Maudie and Benjy, both incapable of physical love, are capable of achieving a love untainted by lust, guilt, fantasy, or narcissism. In these ways, and in several other ways, Maudie takes the same stance as Benjy.

However, Styron cannot leave Maudie in Benjy's stance, because to do so would be to write in continuity with Faulkner. So, where Benjy is given narration, Maudie must be silenced. The articulations of Benjy's thoughts must be undone in Maudie. We are given four points of view in <u>The Sound and the Fury</u>. In <u>Lie Down in Darkness</u> we are given four points of view in the opening chapter alone. Yet there is only one major character whose mind Styron does not enter: Maudie's. <u>The Sound and the Fury</u> begins as a tale told by an idiot. In <u>Lie Down in Darkness</u> the idiot is there; the idiot <u>must</u> be there. However, this stance must end and discontinuity with the property of Faulkner's text must begin. In discontinuing the repetition, in silencing Maudie, Styron silences Benjy's significance and empties out a portion of Faulkner's text. By closely creating a recognizably Faulknerian scenario, Styron openly invites Faulknerian comparisons, but he does so only to highlight his willingness to deviate, to manifest his desire to reformulate the tradition he inherits. Most other borrowings in Styron's novel may be read this way: Styron repeats Faulkner only so that he may deviate from him, thus isolating himself from his precursor and repressing potentially insalubrious elements of Faulkner's achievement. The goal of this imitate-only-to-deviate strategy is to be proclaimed an original in spite of the presence of Faulkner. When a critic proclaims that "Lie Down in Darkness bears Faulkner's imprint, despite Styron's deliberate effort to eliminate it . . . But Styron's novel takes on a life of its own, and its success, indeed a major element of the fictional experience, depends on Styron's movement away from Faulkner and the world view of the twenties,"(29) Styron's revisionary strategy has indeed succeeded.

Rather than cataloguing the many instances of such liberating deviations, let us look, in our final section, at the closing scene of Lie Down in Darkness--the Negro revival--which can serve as a representative example of the revisionary quality of Styron's text of repetition and discontinuity.

III

Faulkner has been both a blessing and a curse to the South--a blessing because he is probably the greatest American novelist of this century and a curse because he was so powerful and influential--that many Southern writers, younger writers who came after him, were influenced even to imitate his idiosyncrasies and his styles and his sentences.(30) (Walker Percy)

It is a general rule that novels which stay close to their literary models have no great value of their own, but Lie Down in Darkness is an exception; in this case the example of Faulkner seems to have had a liberating effect on Styron's imagination. One might even say that his book is best and most personal when it is most Faulknerian. Peyton's wanderings on the day of her suicide are much like those of Quentin Compson on his last day and some of the symbols are the same . . . Yet Styron gets inside her character, makes her more understandable and pitiable than Quentin, and it seems to me that this one passage alone, at least, is better than its model.(31)
(Malcolm Cowley)

I was very much influenced by Faulkner. However, I was aware that, unless I could shake off the obvious in the surface influence, I would be writing more or less imitation Faulkner. I struggled, and I think I've succeeded. I think that, whereas almost any fool could detect an influence of Faulkner in Lie Down in Darkness, I shook the more obvious qualities of Faulkner, and was left with a book which had its own distinctive and original stance. I don't think that the book would have succeeded had it remained heavily under the influence of Faulkner, though I'm more than happy to acknowledge his influence.(32) (William Styron)

As the culmination of Styron's revisionary intentions, the final moments of the novel must above all else be a repetition of Faulkner. Styron exhibits such culminating repetition in the fact that both novels end with Negro revivals headed by visiting Northern preachers. However, the repetition in this chapter extends beyond the surface level and into specific passages of the texts. Note the nearly exact correspondences between the postures of Ella and Dilsey, their relationship to a fading outside world, and their mysterious awareness of time:

> The bus moved on, faster now; black hands waved wildly from
> the windows, toward the sky, toward nothing, in rapture; faint
> from across the bay there was a groan of thunder as the storm
> passed out to sea. Ella sat up stiffly in her seat and rocked
> with the motion of the bus, her eyes glued together: it was as
> if she had become suddenly oblivious of the noise around her, the
> prayers and the laughter and the singing; it was an expression
> neither grieving nor devout but merely silent, profoundly aware:
> of time past and passing and time to come, a look both mysterious
> and peaceful.(33)

> As the scudding day passed overhead the dingy windows glowed and
> faded in ghostly retrograde. A car passed along the road outside,
> labouring in the sand, died away. Dilsey sat bolt upright, her hand
> on Ben's knee. Two tears slid down her fallen cheeks in and out of
> the myriad coruscations of immolation and abnegation and time.(34)

All this strong repetition, all this apparent Faulknerian posturing, makes the discontinuities even more powerful. Where Faulkner's preacher is sincere, Styron's is a charlatan. Where Faulkner's Negroes are moved, Styron's are duped. Styron's Negroes, we are initially lead to believe, are repetitions of Faulkner's heroic and enduring Negroes: we soon see, however, that they are as fully susceptible to the illusions of the modern world as their white neighbors. By making this revelation in the most Faulknerian of his numerous repetitions, Styron challenges Faulkner's text, hoping to strip it of its originality, and of the basis for its claim to be prophetic or religious in meaning. Styron's passage is most powerful when read in relation to the precursor's text, thus confronting the precursor's priority and emptying out its landscape.

I am not alone in recalling Faulkner's text during these final moments of Lie Down in Darkness. Nor am I alone in insisting that the revival serves to show how Styron differs from his precursor. In "William Styron's Southern Myth," Jane Flanders writes: "As in Faulkner, the moral decadence of whites is dramatized by their unthinking dependence on their black attendants and indifference to their humanity. But unlike Faulkner, Styron does not idealize the Negro's religious faith. While the novel's final scene--a religious revival--echoes the end of The Sound and the Fury, the effect is ironic."(35) Richard Pearce insists that the "realistic detail and

the comic irrelevancy of this scene make it a parody of the religious
resolution of <u>The Sound and the Fury</u>."(36) For Rubin, who finds fault
with Styron's treatment, the similarities also point out important differences: "Faulkner's presentation of the Negroes at church, though written
in dialect and presented in a kind of pastoral simplification, is deadly
serious. There is no ironic qualification, no element of condescension
involved [as in Styron's novel]. The variety of religion is simple, but not
ignorant."(37) In a reading that the novelist himself would certainly laud,
Marc L. Ratner affirms Styron's strategy of repetition and discontinuity as
empowering Styron with an originality which is both Faulknerian and
"sharply different from Faulkner":

> Styron presents a scene similar to Dilsey's section in Faulkner's
> <u>The Sound and the Fury</u>. He portrays Ella . . . as an enduring
> figure; but he then proceeds to demonstrate the sheer emotionalism
> of her faith. Her hysteria over Daddy Faith is ironic. Instead of
> the simple preacher of Faulkner's sermon, Daddy Faith is a
> showman, not a healer of souls . . . the dreaming mood of
> spellbound Ella--transfixed by the train in her religious ecstasy--
> gives Styron's ending a prophetic and essentially hopeless tone
> sharply different from Faulkner's note of endurance.(38)

As we can read this final scene, in its suggestive repetition and discontinuity, so too can we read the entire novel, which, because it begins in
repetition and ends in discontinuity, has us speaking of Faulkner's
influence and Styron's originality in the same breath. In a suggestively
resonant passage, Bloom employs the metaphor of night and day to
explain how an anxious writer must fight through continuity with his
precursor and into a posture of his own priority:

> Continuities start with the dawn, and no poet <u>qua</u> poet could
> afford to heed Nietzsche's great injunction: "Try to live as though
> it were morning." As poet, the ephebe must try to live as though
> it were midnight, a suspended midnight . . . The ephebe's first
> realm is ocean, or by the side of the ocean . . . What is instinctual
> in him would hold him there, but the antithetical impulse will
> bring him out and send him inland, questing for the fire of his
> own stance.(39)

If we permit ourselves to meditate on this metaphor, we note how Styron's
novel begins at dawn, by the water, and in a land that is a repetition of
Faulkner's South. Styron's Virginia Negro at the side of the tracks
corresponds to Faulkner's Virginia Negro at the side of the tracks in
Quentin's section. Both Negroes represent moments of homecoming:

> Now the sun is up and you can see the mist lifting off the fields
> and in the middle of the fields the solitary cabins with their slim
> threads of smoke unwinding out of plastered chimneys and the faint
> glint of fire through an open door and, at a crossing, the sudden,
> swift tableau of a Negro and his hay-wagon and a lopeared mule:

the Negro with his mouth agape, exposing pink gums, staring at
the speeding train until the smoke obscures him, too, from view,
and the one dark-brown hand held cataleptic in the air.(40)

I didn't know that I had really missed Roskus and Dilsey and them
until that morning in Virginia. The train was stopped when I waked
and I raised the shade and looked out. The car was blocking a road
crossing . . . and there was a nigger on a mule in the middle of
the stiff ruts, waiting for the train to move. How long he had been
there I didn't know, but he sat straddle of the mule, his head
wrapped in a piece of blanket, as if they had been built there with
the fence and the road, or with the hill, carved out of the hill
itself, like a sign put there saying You are home again.(41)

Thus, Styron's novel begins in a repetition of the Faulknerian South;
however, like the train that speeds by the Negro and leaves him obscured
in its smoke, Styron must move out of the dawn and into a suspended
midnight, where the influence of Faulkner is obscured in the smoke of
Styron's new achievement.

The concluding sentence of Lie Down in Darkness, resounding like a
Faulknerian apotheosis, culminates this metaphor.

Another blast from the whistle, a roar, a gigantic sound; and it
seemed to soar into the dusk beyond and above them forever, with a
noise perhaps, like the clatter of the opening of everlasting gates
and doors--passed swiftly on--toward Richmond, the North, the
oncoming night.(42)

Just as this train, which earlier in the day had ridden into the South, now
blasts out of the South, so too does Styron, who earlier in the text rides
into the landscape and property of Faulkner, now blasts out of that
priority. We can read the final triptych as Styron's vision of his own
poetic aspirations. To achieve his own fiery stance Styron must, like the
train, ride through the heart of his region (Richmond), break out of the
bounds of his region (into the North), and ride on into the realm of his
own suspended midnight (the oncoming night).

In a 1974 interview, Styron insisted that "You cannot become a writer
without falling under influences and being affected by them, in order to
create a universe in your image. The shadow of Faulkner glides over my
first works, but no responsible critic can say that I am a disciple of
Faulkner. I am my own master."(43) In his first novel, Styron begins his
career-long struggle with the gliding shadow of his poetic father, thus
initiating a courageous and salubrious Oedipal confrontation in which the
son achieves, via revisionary repetition and discontinuity, his own originality, his own universe. Thus, what Shaun O'Connell claims for the novel
we can now in turn claim for Styron himself: "the real theme of Lie Down
in Darkness [is] not lost-childhood, not simply lost-beauty, but the

incorrigible human impulse to renew and redeem oneself, to father oneself anew."(44)

But rather than speaking for the novel one last time, we should allow the novel to speak for itself. Recall that the boldest assertion of Bloom's revisionary poetics is that the final achievement of the strong poet is to complete his desire to defeat his old father and create his own, new father. Styron expresses paradoxically destructive and regenerative desire throughout his text, but nowhere more poetically and more assertively than in Peyton's monologue, in a passage that serves both as a confession of Styron's revisionary intentions and as a courageous proclamation of his sinful rebellion from Faulkner's mediating rivalry:

> not out of vengeance have I accomplished all my sins but because something has always been close to dying in my soul, and I've sinned only in order to lie down darkness and find, somewhere in the net of my dreams, a new father, a new home.(45)

Notes

(1) Flannery O'Connor, "The Grotesque in Southern Fiction," in Mystery and Manners, ed. Sally and Robert Fitzgerald (New York: Farrar, Strauss, and Giroux, 1969), p. 45.

(2) Stephen Goodwin, "An Interview with Peter Taylor," in Conversations with Peter Taylor, ed. Hubert H. McAlexander (Jackson: University Press of Mississippi, 1987), p. 8.

(3) Thomas Daniel Young, "A Second Generation of Novelists," in The History of Southern Fiction, ed. Louis D. Rubin, Jr. (Baton Rouge: Louisiana State University Press, 1985), pp. 466-67.

(4) Harold Bloom. The Anxiety of Influence: A Theory of Poetry (New York: Oxford University Press, 1973), p. 10.

(5) Robert Gorham Davis, "A Grasp of Moral Realities," American Scholar 21 (Winter 1951): 116.

(6) Malcolm Cowley, "The Faulknerian Pattern," New Republic, 8 October 1951, p. 19.

(7) Louis D. Rubin, Jr. gives us the most extensive comparison of the two novels in "William Styron: Notes on a Southern Writer in Our Time," in The Faraway Country: Writers of the Modern South (Seattle: University of Washington Press, 1963), pp. 185-230. Rubin's agenda is "to compare the manner in which [The Sound and the Fury] realizes its tragic potentialities with the way in which Styron's novel does." Rubin sees only a "surface similarity," for upon "closer examination Styron turns out to have a significantly different attitude toward many things." Rubin's final conclusion is that we forced Styron and his novel to be "Southern" because we wanted an "assurance that the kind of contribution Faulkner, Wolfe, Warren, and Welty, and others had been making to American fiction for two decades and more was not going to dwindle and die, but

could flourish for another literary generation." My reading of the two novels takes a markedly different comparative approach. Of the many interpretations of Lie Down in Darkness, Frederick Karl's brief but unexplored comment in Modern Fictions 1940-1980: A Comprehensive History and Critical Evaluation (New York: Harper and Row, 1983) comes closest to my argument: "Another view of Styron's career is this: that each novel, located almost a decade apart, was preparation for a succeeding effort in which he would break free of something. We can perceive Lie Down in Darkness as purging Faulkner; Set This House on Fire as exorcising elements of personal guilt; The Confessions of Nat Turner as coming to terms, Styron's own intimate terms, with black/white relationships by way of the legendary rebellious slave; and finally, Sophie's Choice as Styron's apotheosis of his freedom: his choice as embedded in Sophie's" (p. 236).

(8) Melvin J. Friedman, William Styron (Bowling Green: Bowling Green University Popular Press, 1974), p. 3.

(9) J.D. Scott, review of Lie Down in Darkness by William Styron, New Statesman and Nation, 19 April, 1952, 473.

(10) J. William Broadway, "A Conversation with Peter Taylor," in Conversations with Peter Taylor, p. 82.

(11) William Kaufman, "A Conversation with Reynolds Price," Shenandoah 17 (Spring 1966): 8-9.

(12) Rene Girard, Deceit, Desire, and the Novel: Self and Other in Literary Structure, trans. Yvonne Freccero (Baltimore: Johns Hopkins Press, 1965), p. 11.

(13) Cleanth Brooks, "William Faulkner," in The History of Southern Literature, p. 432.

(14) William Styron, "Lie Down in Darkness" in This Quiet Dust and Other Writings (New York: Random House, 1982), pp. 291-92.

(15) David Dempsey, "A Talk with William Styron," New York Times Book Review, 9 September 1951, p. 27.

(16) As this paper will later bear out, Styron's revisionism was not merely a rejection of his influences. Styron's encounter with the Southern literary tradition was a complex response, filled with moments of both rejection and embrasure. In a 1977 interview with Michael West, Stryon "confessed" to his borrowings from another literary giant of the Southern renascence, Robert Penn Warren. (See Michael West, "An Interview with William Styron," in Conversations with William Styron, ed. James L.W. West III [Jackson: Univ. of Mississippi Press, 1985] p. 221). In the following exchange note how Styron insists that his borrowing from a precursor was not merely imitation but a "touchstone" upon which to shape his own original stance.

West: There is one thing I wanted to ask about Lie Down in Darkness. The opening section, which serves to bring the reader rather rapidly into the atmosphere of Tidewater, uses as a vehicle a train ride down to the town of Port Warwick. The peculiar thing about that section is that it is addressed to the reader. But instead of "Dear Reader," it's "You." How did you decide upon using that second-person technique?

Styron: Well, I'll tell you. I confessed it to the man who influenced me, so I might as well confess it to you. It was a direct steal from All the King's Men, the beginning of All the King's Men, which also uses that "you," the second-person technique, to get the book going. Look back at it some time and you'll see, only it's set in Louisiana, in a car going to Willie Stark's home somewhere in the red clay country of Louisiana. Now, if mine had been mere imitation, everybody would have noticed it in two seconds. But it wasn't an imitation. It was my taking what Red Warren had done, mainly the use of that "you," and taking his keen observation of what Louisiana was in his time and bringing it to ride, that same kind of--not the rhythm even, but just the resonance, the touchstone. So I created something quite original by using this wayback as a model.

(17) Dempsey, "A Talk with William Styron," p. 27. For another interesting perspective on Styron's anxiety over Faulkner's presence in his first novel, see Styron's short story "Marriott, the Marine," Esquire, September 1971, pp. 101ff.   The narrator, an ex-Marine and WWII veteran, has been recently recalled for military duty in the Spring of 1951 (much like Styron was). The narrator tells us that he "had also written a first novel, which was about to be published." This novel, which the narrator refers to as "my Southern Gothic Romance," is read by the company Colonel, a man of refined literary tastes. The following exchange occurs: "The subject of literary influences came up and when I admitted, a bit awkwardly, that I feared that my work still betrayed rhythms and echoes of my predecessors--mainly Faulkner and Fitzgerald--he looked amused and said: 'Oh hell, I wouldn't worry about that. It's impossible to be one-hundred-percent original. A writer has to be influenced by someone. Where would Faulkner be without Joyce, after all?'"

(18) William Styron, "Lie Down in Darkness," p. 292.

(19) Flannery O'Connor, "The Fiction Writer and his Country," in Mystery and Manners, p. 29.

(20) Bloom, The Anxiety of Influence, p. 39.

(21) William Styron, Lie Down in Darkness (New York: The Modern Library, 1951), p. 24.

(22) Peter Matthiessen and George Plimpton, "The Art of Fiction V: William Styron," Paris Review, no. 5 (Spring 1954): 48-49.

(23) Shaun O'Connell, "Expense of Spirit: the Vision of William Styron," Critique: Studies in Modern Fiction 8 (Winter 1965-66): 22.

(24) Bloom, The Anxiety of Influence, p. 67.

(25) Styron, Lie Down in Darkness, pp. 185-86.

(26) Bloom, The Anxiety of Influence, p. 80.

(27) Rubin, "William Styron: Notes on a Southern Writer in Our Time," p. 198.

(28) Bloom, The Anxiety of Influence, p. 90.

(29) Richard Pearce, William Styron (Minneapolis: University of Minnesota Press, 1971), p. 11.

(30) William Buckley, Jr., "'The Southern Imagination': An Interview with Eudora Welty and Walker Percy," in Conversations with Eudora Welty, ed. Peggy Whitman Prenshaw (Jackson: University Press of Mississippi, 1984), p. 112.

(31) Cowley, "The Faulkner Pattern," p. 20.

(32) Jack Griffin, Jerry Homsy, and Gene Stelzig, "A Conversation with William Styron," in Conversations with William Styron, pp. 54-55.

(33) Styron, Lie Down in Darkness, pp. 391-92.

(34) William Faulkner, The Sound and the Fury (New York: Random House, 1956), p. 368.

(35) Jane Flanders, "William Styron's Southern Myth," in The Achievement of William Styron, revised edition, ed. Robert K. Morris with Irving Malin (Athens: University of Georgia Press, 1981), p. 111.

(36) Pearce, William Styron, p. 19.

(37) Rubin, "William Styron: Notes on a Southern Writer in Our Time," pp. 205-06.

(38) Marc L. Ratner, William Styron (New York: Twayne, 1972), p. 52.

(39) Bloom, The Anxiety of Influence, p. 79.

(40) Styron, Lie Down in Darkness, p. 10.

(41) Faulkner, The Sound and the Fury. p. 106.

(42) Styron, Lie Down in Darkness, p, 400.

(43) Pierre Dommergues, "William Styron A Paris," Le Monde, 26 April 1974, 19. Quoted in Judith Ruderman, William Styron (New York: Ungar, 1987), pp. 127-28.

(44) O'Connell, "Expense of Spirit: The Vision of William Styron," p. 25.

(45) Styron, Lie Down in Darkness, p. 379.

*From Studies in the Novel 22 (1990): 308-22.

DARKNESS VISIBLE AND INVISIBLE: THE LANDSCAPE OF DEPRESSION IN LIE DOWN IN DARKNESS*

Jeffrey Berman

> "'I'm sick, I said, 'un probleme psychiatrique'"
> Darkness Visible (1)

Darkness Visible (1990), William Styron's extraordinary account of his descent into mental illness, chronicles the development of his depression from its origins in October 1985 to its near-fatal conclusion in December, when the novelist narrowly rejected suicide, hospitalized himself, and initiated the healing process. Styron tells us in the Author's Note that the book originated as a lecture given at a 1989 symposium on affective disorders sponsored by the Department of Psychiatry of the Johns Hopkins University School of Medicine. Like A. Alvarez's The Savage God (1972)(2), Darkness Visible situates the writer's suicide attempt in the larger context of the numerous nineteenth-and twentieth-century artists who have taken their lives. Styron explores the personal, psychological, and literary implications of depression, a mysterious disease that has "yielded its secrets to science far more reluctantly than many of the other major ills besetting us" (p. 11).

The difficulty of writing about depression, Styron notes at the beginning of Darkness Visible, is that it remains "nearly incomprehensible to those who have not experienced it in its extreme mode . . . (p. 7). He returns to this theme at the end of the book, observing that to those who have endured it, "the horror of depression is so overwhelming as to be quite beyond expression, hence the frustrated sense of inadequacy found in the work of even the greatest artists" (p. 83). Styron's brilliance as a writer enables him to describe the indescribable feelings of madness to which he almost succumbed in late 1985: the gloom slowly closing in on him, the growing dread and alienation, the indefinable anxiety that seized hold of him. He singles out, among the most debilitating symptoms of depression, "confusion, failure of mental focus and lapse of memory" (p. 14). At a later stage of the illness his mind was dominated by "anarchic disconnections." There was also a bifurcation of mood: "lucidity of sorts in the early hours of the day, gathering murk in the afternoon and evening" (pp. 14-15). He likens the pain to drowning and suffocation, metaphors also used by Sylvia Plath to describe the suicidal depression in The Bell Jar. Like Plath and others who have written autobiographically or semi-autobigraphically about depression, Styron identifies a "sense of self-hatred--or, put less categorically, a failure of self-esteem" (p. 5) as one of the worst manifestations of the illness. The self-loathing became so virulent that he lost the ability to write, concluding that he was not worthy of receiving the Prix Mondial Cino del Duca, the prestigious French award, given annually to an outstanding humanistic scientist or artist, which had been bestowed upon him when the paralyzing illness struck.

Styron records the other symptoms of depression eroding his will to live: a growing hypochondria, including "twitches and pains, sometimes intermittent, often seemingly constant, that seemed to presage all sorts of dire infirmities" (pp. 43-44); exhaustion combined with sleeplessness, producing a "rare torture" (p. 48); the loss of libido and an indifference to food; and a growing obsession with suicide, to the point where he felt compelled to revise his will and pen a farewell note--a task the novelist was unable to execute. "It turned out that putting together a suicide note, which I felt obsessed with a necessity to compose, was the most difficult task of writing that I had ever tackled" (p. 65). He finally had to abandon the effort because he was unable to reconcile the intention to maintain the "sheer dirge-like solemnity" of the suicide letter with the melodramatic words he heard himself contrive. He also describes a phenomenon experienced by other people suffering from severe depression, the "sense of being accompanied by a second self--a wraithlike observer who, not sharing the dementia of his double, is able to watch with dispassionate curiosity as his companion struggles against the oncoming disaster, or decides to embrace it" (p. 64).

The depression which struck Styron when he turned sixty was not of the manic type, associated with euphoric highs, but of the unipolar form, leading straight down into an abyss. The two physical factors that contributed most to the onset of the illness were fits of anxiety resulting from his body's sudden intolerance to alcohol, a substance he had been abusing for forty years, and a dangerous dependency upon a drug named Halcion, a tranquilizer prescribed to him for insomnia by a physician who was unaware that it could precipitate a major depression, especially in the heavy dosages he recommended. Styron has few good words for the psychiatrists who treated him before and during his six-week stay at Yale-New Haven hospital. The physician he sardonically calls "Dr. Gold" spoke with the dry platitudes of the <u>Diagnostic and Statistical Manual of Mental Disorders,</u> the psychiatric reference work that Styron himself read, during the early stages of the illness, in an unsuccessful effort to cure himself. Dr. Gold prescribed depressants that did nothing to lessen Styron's pain. When the illness progressed to the point where the novelist feared committing suicide, the psychiatrist remained reluctant to hospitalize him because of the "stigma" involved--an attitude that Styron finds appalling. In the hospital he encountered an odiously smug young shrink, with a spade-shaped dark beard (<u>der junge</u> Freud?)" (p. 73), who used group therapy to belittle and bully his helpless patients. None of this speaks well for psychiatrists who, in Styron's view, rarely empathize with a mentally ill person. Conceding that pharmacology and psychoanalysis can help many patients, Styron observes that, for reasons still unclear to him, neither therapy was able to arrest his plunge toward the depths. The real healers for him were the hospital environment--with its enforced safety, solitude, and stability--and time.

Despite the effort to understand the origins of his depression, Styron insists that the illness can never be understood, neither his nor anyone else's. "I shall never learn what 'caused' my depression, as no one will ever learn about their own" (p. 38). Acknowledging that there were probably multiple causes, he singles out one psychological factor that may inhere in all cases of depression, namely, loss, particularly if it leads to incomplete mourning. In Styron's case, childhood loss led to a more massive loss of self in later life, resulting in dependency, infantile dread, and fear of abandonment. He tersely mentions two crucial childhood losses in his own life: the early hospitalization of his father, who battled the gorgon of depression for much of his life; and the death of his mother when he was thirteen, an event with which he had never come to terms.

An "autodidact in medicine" for much of his life, Styron was surprised to learn, upon falling ill, that he was "close to a total ignoramus about depression"--despite the later realization that he was probably always an "incipient depressive" (p. 9). "Until the onslaught of my own illness and its denouement, I never gave much thought to my work in terms of its connection with the subconscious--an area of investigation belonging to literary detectives" (p. 78). After recovering from his illness, he was astonished that his novels had long foreshadowed his suicidal obsession:

Suicide has been a persistent theme in my books--
three of my major characters killed themselves. In
rereading, for the first time in years, sequences
from my novels--passages where my heroines have
lurched down pathways toward doom--I was stunned to
perceive how accurately I had created a landscape of
depression in the minds of these young women, describing
with what could only be instinct, out of a subconscious
already roiled by disturbances of mood, the psychic

imbalance that led them to destruction. (pp. 78-79)

The landscape of depression can be seen in Styron's earliest novel, Lie Down in Darkness, published in 1951. Reading the novel in the light of Darkness Visible, one is struck by the extent to which Styron's fictional characters anticipate the symptoms of clinical depression that he himself writes about nearly four decades later in his memoir of madness: gloom, dread, alienation, and anxiety; confusion, panic, memory loss and anarchic disconnections; feelings of worthlessness and self-hatred; sleeplessness, fatigue, dependency upon alcohol and drugs, and hypochondria. Characters are driven in despair to physicians and analysts who, instead of offering insight and compassion, serve up maddening platitudes and glib diagnoses. Before the novel's heroine jumps to her death from the twelfth story of a Harlem building, she is oppressed by the same feelings of self-loathing, dependency, and abandonment that Styron writes about in Darkness Visible; dwells morbidly upon all the losses in her life; describes the torment of mental illness in ways that are most closely connected to drowning and suffocation; and, perhaps most striking of all, experiences in the final hours of her life the same wraithlike observer that her creator personally experienced thirty-five years later. Although the landscape of depression in Lie Down in Darkness does not prefigure the psychic scenery of Darkness Visible in every detail, the similarities are uncanny.

II

"It's somehow Freudian, he says"
Lie Down in Darkness(3)

Lie Down in Darkness chronicles an American family's inexorable drift toward madness and self-destruction. Milton Loftis is a Virginia attorney in his fifties who is devastated by the suicide of his beloved daughter Peyton. His wife Helen is a nervous, strait-laced woman whose frail health collapses as a result of the earlier death of her older daughter Maudie, born with severe physical and mental disabilities. Maudie's death deepens Helen's bitterness toward life, producing a black depression from which she never recovers. Nor does Loftis psychically recover from Peyton's death. While neither Loftis, Helen, nor Peyton bears a precise resemblance to the portrait of clinical depression Styron presents in Darkness Visible, they experience collectively nearly all the characteristics of their creator's mind-numbing descent into sorrow and madness.

Lie Down in Darkness begins in August, 1945, immediately after the atomic bombing of Hiroshima, but for Milton Loftis a more catastrophic event has just occurred. The novel opens with a train carrying Peyton's coffin home to Port Warwick, Virginia, where the estranged father and mother await its arrival. Juxtaposing past and present, Styron uses flashbacks, interior monologues, and, in Peyton's final fifty-page section, first-person stream of consciousness prose to illuminate the family tragedy. Loftis cannot defend himself against the "bewildering sorrow" of Peyton's loss. "Yesterday he had been happy, but this sorrow--descending upon him as it had the night before--seemed to have confounded him beyond all hope, since, for the first time in his life, he was unable to cut his trouble adrift, to shed it like some startling and unwelcome chrysalis, and finally to explain it away as 'one of those things'" (p. 10). Styron emphasizes the numbing, paralyzing, bewildering nature of sorrow: it is not a passive but an active adversary, a force that seizes control of body and spirit and overpowers the will to live.

Although he does not seem to be constitutionally predisposed to mental illness, as Helen is, Loftis finds himself confronting depression whenever he dwells upon the losses in his life, particularly the death of his mother during early childhood and, of course, Peyton's suicide. Significantly, even before Peyton's death Loftis dwells morbidly upon loss. He recalls the "fog of hostility" hanging over the entire family during the Christmas dinner the year Peyton was eighteen, and this memory evokes earlier holiday celebrations that were similarly grim. "A terrible melancholy seized him; his mind trembled upon loss, upon the sounds of ancient forgotten Christmases . . . " (p. 159). The novel never clarifies these memories, which remain as mysterious and unsettling to us as they do to Loftis. In Styron's world, memory serves mainly as a brooding reminder of loss, and there is danger when his characters meditate on the past. Later, on Peyton's wedding day, Loftis feels "unbelievably depressed and neurotic" (p. 257), yet he cannot explain why he feels this way. He knows only that the "unbearable depression" is destroying his life.

Helen Loftis' struggle against depression begins long before the deaths of her two children--her adored Maudie, whom she has always favored and fiercely protected, and Peyton, with whom she has fought bitterly her entire life. Even when the family is intact Helen is a "hurt" and "neurotic" woman, qualities that seem to increase her husband's attraction to her. Loftis finds "something still imposingly youthful about her in spite of everything--the complaints, the headaches, the moments of eerie and popeyed hysteria . . ." (p. 88). Helen's psychological conflicts take the form of physical complaints, and she becomes as dependent upon sleeping pills as her husband is on alcohol. In her bitterness toward those whom she views as betraying her, she becomes, in the words of one character, a "nest of little hatreds" (p. 105). Not that Helen lacks reasons to be disappointed with life. Her husband's womanizing and alcoholism distress her, as does his capacity for self-indulgence and rationalization; Maudie's disabilities fill Helen with sorrow and guilt; and Peyton's intimacy with her father fuels Helen's jealousy and anger.

Helen's only passion in life is Maudie, who remains childlike and compliant until her death at the age of twenty from military tuberculosis. By favoring Maudie over Peyton, Helen reveals her preference for dependence over independence, compliance over rebellion, control over freedom. In contrast to the saintly Maudie, who resembles the severely retarded Benjy in William Faulkner's The Sound and the Fury, Peyton is self-centered, willful, solipsistic. Peyton is not, however, the "little devil!" (p. 58) that her mother viciously calls her. Helen's criticisms of Peyton are unrelenting. She cannot forgive Peyton for dropping Maudie as a child, even though Maudie herself does not hold her sister responsible, and despite the absence of clear evidence that Peyton intended the accident. Throughout the novel Peyton remains the target for her mother's pent-up anger, anger that prevents the mother from ever really loving her daughter.

"God help me please, I'm going crazy" (p. 124), the panic-stricken Helen thinks to herself after Maudie's fall, acknowledging for the first time her fear of madness. She momentarily considers swallowing ten or fifteen pills of nembutal but rejects the idea as hateful. "[T]he whole idea of insanity was forgotten as too difficult and too gross a thing to contemplate for more than an instant" (p. 124). Helen's mental health continues to deteriorate, producing a cancerous religiosity that sees sin and damnation everywhere. Maudie's death shatters Helen's life, resulting in loss of religious faith and deepening religious faith and deepening hatred toward Peyton. Sinking into suicidal despair, she swallows an overdose of pills, her last thought before drifting into unconsciousness is a mysterious, whispered apology to her father, a West Point officer who had died years ago. Loftis saves Helen from death but cannot rescue her from the wild paranoia engulfing her life. Her dreams become "crowded with enemies, dreams bizarre and frantic, villainous beyond men's wildest imaginings" (p. 283). The most striking symptom of Helen's paranoia is the split between her overidealization of Maudie and her virulent devaluation of Peyton; she elevates the former into an angel and casts off the latter as a devil. The split between over-idealization and devaluation suggests Helen's inability to integrate love and hate, her failure to acknowledge the massive ambivalence she feels toward her family. Her condemnation of Peyton is in excess of anything her daughter deserves, and the accusation that Peyton has "half-killed her own sister through negligence--did kill her in fact, she let Maudie fall!" (p. 286) reveals the irrationality of Helen's thoughts. In their last exchange, Peyton expresses to her mother what is surely the authorial point of view: "You know, I suspect you've always hated me for one thing or another, but lately I've become a symbol to you you couldn't stand," adding, "the terrible thing is that you hate yourself so much that you just don't hate men or Daddy but you hate everything, animal, vegetable and mineral" (pp. 297-298).

In her efforts to find peace with herself, Helen visits Carey Carr, her episcopal minister. As she unburdens herself to him, he recognizes that she is consumed by hatred and guilt. He tells her, significantly, that she has a low opinion of herself and points out that she must love herself before she can love other people. He also suspects that Helen's obsession with evil is the result of infantile emotions rigidly repressed. Priding himself on his intuitive understanding of psychology and his advocacy of free inquiry, he scorns less liberal American religious movements because of their tendency to invoke the devil as scapegoat for disowned sexual and aggressive drives. He welcomes the opportunity to counsel Helen, flattered by her willingness to allow him to be her minister and analyst. Like an analyst, he encourages Helen to share her feelings with him, repeats her statements back to her, and reassures her that everyone has shameful thoughts.

As Helen's visits increase, however, Carey becomes annoyed by her growing dependency upon him, and his tangled erotic feelings toward her prevent him from maintaining the healthy professional distance necessary for a minister or an analyst. His ignorance of clinical concepts of transference and countertransference--the phenomena in which patients and analysts, respectively, project unconscious feelings onto each other--makes him an ineffective counselor. His hostility toward psychiatry also emerges. "He thought that he was enlightened, and he wanted to be, but this business of psychology and such matters was to him maddening and strange: that so potentially strong an ally should still possess no real Godhead and be so indecently inquisitive and expensive, and have no respect for the tender and infinite mutations of the heart" (p. 135). His depression over Peyton's suicide momentarily shatters his faith, almost resulting in apostasy. Two years earlier, during Peyton's wedding, Carey is so unnerved by Helen's paranoid actions that he loses patience with her, exclaiming in exasperation, "I think you're a sick woman. I don't know whether it's proper to call a spade a spade in such a case, but you asked me. There's something wrong with you beyond curing, beyond anything I can do, anyway" (p. 281). He thus implicitly acknowledges his failure as Helen's minister and analyst.

Carey Carr is one of many Styron characters who attempts to cure or heal an individual in distress, to no avail. Not only do these ministers, physicians, or therapists fail, but their motives are suspect: they are naive, insincere, glib, pietistic. Sometimes they are driven to cure others in an effort to cure themselves, a motive that Styron finds particularly suspect in Lie Down in Darkness. As a youth, for example, Carey was overly sensitive and unsure of his masculinity, and exhausted himself by writing hundreds of sonnets that he knew were miserably bad. When he suffered a nervous breakdown, his mother hurried him to a sanitarium. Upon her prompting, he later entered a seminary and emerged a changed man: "He had put on thirty pounds and through a violent struggle had learned how to swim and play softball, and had in general cast out his womanish failings . . ." (p. 100). His passion to save Helen from religious despair derives as much from his own incomplete relationship to God, and from unanalyzed egotism and eroticism, as from the need to offer a helping hand. Thus he is disappointed that Helen's temporary recovery after

Maudie's death was due to Loftis' decision to abstain from drinking rather than to his own powers of religious salvation. Unable finally to understand or empathize with Helen, Carey Carr is one of many members of the helping professions whom Styron undercuts in the novel. Loftis, too, fails in his efforts to "cure" Helen, to "make her well" (p. 97), and Styron demonstrates repeatedly that real cure or recovery can come only from within, not from without.

Like her mother, Peyton Loftis proves to be beyond cure or redemption. The two-page suicide letter she writes to her father on her twenty-second birthday gives us a few clues into her state of mind. Beginning the letter "Dearest Bunny," a name, we later find out, that her great-grandmother used to call him, Peyton tells her father how much she misses him now that she is living in New York City and estranged from her husband, Harry Miller. "After you've lived with someone for a time it leaves a huge gap in your life when they're gone . . ." (p. 34). She recounts to Loftis her growing sleeplessness and morbid thoughts.

They've just started lately it seems. I've had these moments
before, but never for so long--and they're terrible. The
trouble is that they don't--these thoughts--seem to have any
distinctness or real point of reference. It's more like some
sort of black, terrible mistiness like the beginning of a disease,
the way you know you feel when you're catching the flu. (p. 35)

Although Peyton compares her illness to a physical disease, her language, both here and in the convoluted stream of consciousness interior mono-logue at the end of the novel, evokes a symptomatology startlingly similar to Styron's description of clinical depression in Darkness Visible: sleep-lessness, loss of mental clarity, panic and, most striking of all, a sense of drowning. "I feel adrift, as if I were drowning out in dark space some-where without anything to pull me back to earth again. You'd think that feeling would be nice--drowning like that--but it isn't. It's terrible" (p. 35). In the same letter she refers to the "absolute panic" upon seeing her husband and the feeling that "something terrible is happening to me" (p. 36). The letter reveals Peyton's other preoccupations that become more evident later in the novel: an enigmatic reference to an alarm clock she has bought recently, a symbol of her desperate need for order, unity, and perfection: the belief that she has been unkind to the people in her life, whom she fears have now abandoned her; and her growing obsession with death. "I think of Maudie. Why did she have to die? Why do men have to die?" (p. 36). The letter continues but Loftis can read no more of it because "it all became so crazy and confused" (p. 36).

Until Peyton's final monologue, we see only isolated glimpses of her, often from her father's point of view as he agonizes over her death. One of Loftis's earliest recollections is hearing a small voice announce passionately on a dewy spring morning, "Daddy, Daddy, I'm beautiful!" He stares at his nine-year-old daughter who is standing in the grass, gazing into a little mirror and exclaiming: "I'm beautiful, Daddy!" He picks up the budding Narcissus and, "with a sudden, almost savage upwelling of love," presses her against him and murmurs, in a voice choked with desire: "'Yes, my baby's beautiful,' with wonder and vague embarrassment paying homage to this beautiful part of him, in which life would continue limitlessly" (p. 42). Loftis recalls another incident, one Christmas morning nine years later, when he tiptoes into the room where Peyton is sleeping, rouses her with a kiss, spanks her across the bottom and asks: "Who do you love?"--to which she replies, "Me" (p. 155).

In pursuing Styron's suggestion in Darkness Visible that depression usually originates from childhood loss, we are led to contemplate Peyton's own childhood, where we encounter severe Oedipal and pre-Oedipal conflicts. Lie Down in Darkness contains one of the most striking Oedipal father-daughter relationships in twentieth-century American fiction. Not only does Loftis love Peyton more than anyone else in his life, he is always kissing, fondling, or gazing at her as if she were a lover instead of a daughter. Judging from the way he embraces Peyton on her wedding day, one might conclude that he is the aroused groom:

> He shoved the book away and swept her up toward him,
> laughing, kissing her helplessly. She lay tender and
> unresisting against his shoulder; he breathed the perfume
> in her hair, and was stricken by beauty at the sight of a
> gardenia pinned there, nestling just beneath his left eye.
> "Bunny," she said finally, pushing away from him, "you
> are such a demonstrative old bum. Come on, quit it now.
> I've got lipstick on your neck." (p. 249)

Peyton's response to her father's overwhelming desire for her is ambiguous. At times, as in the above passage, she is embarrassed by her father's advances and pushes him away. It is harder for her to separate herself from him when he is drinking, when his lust for her becomes almost uncontrollable. After the wedding is over and Peyton prepares to leave with her husband for New York City, Loftis, driven by mad desire and sodden despair, makes one last effort to cling to her. "He bent down to kiss her. She didn't move when he kissed her cheek, her ear, her hair. He kissed her on the mouth. 'Don't--' she whispered, pushing him away" (p. 299). At other times, Peyton encourages her father's erotic advances in order to manipulate him into giving in to her wishes, as when she succeeds in getting him to buy her a car on her sixteenth birthday. "'Come on, honey, buy me a car.' She pressed a big smear of lipstick on his neck" (p. 90). He himself believes that it was "unfair of Peyton to seduce him" (p. 252) into giving her, on her wedding day, a half-pint of whisky he had secretly stored in a cough-syrup bottle sometime after Maudie's death eight months before, when he decided to give up drinking. Unable to resist Peyton's request for whisky, he begins drinking again at the wedding--with disastrous results, since his body has grown intolerant to alcohol.

During the wedding ceremony, Loftis cannot take his eyes off his daughter's body. "Peyton's dress was drawn tightly against her hips; he could see them, the two crescent shadows that a tight girdle makes when you look at a woman's behind, joining above like a curved Dutch roof: it was too obvious, or something; she should have dressed more demurely" (p. 257). The more the father pursues her, the more the daughter recoils. "Please don't smother me," she tells him crossly, just don't smother me, Bunny!", adding: "You'd love me half to death if you could" (pp. 254-55). Helen overhears Peyton's rebuke of Loftis and, in a fit of insane jealousy and rage, ironically accuses her of being a "shameless little seducer" (p. 286).

Threatened by Peyton's beauty, youth, and intimacy with her father, Helen has long seen her daughter as a seductress; yet Helen is blind to her husband's aggressive pursuit of Peyton. The father's incestuous attraction to his daughter is hinted at earlier in the story when Loftis, in response to Peyton's being "pinned" to Dick Cartwright, gives her his University of Virginia ring, as if he were the betrothed. "Look at Daddy, I love him so," Peyton later tells her ex-boyfriend. "'But he lost me and he doesn't even know it.' She took the ring out of her pocket and looked down at it. 'The dear. I think we've got a Freudian attachment'" (p. 224). Loftis has invoked the same psychoanalytic theory to explain the intense family dynamics; earlier in the novel, his mistress Dolly Bonner ruminates over the family tragedy and recalls something he once told her:"It's somehow Freudian, he says" (p. 71).

It is impossible to know precisely whether Loftis and Peyton have actually committed incest together and, if so, the circumstances.(4) There are moments in the novel when both characters brood darkly over a distant memory involving the other, the language intimating each time an erotic encounter. At one point Loftis recalls walking one summer day with his young daughter to a church, where they climb the creaking stairs and stand at the belfry door. Suddenly the church bells begin to chime, deafening them, and the frightened Peyton bursts into tears and clings to her father. The intensity of his desire for her, as the following passage suggests, would hardly be reassuring to a young girl:

> He smooths dust from her skirt, saying, "Peyton, don't be
> scared," and then kisses her. The weeping stops. Beneath
> his cheek he can feel cool, tiny beads of sweat on her brow.
>
> He doesn't know why his heart pounds so nor, when he kisses
> her again, in an agony of love, why she should him him so
> violently away with her warm small hands. (p. 277)

In an even murkier passage describing Peyton's wedding, Loftis, gazing at his daughter's body, closes his eyes and begins to recall an ancient memory so horrifying in its animality that he is forced to break off the thought and return to a safer object of lust, his mistress Dolly:

> He let his eyes close, began to perspire, and thought of the

blessed release whisky might give. Yet it was only this; his
eyelids slid open, he saw Peyton, those solid curved hips
trembling ever so faintly; he thought desperately, hopelessly
of something he could not admit to himself, but did; of
now being above--most animal and horrid, but loving--
someone young and dear that he had loved ever since he
was child enough to love the face of woman and the flesh,
too. Yes, dear God, he thought (and) he thought dear
God, what am I thinking?) the flesh, too, the wet hot
flesh, straining like a beautiful, bloody savage. He thought
vaguely of Dolly, wondering why she was not here. (p. 258)

Whatever the meaning of this passage, Loftis is consumed by dark
desire for his daughter, and she, too, is tormented by an ancient memory
involving her father. Toward the end of her monologue she recalls a fierce
battle with her husband over her repeated sexual infidelities with men
whom she meets on the street. As she tries to tell Harry that she has
derived no joy from the sordid affairs which bring only pain and humiliation, her mind travels back beyond "dreaming of memory" to dwell upon
a terrifying memory in which she hears herself pulling away from her
father and crying out the word "no":

[C]ouldn't he see, couldn't I convince him of, instead of
joy, my agony when I lay down with all the other hostile men,
the gin and the guilt, the feathers that rustled in the
darkness, my drowning? Then I would say: oh, my Harry,
my lost sweet Harry, I have not fornicated in the darkness
because I wanted to but because I was punishing myself for
punishing you: yet something far past dreaming or memory,
and darker than either, impels me, and you do not know,
for once I awoke, half-sleeping, and pulled away. "No,
Bunny," I said. That fright. (p. 359)

Fright motivates Peyton to visit a Newark psychiatrist named Dr. Irving
Strassman. Before seeing him, she has expressed interest in psychoanalysis, telling Harry upon meeting him that "Maybe I need to be analyzed"
(315). Yet when she does meet Strassman, Peyton is distinctly hostile. "I
don't think I like you," she says, adding, for further insult, "I think I'm
more intelligent than you." Strassman counters, belligerently: "Perhaps so,
but certainly less stable" (p. 330). The therapy never progresses beyond
this impasse--Peyton is a recalcitrant patient and Strassman an antagonistic
analyst. Like Dr. Gold in Darkness Visible, Dr. Strassman reflects Styron's
belief that psychiatrists are generally remote, ineffectual, unimaginative.
"Be calm. Be calm" (p. 329), Strassman blandly tells his patient and then
labels her "dangerously abstracted" (p. 330), a term she mockingly repeats
to herself. When Peyton offers him a promising clue to her illness, telling
him that "all hope lies beyond memory, back in the slick dark womb," Dr.
Strassman can only respond, "That's what I mean, your abstraction" (p.

355), upon which she reasonably concludes that he cannot help her and breaks off therapy.

Suicide, like all complex acts, is overdetermined, and we may discern several motives behind Peyton's leap into oblivion, beginning with the wish to punish herself for allowing Maudie to fall as a child. Peyton comes to accept Helen's accusations that has tried to harm her sister, and Peyton's guilt toward Maudie is undeniable. Several times in the story Helen brings up this incident, always for the purpose of hurting Peyton, and Peyton repeats her mother's accusation to Strassman, who inexplicably refuses to pursue it. By viewing herself as a bad daughter and a cruel sister, Peyton comes to accept her mother's judgment of her as vicious and evil. Peyton's suicide represents, in terms of ego psychology, an internalization of her mother's murderous rage. By killing herself Peyton is (1) confirming her mother's judgment that she is unfit to live, (2) symbolically destroying the mother who has rejected her, (3) punishing herself for harboring murderous feelings, and (4) ridding herself of a hateful inner adversary.

Had Dr. Strassman read Freud's classic essay "Mourning and Melancholia" (1917), he would have also recognized the relationship between Peyton's depression and object loss. "The distinguishing mental features of melancholia," Freud writes, "are a profoundly painful dejection, cessation of interest in the outside world, loss of the capacity to love, inhibition of all activity, and a lowering of the self-regarding feelings to a degree that finds utterance in self-reproaches and self-revilings, and culminates in a delusional expectation of punishment"(5)--symptoms that unerringly characterize Peyton's illness. Not only does Peyton punish herself for Maudie's fall and eventual death, she also punishes herself because of her rage toward a mother who has never loved her. Unloved by her mother, Peyton has been the target of excess love--or rather lust-- from her father. The incestuous relationship has affected her in ways that she cannot begin to fathom. If, as seems likely, father and daughter actually committed incest in the distant past, this would help to explain Peyton's sexual acting out and frigidity, the need to punish herself masochistically by entering into affairs with men who reinforce her feelings of self-loathing. Childhood incest would also help to illuminate Peyton's fixation on a past memory she can neither remember nor forget; the repeated flashbacks involving her father, ending in her anxious "no!"; the emotional instability, panic attacks, promiscuity, and self-hatred accompanying her relationship with men; the fear that she is pursued by angry, stinging bees, a recurrent image that may be a displacement of her relentless pursuing phallic father; and the ever-present pains in her womb, a physical and psychic reminder of the fear and revulsion engendered by a shameful act.(6)

Additionally, although the term was not in existence in 1951, when Styron completed Lie Down in Darkness, many of Peyton's symptoms are similar to those of post-traumatic stress disorder--a psychologically distressing event, outside the range of ordinary human experience, that produces recurrent and intrusive recollections of a traumatic incident, along with intense fear, terror, and helplessness. Peyton's flashbacks and distressing recollections of the past, her sexual numbness and emotional anesthesia, her feelings of detachment and estrangement from others, and her sense of a foreshortened future are all characteristic of this disorder.(7)

Climbing the staircase of the Harlem building from which she leaps to her death, Peyton experiences an inner observer watching her every action. "I stood erect: Did I have a companion? I felt that someone was watching me, myself perhaps; at least I knew I was not alone" (p. 367). This wraith-like observer may be viewed as a manifestation of psychic splitting. In a clinical article called "The Devices of Suicide," John Maltsberger and Dan Buie suggest that in many suicides there is a "hostile introject" or killer self that orders a person to die.(9) This destructive introject is a person, often a parent, who becomes internalized within one part of the self and succeeds in persecuting the other part of the self. In less psychological states the hostile observer is experienced not as a killer self but as a chronically nagging conscience, making relentlessly perfectionistic or omnipotent demands upon the self--a state of mind that Styron's major characters know all too well.

The description of Peyton's wraithlike observer eerily foreshadows Styron's account of his own inner observer forty years later in Darkness Visible. Not that the author and his fictional character experience the identical depression: there is a euphoric quality to Peyton's interior monologue in Lie Down in Darkness that is absent from the gray landscape of depression in Darkness Visible. Peyton's monologue contains some of the most poetic descriptions of a suicidal consciousness found anywhere in literature; her suicide recalls, in its lyrical and dramatic intensity and haunting birdlike imagery, Septimus Warren Smith's Icarian plunge to his death in Virginia Woolf's Mrs. Dalloway.

But unlike Septimus' death, which is motivated mainly to avoid being institutionalized by his psychiatrist-jailers, Dr. Holmes and Sir William Bradshaw, symbols of a repressive culture, Peyton's suicide seems to be motivated by the desire both to end the self-punishing guilt that is darkening her life and to discover a more positive father surrogate, of whom she has long been in pursuit. In language that evokes Stephen Dedalus' search for a father figure in A Portrait of the Artist as a Young Man and Ulysses, Peyton tells Harry that she has sinned "only in order to lie down in darkness and find, somewhere in the net of my dreams, a new father, a new home" (p. 362).

Peyton is also in quest of a mother figure, a pre-Oedipal theme which has remained largely ignored by critics. Peyton has never had a loving, attentive mother; psychologically speaking, she has been abandoned by Helen from birth. Maternal loss figures as prominently in Peyton's depression as Oedipal fixation. Ironically, Peyton is her mother's daughter: both women are incapable of loving others or themselves, are in precarious mental health, accuse their husbands of neglecting them, regard sex as torture, and are governed by sinister moods they can neither understand nor control. "You're a Helen with obsessions directed in a different way" (p. 337), Harry tells her. Like her mother, Peyton has been searching for a rescuer. "You left me just like you always do," she reproaches her husband. "When I needed you. Why didn't you come and rescue me?" (p. 304). In the end, Peyton proves as needy and dependent as her mother, as obsessed with guilt, sin, damnation, and martyrdom.

As Lie Down in Darkness closes, we are left with the image of a dead and dying family. Maudie and Peyton are in the earth, and Loftis and Helen are beyond recovery. Loftis becomes so enraged by Helen's refusal to take him back that he tries to choke her after Peyton's funeral; years later, Carey Carr cannot forget the sudden eruption of horrifying violence. The last few pages of the novel describe a black evangelical speaker named "Daddy Faith," a smiling, avuncular man who holds out the promise of everlasting peace to the mesmerized masses gathered for baptism. "Who loves you, my people?" he asks, to which they respond, "You, Daddy! Daddy Faith! You love us! You, Daddy!" (p. 378). As Marc Ratner has noted, Daddy Faith is a "showman, not a healer of souls"(8), and it is difficult to find convincing affirmation in the final pages of the novel. As the baptism ends and the crowd disperses, a train rumbles past Port Warwick, on its way to Richmond, thus closing the last page of the Loftis family.

III

"my writing had kept serious emotional distress safely at bay"
--Sophie's Choice (10)

Peyton, Helen, and Milton Loftis figure prominently in Styron's real life, constituting the landscape of depression that may be seen in his later writings. In Sophie's Choice (1979), Stingo, who is largely Styron himself(11), tells us that the inspiration behind his first novel Inheritance of Night (the original title of Lie Down in Darkness) was a letter he received from his father in 1947 informing him of the recent death of a beautiful twenty-two year-old woman, Maria Hunt, with whom Stingo had been hopelessly in love during his early adolescence. In as essay on Lie Down in Darkness appearing in the volume This Quiet Dust (1982), Styron describes this woman as the "source of my earliest and most aching infatuation."(12) Maria Hunt had killed herself, Stingo discovers, by leaping from the window of a Manhattan building; as it turned out, she had lived around the block from him in Greenwich Village. She had come from a tragic household, according to Stingo's father, with a father who was a "near-alcoholic and always at loose ends" and a mother who was "pretty unremitting and cruel in her moral demands upon people," particularly upon her daughter (Sophie's Choice, p. 44).

Maria Hunt's death gave birth not only to Peyton Loftis but to her future avatar, Sophie Zawistowska, who commits suicide with her psychotic lover at the close of Sophie's Choice. Although the character Sophie was based on a real Polish survivor of Auschwitz whom Styron knew briefly while living in New York City immediately after World War II, she also seemed to be an incarnation of Maria Hunt. "And what is still ineffaceable about my first glimpse" of Sophie, Stingo observes, "is not simply the lovely simulacrum she seemed to be of the dead girl but the despair on her face worn as Maria surely must have worn it, along with the premonitory, grieving shadows of someone hurtling headlong toward death" (p. 46).

At the same time, Lie Down in Darkness is a "mirror" of Styron's family life, as the novelist concedes in a December, 1982, interview in the New York Times Book Review. Helen Loftis was modeled on his stepmother, "as close to the wicked stepmother image as one can possible imagine," while Milton Loftis was modeled on his father.(13) "The basic torment between Peyton and her family was really a projection of my own sense of alienation from my own tiny family--that is, my father, whom I really loved and this strange woman who had just come on the scene and who--I think I'm speaking as objectively as I can--was really trying to make my life a hell." Writing Lie Down in Darkness was a "form of self-psychoanalysis," he adds, "which freed me from any need to go to a shrink."

Styron's other father figures, while more sympathetically portrayed than Milton Loftis, are cut from the same cloth as Styron's own father.(14) The shadowy figure in Styron's life whom future biographers will need to discuss is the absent mother, whose death when he was thirteen represented, as he writes in Darkness Visible, one of the crucial determinants of later depression. Judith Ruderman notes in her 1987 book that soon after the future novelist was born, Styron's mother developed cancer, underwent a series of operations, and remained an invalid for the rest of her life.(15)

A portrait of the mother appears in the largely autobiographical "A Tidewater Morning," published in Esquire in August, 1987.(16) Originally intended as the introductory chapter of a novel that has not yet appeared, the story describes a thirteen year-old boy's grief as he watches his mother, riddled with cancer, die. The mother's monstrous suffering most visibly affects the father, but the son is also affected. It seems probable that the illness produced in the young boy a desire to rescue his mother from death; when the rescue fantasy ultimately failed, feelings of guilt and helplessness emerged. This may be one of the sources of the pervasive rescue fantasies of Styron's characters, who similarly fail to save loved ones from illness and death.

There are glimpses of the idealized mother in at least two of Styron's novels. In <u>Lie Down in Darkness</u> Milton Loftis momentarily reflects upon his mother, who died when he was very young. "The sunlight sifted downward through gently rustling blinds and somewhere infinitely far above, it had seemed, there was his mother's vacant, hovering face, unseen and finally unknown because she died before he could picture in his consciousness those features his father later said were refined and lovely" (p. 12).

Another image of the lost mother emerges in <u>Sophie's Choice</u> as Stingo recollects an unforgivable crime he committed against her when he was twelve, a year before her death. Suffering from terminal bone cancer which incapacitated her, his mother was confined to a bed or a chair, from which she would pass the day reading. Stingo's responsibility during the chilly winter months was to hurry home after school and see to it that the fireplace was well fueled. One particularly frigid afternoon he "abandoned" her by accepting a schoolmate's invitation to ride in his new Packard-Clipper. Arriving home hours later, long after the fire had died out, Stingo found his father massaging his wife's numbed hands, both parents silently reproaching their neglectful son. Later the father marched his wayward son to the woodshed, where he received his just deserts by shivering for the rest of the evening. Stingo recalls how he would have willingly frozen to death in order to expiate his heinous crime, one which was "ultimately beyond expiation, for in my mind it would inescapably and always be entangled in the sordid animal fact of my mother's death" (p. 297).

Daniel Ross, in his perceptive psychoanalytic interpretation of Stingo's dreams, notes that Styron's narrator is oppressed by guilt over the failure to rescue the three most important women in his life--his mother, Maria Hunt, and Sophie. The guilt is heightened by the fact that Stingo waits so long before he finally writes about the story which Sophie entrusted to him years earlier. "It is certainly a curious fact," Ross writes, "that a storyteller as gifted as he would withhold so dramatic a tale for a quarter of a century, especially when, as I have suggested, Sophie seems to have bequeathed the story to him as a special gift, the surviving offspring of their relationship."(17) When Stingo does tell the story, he does so with the "compulsive obsessiveness of the Ancient Mariner, insisting repeatedly on the necessity of speaking the unspeakable . . ." (Ross, pp. 144-45).

The analogy to the Ancient Mariner, with its implication of narrating a harrowing experience for the purpose of therapeutic relief, is particularly appropriate. Stingo himself recognizes that the writing of his first novel helped preserve his sanity: "my writing had kept serious emotional distress safely at bay, in the sense that the novel I was working on served as a cathartic instrument through which I was able to discharge on paper many of my more vexing tensions and miseries" (<u>Sophie's Choice</u>, p. 438). By contrast, the inability to write has the most dire consequences for the creative artist. Elsewhere Styron has characterized writer's block, from which he periodically suffers, as "one of those despairing moments when you're drowning"(18)--an image that he associates with suicide.

For a writer who has long been mistrustful of psychoanalysis, and who has satirized the spirit of Freudianism in two of his novels, Styron may be surprised to discover that he believes powerfully in the therapeutic nature of artistic creativity. "When I'm writing," he revealed in his Paris Review interview published in Writers at Work (1958),

> I find it's the only time that I feel completely self-possessed, even when the writing itself is not going too well. It's fine therapy for people who are perpetually scared of nameless threats as I am most of the time--for jittery people. Besides, I've discovered that when I'm not writing I'm prone to developing certain nervous tics, and hypochondria. Writing alleviates those quite a bit.(19)

Styron goes on to say in the same interview that while much of the morbidity and depression of modern life arises from the explosive increase of scientific knowledge of the self associated with Freudianism, the "good writing of any age has always been the product of someone's neurosis, and we'd have a mighty dull literature if all the writers that came along were a happy bunch of chuckleheads" (282).

Styron is one of those artists in the tradition of what I have called elsewhere "writing as rescue,"(20) and it is now clear that a central driving force behind his creativity is the need to master psychic conflicts and heal himself. He belongs to that group of novelists like Joseph Conrad, Virginia Woolf, and Ernest Hemingway, whose fictional characters reveal their authors' lifelong preoccupation with self-destruction. In For Whom the Bell Tolls Robert Jordan expresses his creator's belief that writing enables one to discharge potentially paralyzing anxieties: "you will get rid of all that by writing about it. . . . Once you write it down it is all gone."(21) In comparing him to Woolf and Hemingway, I am not implying, of course, that Styron will share their fate. Significant advances in treating depression have been made since Hemingway's suicide in 1961, and Styron himself points out in Darkness Visible that "one need not sound the false or inspirational note to stress the truth that depression is not the soul's annihilation; men and women who have recovered from the disease--and they are countless--bear witness to what is probably its only saving grace: it is conquerable" (p. 84).

There is nothing breezily optimistic about Styron's writings, and he is not naive enough to believe that writing always enables one to ward off serious mental illness, or that reading about a real or fictional character's suicide is an antidote to madness. And yet, by writing about his nightmarish struggle against depression, Styron has not only succeeded in keeping his emotional stress safely at bay for most of his life, he has raised one more eloquent voice against the forces of despair. In the forty years since the publication of <u>Lie Down in Darkness,</u> Styron's writings have grown more profound, more compassionate, and he writes about madness now with the authenticity of one who has experienced it. There is an almost evangelical fervor to <u>Darkness Visible</u> that Styron might have treated satirically forty years earlier in <u>Lie Down in Darkness</u>. "It may require on the part of friends, lovers, family, admirers, an almost religious devotion to persuade the sufferers of life's worth, which is so often in conflict with a sense of their own worthlessness, but such devotion has prevented countless suicides" (<u>Darkness Visible,</u> p. 76). In the words of the Reverend Carey Carr or Peyton's psychiatrist Dr. Strassman or Daddy Faith, this message would have been ironically undercut, but in <u>Darkness Visible</u> it is conveyed with humility and but in <u>Darkness Visible</u> it is conveyed with humility and truth. A more empathic book than <u>Lie Down in Darkness,</u> <u>Darkness Visible</u> is the work of a man who has plunged into the depth of depression and emerged stronger and wiser. Whereas Milton, Helen, and Peyton Loftis are unable to heal themselves. Styron's own life and art affirm the possibility of surviving the landscape of depression and transmuting it into profoundly moving literature.

Notes

(1) William Styron, <u>Darkness Visible</u> (New York: Random House, 1990), p. 15. Future citations will be from this edition and will appear in the text.

(2) A. Alvarez, <u>The Savage God: A Study in Suicide</u> (New York: Random House, 1972).

(3) William Styron, <u>Lie Down in Darkness</u> (New York: New American Library, 1978), p. 71. Future citations will be from this edition and will appear in the text.

(4) New evidence that Milton Loftis and Peyton have actually committed incest appears in the publication of <u>Inheritance of Night,</u> the unfinished predecessor of <u>Lie Down in Darkness.</u> James L.W. West III points out, in his Introduction to <u>William Styron: Inheritance of Night</u> (Durham: Duke University Press, 1993), that a character named Marcus Bonner, a childhood classmate of Peyton's, is "filled with an enormous contempt" toward Milton Loftis as a result of something she had told him "one night in New York in a fury of grief and drunkenness." Peyton confessed "things he refused to believe until later when, carefully retrieving in his memory all those curious and unnamed gestures of the past, he came to know that the things she told him were true indeed." From these statements West concludes that Peyton "had told Marcus of some kind of incestuous relationship between herself and her father--whether sexually consummated or not, one cannot tell from the surviving drafts" (xiv). West suggests, additionally, that this incestuous element may have been omitted from Peyton's final interior monologue in <u>Lie Down in Darkness</u> at the

insistence of Styron's publisher, Bobbs-Merrill, in 1951. I am grateful to Daniel Ross for bringing this new evidence to my attention.

(5) Sigmund Freud. "Mourning and Melancholia." The Standard Edition of the Complete Psychological Works of Sigmund Freud, James Strachey. ed. (London: The Hogarth Press. 1957), Vol. 14. 244.

(6) There may be a connection between the clock Peyton carries around with her everywhere during her last days, which she smashes just prior to her death, and the pains in her womb, evoking revulsion with sex. Freud argues in the Introductory Lectures on Psychoanalysis (1916-17) that clocks and watches often symbolize in dreams menstruation and other periodic biological processes. See volume 16 of The Standard Edition of the Complete Psychological Works of Sigmund Freud (London: The Hogarth Press, 1963), 266. For a clinical definition of post-traumatic stress disorder, see the Diagnostic and Statistical Manual of Mental Disorders, 3rd ed., revised (Washington, D.C.: American Psychiatric Association, 1987), 247-250.

(7) For a clinical definition of post-traumatic stress disorder, see the Diagnostic and Statistical Manual of Mental Disorders. 3rd ed.. revised (Washington, D. C.: American Psychiatric Association, 1987), 247-250.

(8) John T. Maltsberger and Dan H. Buie, "The Devices of Suicide," International Journal of Psycho-Analysis, vol. 7 (1980), 61-72.

(9) Marc L. Ratner, William Styron (New York: Twayne, 1972), 52.

(10) William Styron, Sophie's Choice (New York: Random House, 1979), 438. Future citations will be from this edition and will appear in the text.

(11) To cite some of the parallels between Styron and Stingo, whose names are near anagrams, both were born in Tidewater, Virginia in 1925, lost their mothers at the age of thirteen, enlisted in the United States Marines during World War II after which they completed their education at Duke, worked briefly for McGraw-Hill publishers, wrote similar first novels based on their infatuation with a woman who later committed suicide and a later novel about Nat Turner which provoked sharp controversy, and met a Polish survivor of Auschwitz whose story they later immortalized. There are also some less obvious similarities between Stingo and Peyton. Peyton's obsession in Lie Down in Darkness with being inside a clock parallels a remark Stingo makes in Sophie's Choice when he talks about dreaming of an old clock belonging to his grandparents. "I would think of myself inside the clock--imagine anything so crazy from a child!--where I would just float around on a spring and watch the levers moving and the various wheels turning and see the rubies, red and bright and as big as my head. And I would go to sleep with this clock in my dreams" (p. 80).

(12) William Styron, This Quiet Dust (New York: Random House, 1982), 290.

(13) "Interview with William Styron," New York Times Book Review, 12 December 1982, 26.

(14) For a discussion of Styron's fictional father figures, see John Kenny Crane, The Root of All Evil (Columbia: University of South Carolina Press, 1984).

(15) Judith Ruderman, William Styron (New York: Ungar, 1987), 2.

(16) William Styron, "A Tidewater Morning," Esquire, August 1987, 85-96.

(17) Daniel W. Ross, "A Family Romance: Dreams and the Unified Narrative of Sophie's Choice," The Mississippi Quarterly, 42 (Spring 1989), 144. All citations are from this essay.

(18) James L. W. West, Conversations with William Styron (Jackson: University Press of Mississippi, 1985), 238. Compare the life or death significance writing has for Styron to a remark made by Kafka in a letter to Max Brod: "a non-writing writer is, in fact, a monster courting insanity." Quoted by Ernst Pawel, The Nightmare of Reason: A Life of Franz Kafka (New York: Farrar, Strauss, Giroux, 1984), 97.

(19) Malcolm Cowley, ed., Writers at Work: The Paris Review Interviews (New York: Viking, 1958, rpt. 1973), 272. All citations are from this essay.

(20) Jeffrey Berman. Joseph Conrad: Writing as Rescue (New York: Astra Books, 1977).

(21) Ernest Hemingway, For Whom the Bell Tolls (New York: Scribners, 1940), 165.

*Written for this collection.

THE LONG MARCH

WILLIAM STYRON*

Richard Pearce

In his neglected novella, <u>The Long March,</u> . . . Styron sacrificed range to find a form which expressed the human situation with conciseness and clarity, and in which he could affirm the values of Christian humanism in a way that was consistent with his vision.

At one point the protagonist describes the most frightening experience in his life:

"We were drunk, you see, polluted, all of us. I think there were five of us, all of us boots just out of Dago. Kids. We were on the tenth floor of this hotel and in this room and I believe we were about as drunk as anyone could get. I remember going in to take a shower in the bathroom. It was late at night, past midnight, and after I took this shower, you see, I came out into the room buck naked. Two of those drunk guys were waiting for me. They grabbed me and pushed me toward the window. I was so loaded I couldn't battle. They pushed me out the window and held me by the heels while I dangled upside-down buck naked in space, ten floors above the street." He paused and sucked at a beer can. "Can you imagine that?" he went on slowly. "How I felt? I got stonesober in a second. Imagine being that high upsidedown in space with two drunks holding onto your heels. I was heavy, man, just like now, you see. All I can remember is those teeny-weeny lights below and the tiny little people like ants down there and those two crazy drunk guys holding onto my wet slippery ankles, laughing like hell and trying to decide whether to let go or not. I just remember the cold wind blowing on my body and that dark, man, infinite

darkness all around me, and my ankles beginning to slip
out of their hands. I really saw Death then, and I think
that all I could think of was that I was going to fall and
smash myself on that hard, hard street below. That those
crazy bastards were going to let me fall. I was praying, I
guess. I remember the blood rushing to my brain and my
ankles slipping, and that awful strange noise. And I was
reaching out, man, clutching at thin air. Then I wondered
what that noise was, that high loud noise, and then I
realized it was me, screaming at the top of my voice, all
over San Francisco."

Here Styron found a metaphor of the human situation toward which he
had been reaching in Lie Down in Darkness, which he was to express
more diffusely in Set This House on Fire, and which would even inform
The Confessions of Nat Turner; it recalls his experience as a marine
recruit "shanghaied into the 'clap shack.'" In an environment that is urban,
military, and dark, man is surprised, ambushed, senselessly assaulted--not
to the end of defeat or destruction, not to any end at all. He is suddenly
and capriciously turned upside down, turned from a man with potentials
of dignity and heroism into a helpless clown acutely aware of life's terror.
This terror is caused not by a hostile power or even by an indifferent
universe, but by a wanton sporting with individual life.

. . .

The Long March is similar in many ways to Melville's Billy Budd. In
both works the thematic conflict is between the innocent individual and
the representative of social necessity. In both works social law is made
manifest in a military order. In both works the hero's instinctive reaction
to human injustice has immediate destructive consequences for his associates and for himself. Both works end in a martyrdom that is in fact
socially just. But the difference between The Long March and Billy Budd
is signal; the view of life after World War II is sharply differentiated from
that of earlier periods. Melville dramatizes the tragic price of human
preservation and social harmony; Captain Vere, as he condemns Billy, is
deeply aware of this price. Colonel Templeton knows that military order
and soldierly discipline are necessary on the battlefield, but despite his
sensitivity, integrity, and realistic logic, the end he serves is not a human
harmony, as it was with Vere. In fact the end is obscured from the
sightlines of the novella.

The kind of war depicted in The Long March is just the kind of
purposeless and pervasive war we have come to know so well in the
second half of the twentieth century. For this is not World War II, the
justice of which could guarantee some meaning to death and destruction.
It is not even the battleground of the Korean War, where, despite the
senselessness, there was still an identifiable enemy. This is a marine
training maneuver. The enemy "was labeled Aggressor, on maps brightly

spattered with arrows and symbolic tanks and guns, but although there was no sign of his aggression he fled them nonetheless and they pushed the sinister chase, sending up shells and flares as they went."

Captain Mannix, a Brooklyn Jew, and Lieutenant Culver, from whose viewpoint the story is told, are veterans of World War II who, having adjusted to the postwar prosperity, and being now too old and flabby for effective service, have been called back to train for the Korean War by the unreasonable and impractical mechanism of the reserve system. The book opens with an accident. Two mortar shells have misfired and exploded among a group of lunching recruits: "One noon, in the blaze of a cloudless Carolina summer, what was left of eight dead boys lay strewn about the landscape, among the poison ivy and the pine needles and loblolly saplings." In the first sentence Styron pictures the irrational violence exploding from beneath the placid surface of life, expressing explicitly and with sharper clarity a view that he had begun to conceive in his story of Peyton Loftis, and which would dominate the world of Cass Kinsolving.

Styron drew on his own experiences in 1950, when he was recalled to marine duty during the Korean War and compelled to participate in a forced training march. Within a realistic framework he develops the contradictory irrational potential--the destructive irrationality and an irrational affirmation--with the aid of comic devices. The central conflict is caused not by a direct and clearly embodied hostility, as it is in Billy Budd, but by Colonel Templeton's impersonal and apparently irrational order for a thirty-six mile forced march. Mannix's determination to assert the value of his own person and of his men in the featureless face of the Marine Corps is also irrational; and Lieutenant Culver finds himself in a situation similar to Peyton's, caught between warring powers which cannot be ethically distinguished. Captain Mannix tries to achieve his end in an action that is doubly irrational: he will defy the colonel by driving his men to achieve the impossible, which is to complete the march. And his defeat is accomplished far less in the prospective court-martial than it is in the picture of the heroic captain turned into a clown, gratuitously wounded by a nail in his shoe, "toiling down the road with hobbled leg and furious flailing arms." And even more by the irony of his being turned into Templeton's accomplice: "You're goddam right, Jack. . . . My company's going to make it if I have to drag in their bodies."

The world is surely upside down when we see Mannix, with his compassion and sense of justice, fulfilling the role of Satan and Templeton assuming the role of priest. This is indeed the kind of hell Mannix saw as he dangled high up in space with two drunks holding onto his slippery heels. And in the confrontation between Mannix and Templeton Styron creates a modern version--or inversion--of the confrontation in Dostoevski's "Grand Inquisitor."

Still, we come to realize that this has all been a preparation for a final inversion. The Long March ends with a comic recognition. Back in their quarters Mannix, coming out of the showers, encounters the Negro maid, who looks at him and says, "Oh my, you poor man. What you been doin'? Do it hurt? . . . Oh, I bet it does. Deed it does." Mannix looks at her silently, blinking, as she repeats, "Deed it does." And "almost at precisely the same instant, the towel slipped away slowly from Mannix's waist and fell with a soft plop to the floor; Mannix then, standing there, weaving dizzily and clutching the support at the wall, a mass of scars and naked as the day he emerged from his mother's womb, save for the soap which he held feebly in one hand. He seemed to have neither the strength nor the ability to lean down and retrieve the towel and so he merely stood there huge and naked in the slanting dusty light and blinked and sent toward the woman, finally, a sour, apologetic smile, his words uttered, it seemed to Culver, not with self-pity but only with the tone of a man who, having endured and lasted, was too weary to tell her anything but what was true. 'Deed it does,' he said."

As the story progressed Mannix had become more and more ridiculous, and, more destructive and fanatic than even Colonel Templeton. But with the shift in tone, tempo, and perspective in the final scene, he is reestablished as humane and heroic. We end the book with contradictory views of Mannix, and with the non-rational experience of having come to a deep understanding of the very values which were abrogated by Templeton and the facts of reality. Styron achieved this effect by a double inversion. First he turned the world upside down to convey the full terror of a world governed by capricious forces, and to show man senselessly surprised, ambushed, reduced, and humiliated. Here Styron was following in the long tradition, revived in the 1950's, of writers who evoked the incongruous terror and the gratuitous surprises of an absurd universe through comic means. Then, again, he turned the world upside down to illuminate old values in a new light. Here the comedy works to surprise us, through inversions of accepted views, into a fresh awareness: "Christ on a crutch" turns out to be a kind of Christ after all.

*From <u>William Styron</u>: 19-24.

STYRON'S FAREWELL TO ARMS: WRITINGS ON THE MILITARY*

Judith Ruderman

At the age of seventeen Styron joined the Marine Corps, serving altogether for more than three years in two different wars, as both an enlisted man and an officer. Although his initial infatuation with the military calling in general, and with marines in particular, quickly cooled, Styron's interest in the military has never diminished. War and the men who wage it figure importantly in most of Styron's works. Except for The Confessions of Nat Turner, set in the nineteenth century, all of Styron's major novels deal to some extent with the wars in which the writer himself participated. . . . World War II and the bombing of Nagasaki form the global background against which the Loftis family plays out its domestic tragedy in Lie Down in Darkness. Cass Kinsolving is mental breakdown during World War II brings him into the care of a military psychiatrist, Slotkin, whose values Kinsolving will later adopt as a standard bearer in more personal battles. The Nazi persecution of non-Aryans is the horror that forces Sophie's choice in the novel of that name, and reinforces the dark vision of life that will forever color Stingo's art.

. . .

Lieutenant Culver of The Long March, like many of Styron's protagonists, looks nostalgically from a chaotic present into an Edenic past. He has left behind a law practice, his family, and the strains of Haydn, Bach, and Mozart reverberating through peaceful Sunday afternoons in New York City. Now his companions are his fellow marine reservists in the Headquarters and Service Company in rural North Carolina, his comfortable existence exchanged for endless maneuvers during frigid nights and torrid days in training for possible combat in Korea. The surrealist pursuit of an imaginary enemy, the relentless exhaustion, and the isolation from all ordinary endeavors fill Culver with confusion, apprehension, and dismay. This sense of disorder and chaos is replicated in Styron's narrative technique, which substitutes flashback for a chronological sequence of events. The first two chapters of the novella proceed by means of flashbacks to present the central event in the novel: not the long march of the title, as one might suspect, but the event that causes the march to take on its utmost meaning--that is, the accidental short firing of rounds that kills eight soldiers in the next battalion.

Chapter 1 begins at the scene of carnage, with the bodies strewn about and Lieutenant Culver off to the side vomiting at the sight. The rest of the chapter relates, through flashback, how Culver came to be in marine camp, and what he left behind. Chapter 2 starts at the moment when Culver and his company are eating lunch in a command post and hear the explosion off in the distance. The rest of the chapter focuses on the order for the long march and introduces the antagonists, Colonel Templeton and Captain Mannix, whose personalities are adumbrated mainly through flashbacks. Chapters 3 and 4 deal with the march itself--a thirty-six mile, thirteen-hour trek at two-and-onehalf miles per hour. No lengthy flashbacks occur here, for the agonizing present blots out thoughts of anything but blind, dogged survival. Yet even here, near the beginnings of chapters 3 and 4, the explosion and deaths figure prominently, hovering at the fringes of Culver's consciousness and accounting, in Culver's mind, for Captain Mannix's moody behavior. The final chapter, a postmarch coda, also begins with mention of the dead marines. They function as a leitmotif in this story, a picture returning to the main characters' minds, as to the reader's, "with the unshakable regularity of a scrap of music."

The novella, then, focuses on a tragedy: the slaughter of eight young marines through what would come to be known in the Vietnam War as friendly fire. Because of this accident, and because of the stateside setting in a noncombat situation, the characters wonder about the identity of their real enemy. Who is the invisible aggressor whom the reservists relentlessly stalk, against whom the commanding officers ceaselessly warn? The state of exhaustion in which the reservists perpetually exist, for they are woefully out of shape, softened by the good life back home, makes the answer to that question unclear to Culver, who plays the role of Everyman in this story. Through Culver's eyes the reader views the man who plays the role of the tragic hero, the platoon leader Al Mannix. A man of mythological proportions, compared implicitly to Atlas and to Christ, Mannix identifies the enemy as the military system itself and proceeds to knock his head against the nature of things in an effort to beat the system. Through this effort, which is ridiculous and even aberrant by standards of sanity and propriety, Mannix wrests control over his life from the powers-that-be and asserts the humanity of the boys who died as well as of the reservists he leads.

The story of Mannix's perverse rebellion cannot be understood unless the nature of military service as Styron views it is first delineated. Styron does not regard the military as an inherently evil profession, but ever suspicious of institutions, he considers it to be a bureaucracy that stifles individuality. The reservists in H & S Company must all be treated alike, as marines; all-important is the espirit de corps that bonds the many into the one. In that sense the men are nonentities rather than fully realized human beings. Sergeant O'Leary, a marine regular, is said to be grafted onto the military system like a piece of skin, and therefore molded into the image of marine. The reader is reminded that the outcome may be similarly dehumanizing: the eight dead marines look as if they've been sprayed from a hose, turned into mere shreds of skins and bone that seem never to have been alive at all. Because the reservists have known freedom, they are especially resistant to the authority wielded by Colonel Templeton and his officers.

This authority manifests itself most forcefully in Colonel Templeton's order for a thirty-six-mile march that will toughen the reservists, prepare them for actual combat, and make them more like the regulars. The order and the subsequent march fill Culver and Mannix with revulsion and fear, not merely because they doubt their ability to withstand the heat and the pain, but, more importantly, because they are loath to relinquish their free will: "How stupid to think they had ever made their own philosophy; it was as puny as a house of straw, and at this moment--by the noise in their brains of these words, you will--it was being blasted to the winds like dust. They were as helpless as children." The military reduces the fighting men to the state of children, belittled as it were, with the commanding officers as powerful parental figures determining the course of their charges' lives-fathers, maybe, or even priests, invested with a quasi-divine authority. Culver, calling "Bundle Able" on the radio at Colonel Templeton's request, feels "juvenile and absurd, as if he were reciting Mother Goose." Mannix has only contempt for this code language of military communication that replaces ordinary conversation with boy-scout passwords. Major Lawrence, subservient to the colonel, looks to Culver like a five-year-old child, and speaks to the colonel in the third person as if Templeton were an imperial ruler and the major his subject.

Other figures of speech, more emotionally charged than the references to children, hint at the odious status of the soldiers. Captain Mannix is compared at one point to a shackled slave, and at another to a chain-gang convict. By these means Styron conveys the idea that the military imprisons the individual and subordinates him to the system. Quite simply, the marines are not free men. Mannix despises Templeton for the authority that Templeton wields, not only because authority is anathema to this rebellious individual, but also because Mannix is all too aware of the fallibility of those who wield the power. The accidental misfiring of the missiles and the resultant death of the eight young marines may well have been caused by the decision to use old shells stored on Guam since 1945. Such disregard for the consequences of decisions bespeaks a lack of connection between those who give the orders and those who do the fighting. This lack of communication between commander and com- manded--indeed, between men in general--is symbolized by the incident that Mannix relates to Culver from his buck-sergeant days during World War II. Pinned down in his shell hole under heavy fire from the Japanese, Mannix screams desperately into the telephone for assistance. Each time he hollers for aid he gets hit by another piece of shrapnel. Just before losing consciousness he notices that the telephone wires have all along been severed. There has been no lifeline between him and others. Instead, he's on his own, to succeed or fail on his own powers along with the luck of the draw. Even the radio over which Lieutenant Culver tries to make contact with Able Company emits only a banshee wail of signals, "Like the cries of souls in the anguish of hell." No call to that company gets through, so isolated and uprooted are uprooted are these men. Alienated from his God, estranged from his fellows, the individual cannot count for aid and comfort on the ministrations of anyone else; he had best rely on himself.

And so, because the dead soldiers could not take control over their lives, Captain Al Mannix takes control over his. He does not opt out of the marines, for he has made his commitment. (This is, after all, the Korean War in the conformist 1950s; the next war, in the next decade, would tell a different tale.) Rather, he chooses to exert the full force of his individu- ality within the strict parameters of the military system. If Colonel Templeton, nicknamed Old Rocky because of his obdurate nature, can order thirty-yearold, out-of-shape reservists to march for thirteen hours, then Captain Mannix can find his own way of being an immovable object. He finds it in a rebellion in reverse--that is, in seeing the march through to its end and exhorting his company to do the same. Mannix accomplish- es this task under especially grievous conditions; added to the fatigue and heat suffered by all the marchers is the discomfort of a nail sticking up from his boot into his foot, resisting his best efforts at removal. Marching for Mannix becomes a true torture, and thus a true test of his human capacity to endure. The nail and the injury it causes provide Mannix with an escape from the forced march if he wants it: Templeton commands him to ride in on the truck. But Mannix chooses to obey the first command to march, rather than the second one, and thereby enacts his perverse rebellion. This "one personal insurrection" cannot hope to accomplish much good. Indeed, it turns Mannix into a taskmaster, bullying his men into completing the march with him. It injures his foot and makes every step a crucifixion. It gets him confined to quarters, and perhaps even court-martialed, after cursing the colonel. But if this insurrection is absurd it is not therefore without value. In fact, it does get Mannix from point A to point B on his own terms. And he does indeed carry some of his company on his back, Atlas-like, completing his superhuman task almost like a god rather than a man, elevating his men in spite of themselves. By refusing to drop out or to let them drop out (though two-thirds of them eventually do), he asserts the dignity and worth of human life and thereby wrests control for the individual from dominating outside forces. Though comical, caricatural, and even bizarre, Mannix's gesture attests to the durability of the human spirit.

If Mannix is not necessarily to be considered a fool, is he therefore to be considered a hero? Styron thinks so. In the midst of senseless slaughter and a senseless, seemingly endless march, in a war presaging the "force-less, soulless, pushbutton wars of the future,(1) one indefatigable man with an indomitable will imprints his features on the action. By so doing he fights the battle of the luckless marine whose face had been blasted out of sight while he waited for his lunch. Templeton's own face is likened to a mannequin's, betokening his lack of humanity, and the loaded pearl-handled revolver he wears on his hip is a sign of the military's potential to turn humans into inert matter in one moment, as the short rounds did to the men on the chow line; the forks and spoons of the dead soldiers were turned into pathetic metal flowers, completing the inhuman and unnatural picture. Mannix is ennobled by his suffering, which personalizes the impersonal order to march and dehumanizes the dehumanizing task of carrying out this order. His rebellion therefore sets the world in order, if only temporarily. The reader recalls the episode related by Mannix to Culver about his most harrowing experience during World War II. On a spree out of boot camp, on the tenth floor of a hotel in San Francisco, Mannix had been suspended for several long minutes naked and upside down from the window by a couple of drunken marines. The utter helplessness and disorientation of the situation were too horrible for bearing. Human existence, Styron implies, is often an upside-down view into the abyss. Any attempt to set the world rightside up and to provide something to hold onto is a laudable, even heroic task.

Throughout the novella Styron draws attention to Mannix's body. Whereas the other characters are clothed and protected, Mannix is often pictured naked and vulnerable. One is aware of his fleshiness, his mortality; he is massive and hairy, larger than life. Mannix points out to Culver the many scars covering his entire body. He seems almost a mass of wounds, and he shows them off not proudly but matter-of-factly, as if to say, this is what it means to be alive. He is wounded and suffers because he dares. His emotions are not controlled, his responses are not pro-grammed. Mannix is a man, not a machine.

The final scene of the novella drives home this point. Mannix has showered after his long march and proceeds down the hall draped only in a towel, clutching the wall for support and dragging his maimed leg behind him. His suffering is described as gigantic, befitting this man's physical and spiritual proportions. He meets the black maid, whose sympathy for his condition is immediate and genuine as she asks him if he is in pain. He communicates a complex set of emotions to the maid without jargon, without lies, almost even without words. As he struggles to remain upright the towel falls away, and for one last moment he stands naked and exposed, his body a mass of scars. Tomorrow Mannix may be court-martialed, his world turned topsy turvy again. But for today he has made it through, vulnerable and suffering as ever, but still standing. And that, at least for now, is triumph enough.

Notes

(1) From the Introduction to the Norwegian edition of The Long March, in This Quiet Dust (New York: Random House, 1982), p. 300.

*From William Styron: 71-78. Reprinted by permission.

SET THIS HOUSE ON FIRE

THE QUARREL WITH TIME IN AMERICAN FICTION*

Thomas F. Curley

Ever since the appearance of William Styron's The Long March, one of the best novels of this decade, I had been waiting, with everyone else who is interested, for Styron's next book. Set This House on Fire is a surprise. Running more than five hundred pages, Set This House on Fire is a character study in depth of two men, Mason Flagg and Cass Kinsolving, narrated by a friend, Peter Leverett, who sets out, after the fact, to discover the reality behind the apparent suicide of Flagg and the murder of a young Italian girl whom Flagg had raped shortly before his death. The events are violent but less important to the burden of the book than the characters of Flagg and Kinsolving. As it turns out, Kinsolving killed Flagg; and the girl, though she was raped by Flagg, did not die by his hands, as had been given out, but by the village idiot. . . . Styron [is a] traditional [novelist], first because the characters take precedence over the events, and second because the very detail with which he imagines his characters implies a confidence in the ability, by sheer force of the imaginative power, to come to a knowledge of good and evil. There is nothing of the abstract in this book. Each scene is carefully built up and the sensations of the characters are enumerated, described, followed one by one with an eye (and ear) alert to every nuance. And at the end? At the end, one knows that this book is book is more about Cass Kinsolving than Mason Flagg, that it is his long agony, at the end of which, finally emerging from the demented weakness of drunkenness, he is saved from self-destruction by the ability to choose being rather than nothingness, the day-to-day ecstasy of being himself, not forever, but for a time. But not only that. Along with the choice is a vision of America Kinsolving has after a number of expatriate years in Europe. He wants to go back.

To be brief, <u>Set This House on Fire</u> is not the kind of book I expected from Styron; maybe I should say it is not the kind of book I wanted; but of its kind, it is very good, especially in the detail and thoroughness of characterization. Or rather, . . . I think Cass Kinsolving should have been destroyed by Flagg. As Styron wrote it, Kinsolving blundered into salvation. I know that's the way it is; but it's not the way it should be. And that, as clear as I can make it, is my prejudice and my gripe.

*From <u>The American Scholar</u> 29 (1960): 558, 560. Reprinted by permission.

STYRONIC MANNER*

Charles Monaghan

. . . In Mr. Styron's second novel, his romantic proclivities are the undoing of what might have been a brilliant work. His hero is an expatriate artist who is always drunk and apparently never sleeps, a perfect subject for the Styronic technique. The artist, Cass Kinsolving, falls under the influence of a millionaire upper-bohemian and pseudo-intellectual, Mason Flagg, who has come to Italy to write a play.

Kinsolving degrades himself to obtain money and liquor from Flagg, and finally comes to emotional maturity by murdering him. The novel fails because we never get to know Kinsolving--he is veiled by a fog of liquor and romantic bombast. Not knowing Kinsolving, we find his redemption meaningless. The best parts of the book come when Flagg and his array of cronies are centerstage and the brooding Kinsolving is in the wings.

Mr. Styron seems to sense that his attempt to portray Kinsolving's regeneration does not rise naturally from his characterization of the wandering artist. He tries, therefore, to beef up the novel with philosophical "ideas." The result is bathetic. A few pages from the end of the work, the words "being" and "nothingness" begin to appear with increasing regularity, sledge-hammer hints that this is meant to be an existentialist novel.

The final moral is over-obvious and drops like a lead weight from Kinsolving's mouth: "As for being and nothingness, the one thing I did know was that to choose between them was simply to choose being, not for the sake of being, much less for the desire to be forever--but in the hope of being what I could be for a time." Yes, Virginia, it's true: being is better than nothingness.

*From <u>Commonweal</u> (July 22, 1960): 380. Reprinted by permission.

THE ABSURD HERO IN AMERICAN FICTION: UPDIKE, STYRON, BELLOW, SALINGER*

David D. Galloway

. . . There is a contrast between the prose styles of Lie Down in Darkness and Set This House on Fire. In the former book Styron was largely concerned with a somewhat static enumeration and articulation of the various absurdities of modern life, while in the latter his involvement is direct and energetic. The two novels reflect stylistically the different impulses from which they were written. In Lie Down in Darkness Styron avoided any passionate moral commitment, but in Set This House on Fire his commitment was specifically and passionately an affirmation, through the attempted creation of a tragic hero, of the order of the universe.

In Set This House on Fire, as in his first two books, Styron has given considerable time to establishing the absurdity of the environment in which his characters are placed. Like his earlier work, this novel suggests an environment dominated by a profound desuetude of order and value, and again the action centers around the events of a single day. Unlike the day described in Lie Down in Darkness, that in Set This House on Fire does not simply centralize what would otherwise be the chaotic action of the book, but contains the central action of the novel. Set This House on Fire opens, several years after the tragic events which occurred in Sambuco, Italy, with the reminiscences of Peter Leverett, the fairly detached observer of the results of the two acts of horror which occurred on that day. Leverett serves much the same function in the novel that Nick Carraway served in The Great Gatsby, that of synthesizer and commentator. He does not, as did Nick, tell the story solely through his own reminiscences (the story is so much bigger and more complex that a single-narrator retelling would be virtually impossible), but he does provide the catalyst which induces Cass Kinsolving to fill in the gaps in his own knowledge of that day in Sambuco and offer a passive but critical commentary on the other characters. Peter Leverett further resembles Carraway in that he represents to some degree the older values of rural America and remains the only uncorrupted male character in the book.

Remembering, even with only the most vague knowledge, the events that had turned his day in Sambuco into one of almost unrelieved horror, Peter Leverett is tortured by dreams:

> One of them especially I remember; like most fierce
> nightmares it had the habit of coming back again and
> again. In this one I was in a house somewhere, trying to
> sleep; it was dead of night, wintry and storming. Suddenly
> I heard a noise at the window, a sinister sound, distinct
> from the tumult of the rain and the wind. I looked outside
> and saw a shadow--the figure of someone who moved, an
> indefinite shape, a prowler whose dark form slunk toward
> me menacingly. Panicky, I reached for the telephone,
> to call the friend who lived nearby (my best, my last,
> dearest friend; nightmares deal in superlatives and
> magnitudes); he, somehow, I knew, was the only one
> dear enough, close enough, to help me. But there was no
> answer to all my frantic ringing. Then, putting the phone
> down, I hear a tap-tap-tapping at the window and turned
> to see--bared with the malignity of a fiend behind the
> streaming lass--the baleful, murderous face of the
> self-same friend. (Set This House on Fire, pp. 5-6)

This first note of horror which the book strikes comes like a fearful prelude to the story, gothicly foreshadowing the violence which follows. Leverett knows that he will be haunted by such dreams until and unless he is able to find some order within the chaos of his day in Sambuco, and especially in the almost surrealistic episodes which occurred on the day of his arrival. He is fully confident that such an order exists if only he can find the key. Motivated by the desire to determine this order and to locate the moral responsibility for two inadequately related acts of violence, Peter Leverett journeys south, stopping briefly in Virginia, the source of those older values which he represents. His intention at this time is to visit Cass Kinsolving, the only person alive who might help him piece out a complete story: his stop is significant as an almost ritualistic preparation for the ordeal of discovery he is soon to undergo with Cass Kinsolving. As he prepares to leave Virginia, Peter thinks:

> In times of stress and threat, I've heard it said, in times
> of terror and alarms, of silence and clinging, people tend
> to hold on to the past, even to imitate it: taking on old
> fashions and humming old songs, seeking out historic
> scenes and reliving old ancestral wars, in an effort to
> forget both the lack-luster present and a future too weird

and horrible to ponder. Perhaps one of the reasons we
Americans are so exceptionally nervous and driven is
that our past is effaced almost before it is made present;
in our search for old avatars to contemplate we find only
ghosts, whispers, shadows: almost nothing remains for us
to feel or seem or to absorb our longing. That evening
I was touched to the heart: by my father's sweetness
and decency and rage, but also by whatever it was within
me--within life itself, it seemed so intense--that I knew
to be irretrievably lost. Estranged from myself and from
my time, dwelling neither in the destroyed past nor in the
fantastic and incomprehensible Present, I knew that I
must find the answer to at least several things before
taking hold of myself and getting on with the job. (pp. 18-19)

. . .

From Leverett's point of view the disintegration of all apparent order
began on the day he left Rome for a visit with his wealthy, oversexed,
arrogant, but somehow gracious friend, Mason Flagg, whose name is
perhaps suggestive of his flamboyant manner. Leverett dates the events
which occur in Sambuco from the moment he left Rome. Setting out at
night, he is forced to sleep in his car, fighting intense heat and swarms of
mosquitoes. Later, almost driven off the road by a speeding Alfa Romeo,
Leverett himself begins to speed, and he is doing over sixty miles an hour
when he smashes into a motorscooter bearing a one-eyed, accident prone
Italian peasant. After being upbraided by the peasant's mother for wartime
raping, stealing, bombing, and looting, Leverett, suffering from extreme
nervous exhaustion, proceeds toward Sambuco in his wrecked car. The
speedy building up of absurd incidents creates a tone of high comedy
which finally becomes hysteria and ends only after sounding a note of
total horror.

When Leverett reaches Sambuco, after a dreamlike encounter with Cass
and his wife, it is only to blunder into the apparently serene village square
to find himself in the middle of a movie set, intimidated by arc lights and
cameras and outraged directors. Styron has achieved here a masterful
comic tone, and with it has established the absurdity of this environment
by introducing into the beautiful ancient village a movie crew engaged in
the filming, in modern dress and with numerous unsuccessful scripts, of
a costume novel about Beatrice Cenci. Assembled to work on the film is
perhaps the greatest single collection of neurotics since Nathaniel West's
Day of the Locust. The Hollywood phantasmagora offered Styron, as it
offered West, a kind of microcosm of the world's distortions and illusions;
and the description of the half-American, half-Italian cast brought together
for the movie creates the nightmarish humor of the surrealist jokesmith
without necessitating the manipulation of environment which surrealistic
imagery usually presupposes.

It is Cass Kinsolving who forms the dramatic center of this novel, and Cass's only involvement with the movie crew is in the fact that Mason Flagg forces him to perform disgusting pantomimes for their amusement. Like John Updike's Rabbit, Cass is continually running. Slotkin, a "kindly old Navy brain doctor," once told him, "'You will be running all your life (p. 314). What Cass is running after is something which had indeed flowed right on out of me, and which to save my very life I knew I had to recapture'" (p. 278). On the day he gratefully surrendered his chastity to a teen-age religious fanatic and nymphomaniac, she had referred to his orgasm as the loss of the divine spirit; Cass later accepts her description as one of particular significance. Commitment to an absurd marriage with a blissfully irresponsible, totally disorganized, and wholly devout Catholic (Cass comes from a staunch Episcopal family) hardly seems to have aided his search, and further agonized by his failures as a painter, Cass has become an alcoholic and acquired the added tortures of an ulcer. Cass had caught Mason Flagg in what was perhaps the only painful faux pas of his career, and the wealthy American embarked with such severity on a program of degrading and dehumanizing the young painter that the threatened to destroy him completely.

Largely as a result of Flagg's tortures, Cass has lost almost all touch with reality, a loss which would have been complete were it not for his intense love for an Italian peasant, Francesca, and his friendship with a semi-Fascist policeman, Luigi. It is chiefly Luigi who reminds Cass of his responsibilities--not necessarily to his family--but to himself as a man and, consequently, to life itself . . . . Trying to halt Cass's course of alcoholic annihilation, Luigi argues:

> "I'm not a religious man . . ., and this you well know.
> However, I studied among the humanist philosophers--the
> Frenchman Montaigne, Croce, the Greek Plato, not
> to speak, of course, of Gabriele D'Annunzio--and if
> there's one thing of the highest value I've discovered,
> it is simply this: that the primary moral sin is self-
> destruction--the wish for death you so painfully and
> obviously manifest. I exclude madness, of course. The
> single good is respect for the force of life. Have you
> not pictured to yourself the whole horrible vista of
> eternity? I've told you all this before, Cass. The absolute
> blankness, il niente, la nullita, stretching out for ever
> and ever, the pit of darkness which you are hurling
> yourself into, the nothingness, the void, the oblivion?
> Yet are you unable to see that although this in itself is
> awful, it is nothing to the moral sin you commit by
> willing yourself out of that life force . . . . (pp. 195-96)

Luigi's statement that the primary moral sin is self-destruction might almost have been taken from the pages of Camus's Myth of Sisyphus, for

Camus's entire argument in that essay is eventually concerned with the problem of suicide and the subsequent affirmation of life itself. Sisyphus, it should be remembered, was sentenced to his unending task precisely because of his persistent commitment to life. Since Cass has lost virtually everything of value and since life appears to him to be hopeless, meaningless, and absurd, he has no desire to live; but through his very fall he is to realize the meaning of life, and through Luigi's intervention he will be given the chance to live it.

It is in Sambuco that Cass first begins to have the "visions" which will eventually assist him in rising to the heights of an absurd hero. The first of these visions is recorded in a diary kept fitfully during his early days in Sambuco:

> "What saves me in the last analysis I have no way of
> telling. Sometimes the sensation I have that I am 2 Persons
> & by that I mean the man of my dreams and the man who
> walks in daylight is so strong and frightening that at
> times I am actually scared to look into a mirror for fear
> of seeing some face that I have never seen before." (p. 361)

This "stranger who at certain seconds comes to meet us in the mirror" (Camus, The Myth of Sisyphus, p. 11) later reappears to Cass: "Then-- wonder of wonders--he had withdrawn from himself. Standing aside, clammy and wet with horror, he saw his other self, naked now, step into the shower and, with the numb transfixed look of one already dead, turn on all the faucets full blast (368). The other self has actually turned on jets of gas. This dream, like the vision of horror in the mirror, comes to Cass immediately before he meets Mason Flagg, and as Flagg begins to dominate him there is doubt that the visions will ever be productive of true rebellion; in fact, it is only the most severe circumstances which shake Cass out of the chain into which he has sunk. Without Luigi, he would long before have been crushed by the weight of his desire for "'a long long spell of darkness'":

> He recovered himself momentarily, focusing upon me his
> hot drowned eyes. "Yes, I'll tell you how you can help
> old Cass," he said somberly. "Now I'll tell you, my
> bleeding dark angel. Fetch him the machine, fetch him the
> wherewithal--a dagger, see, a dirk, well honed around
> the edges--and bring it here, and place it on his breast-
> bone, and then with all your muscle drive it to the core."
> He paused, swaying slightly from side to side, never
> removing his gaze from my face. "No bullshit, Pete. I've
> got a lust to be gone from this place. Make me up a nice
> potion, see? Make it up out of all these bitter-tasting,
> deadly things and pour it down my gullet. Ole Cass has
> had a hard day. He's gone the full stretch and his head
> aches and his legs are weary, and there's no more weeping

in him." He held out his arms. "These limbs are plumb
wore out. Look at them, boy. Look how they shake and
tremble! What was they made for, I ast you. To wrap
lovely ladies about? To make monuments? To enfold within
them all the beauty of the world? Nossir! They was made
to destroy and now they are plumb wore out, and my
head aches, and I yearn for a long spell of darkness. (p. 238)
Camus stated that his aim in examining the absurd was
. . . to shed light upon the step taken by the mind when,
starting from a philosophy of the world's lack of meaning,
it ends up by finding a meaning and depth in it. The most
touching of these steps is religious in essence; it becomes
obvious in the theme of the irrational. But the most paradoxical
and most significant is certainly the one that attributes
rational reasons to a world it originally imagined as devoid
of any guiding principle. (Sisyphus, pp. 31-32)
Cass Kinsolving's world was devoid of any guiding principle from the
moment Mason Flagg came to Sambuco and tossed him the first bottle of
whiskey--a bottle that was to enslave him; but even as he is losing all
perspective, Cass is laying a firm basis for its re-establishment through his
love for the peasant girl Francesca. He has walked with her back into the
primitive, timeless valley where she was born, and has tried to save the
life of her tubercular father. Helping Michele has given Cass something
to live for, and while his mind is still too tormented to be able to realize
fully the significance of this experience, the seeds of self-regeneration are
planted:
On some wet black shore, foul with the blackness of
death's guilt, he was searching for an answer and a key.
In words whose meaning he did not know he called out
through the gloom, and the echoed sound came back to
him as if spoken in an outlandish tongue. Somewhere,
he knew, there was light but like a shifting phantom it
eluded him; voiceless, he strove to give voice to the cry
which now, too late, awakening, he knew: "Rise up, Michele,
rise up and walk!" he roared. And for the briefest space
of time, between dark and light, he thought he saw the man,
healed now, cured, staunch and upright, striding toward
him. O rise up Michele, my brother, rise! (STHF, p. 425)
Cass knows that he has tried to give Michele something he does not really
possess himself, that in rejecting life he has lessened his own ability to
give life to others, and he thinks with sudden horror, "Michele will die
because I have not given. Which now explains a lot . . . hell is not giving"
(p. 453).

Cass's nostalgia, his desire to give, and his blind rage for justice will,
however, finally cause him to break out of the weary chains in which

Mason has bound him. "Every act of rebellion expresses a nostalgia for innocence and an appeal to the essence of being. But one day nostalgia takes up arms and assumes the responsibility of total guilt; in other words, adopts murder and violence" (Camus, The Rebel, p. 105). Circumstances conspire to make all of Cass's stage sets collapse, and finally, jarred from his alcoholic chrysalis, he is able to perform a conscious, overt act in the name of order and value. Ironically, this act--the murder of Mason Flagg--is a profound moral wrong--not just because Cass has misjudged circumstances, but because he has a sudden realization of Flagg's humanness, and through that an insight into the meaning of life.

While the absurd hero may take many forms, underlying them all is the fundamental struggle with the environment--the refusal to surrender personal ethics to environmental pressures. The tragic hero is perhaps the most intense example of the absurd, for his opposition is directed against the moral order of the universe itself. His "disproportion," while a strong affirmation of individual will, is nonetheless of such a nature that, at some point, it will be broken. This breaking or fall of the tragic hero is in itself an affirmation of the logos of the universe, of the fact that the world is governed by "rational reasons." Life may appear cruel to the tragic hero, but this apparent cruelty is necessary to affirm the existence of moral cause and effect in the world. In the fate of the tragic hero a pattern is given to experience, and that pattern is visible not alone to the hero himself, but to the observer of his fall. The optimism inherent in tragedy is the result of this affirmation of a moral order and the assertion that man has not only sufficient power to challenge that order but sufficient nobility to achieve wisdom through his fall. It is absurd to come into collision with the universal law of righteousness (or, like Ahab, with the universal law of unrighteousness), but it is also the height of heroism. Perhaps the most significant reason for the failure of modern authors to create tragedy in its classical fullness is simply that tragedy demands for its full implementation a belief in a moral order superior to the individual. Without such a belief the ultimate tragic creation, the tragic hero, is inconceivable. In Set This House on Fire Styron has perhaps come closer than any other modern author to actualizing this creation.

One of the earliest facts which we learn about Cass is that he is a psychotic, dismissed uncured from a Navy hospital. He is frequently violent in public, he abuses his family, and he goes through the ritual of degrading songs and gestures whenever Mason Flagg demands this payment. We also learn near the beginning of the novel that upon his discharge from the hospital Cass was presented with a two-volume edition of Greek drama (p. 129). Cass refers at length to Oedipus, and in the course of the evening tragedy preceding his murder of Mason, he quotes at length from the tragedy. Such passages alone suggest that Cass is meant to be compared to a classical tragic hero, and on the brink of his fall he seems to grasp the drama which he is now destined to play out:

"Hold on! Let me tell you what we'll do. Together you
and me we'll pull a Prometheus on 'em. We'll bring back
tragedy to the land of Pepsi-Cola and the peanut brittle
and the Modess Because. That's what we'll do, by God!
And we'll make the ignorant little buggers like it. No more
popcorn, no more dreamboats, no more Donald Duck, no
more wet dreams in the mezzanine. Tragedy, by God'
that's what we'll give 'em! Something to stiffen their
spines and firm up their joints and clean out their tiny
little souls. What'll you have? Ajax? Alcestis? Electra?
Iphigenia? Hoo-boy!" Once more his hand plunged into
the neck of his T-shirt. I would not be the murderer of
my mother, and of thee too. Sufficient is her blood. No,
I will share my fortune live with thee, or with thee die:
to Argos I will lead thee . . .'" (pp. 118-19)

What Cass does not know at this time, but what he will learn as a participant in the tragedy of the following day, is a fundamental lesson of all
tragedy: ". . . the harder you kite upward like that the harder you hit the
ground when you fall" (p. 267).

Cass . . . had not only the opportunity but also the ability to become "a
good family man, striving for the sunny ideal of mens sana" but he
rejected this alternative in deference to "that necessary part of the self
which saw the world with passion and recklessness, and which had to be
flayed and exacerbated and even maddened to retain its vision (pp.
296-97). It is because of this passion and recklessness that Cass finds
himself in a situation in which he must sin, albeit unwillingly. W.H.
Auden has argued that the tragic situation in which a character appears to
have no choice but to sin is actually "a sign that he is guilty of another sin
of hybris, an overweening self-confidence which makes him believe that
he, with all his arete, is a god who cannot be made to suffer." Perhaps the
most common instance of hybris is man's failure to recognize human
limitations, in trying to operate with presumably complete knowledge and
control when, of course, the effects of his actions can never be known in
their entirety. Oedipus presumes to act as though he could totally control
the results of his actions, and his final symbolic blinding is a recognition
of his limitations, of what the Greeks would have recognized as ate.

Presuming to be godlike, the tragic hero often takes upon himself the
responsibility of becoming a judge. Such was Oedipus' impetuous attack
on his own father. Cass, too, demonstrates a lack of control, and we have,
in his participation as a boy in the destruction of the Negro cabin, an
example of the kind of hybris which we see when Oedipus strikes his
father. Cass does not appear to know what made him participate in the
willful destruction of all which this family owned or revered, but he
suggests it in his observation that "all the cliches and shibboleths I'd been
brought up with came rolling back--a nigger wasn't much more than an

animal anyway" (p. 378). It is the overweening, blind pride of a white Southerner which makes him strike the face of the humanistic moral universe. The tragic hero presumes to act like a god, sitting in judgment as Cass had done in his treatment of the Negro. Cass must bear the guilt and shame of this episode, must be half-smothered for his blind violation, and he later notes to Peter Leverett that "this figured in what happened to me there in Sambuco" (p. 379). The essential, final ingredient of the tragic hero is that he must realize his own blindness, his own limitations, and accept the obligations of his guilt. At the point of Cass's recognition Styron becomes particularly specific:

> Cass fell silent again. Then he said: "But to kill a man,
> even in hatred, even in revenge, is like an amputation.
> Though this man may have done you the foulest injustice
> in the world, when you have killed him you have removed
> a part of yourself forever. For here was so-and-so. Here
> was some swine, some blackguard, some devil. But what
> made him tick? What made him do the things he did? What
> was his history? What went on in his mind? What, if you
> had let him live, would he have become? Would he have
> stayed a swine, unregenerate to the end? Or, would he
> have become a better man? Maybe he could have imparted
> to you some secrets. You do not know. You have acted
> the role of God, you have judged him and condemned him.
> And by condemning him, by killing him, all the answers
> to those questions pass with him into oblivion. Only you
> remain--shorn of all that knowledge, and with as much
> pain as if somehow you had been dismembered. It is a
> pain that will stay with you as long as you live. . . (p. 446)

It is through Peter Leverett that the scene in Sambuco is first set for tragedy. The macabre experiences of his trip lend the feeling of a surrealistic dreamscape to his arrival. The deserted square almost assumes the character of a stage awaiting its actors, and the personalities of the movie folk clustered beneath the lights (p. 57), as they unfold in the following chapters, help to reaffirm the feeling that we are watching something performed in the theatre. From the moment of Leverett's arrival at Mason's palace, when he observes that a confusing amber light played over the scene (p. 99) until his horrified viewing of the act that Cass performs for Mason, this theatrical feeling becomes increasingly frenzied and helps to prepare the reader for the scenes which follow.

Mason Flagg has raped Francesca, the graceful peasant girl who represents for Cass all the beauty and value which have gone out of his life. Cass knows of the rape and has determined to be revenged on Flagg, but before he can formulate a plan he learns that Francesca has been raped a second time, and that this time she has also been hideously, fatally mutilated. Never questioning Mason's guilt, Cass tracks and brutally murders the young American dilettante. This "justice is executed against a classical setting: before a ruined villa with a sagging facade and blasted columns" (p. 463), a kind of temple bearing the inscription DUM SPIRO SPERO, the adopted motto of Cass's home state, South Carolina. As if to illustrate and support the argument of tragedy, Styron repeatedly suggests classical episodes and settings. Earlier in the novel, when Cass considered ways of breaking free of Mason, he had looked out to sea and observed "above Salerno, aloft, unbelievably high in space . . . a mist, a churning rack of cloud, terrible and only faintly discerned, as of the smoke from remote cities sacked and aflame: he gave a stir, touched on the shoulder by an unseen, unknowable hand" (p. 406).

The tragedy that takes place in Sambuco first comes to Leverett through a series of wailing cries similar to those which might be made by the chorus in a Greek play. The first words of explanation which he hears are "'Quelle horreur! Quelle tragedie'" (p. 219). Pressed for more details, the money-conscious hotel owner, Windgasser, can only mutter, "'Overpowering twagedy, my God. It's like the Gweeks, I tell you, but far worse!'" (p. 220). Describing the crowded square into which he runs, Leverett notes that "A squad of carabinieri entered in a riot truck, stage right . . ." (p. 221), and when the horrifying events of the day are over, Cass comments to Leverett, "Exeunt omnes. Exit the whole lousy bunch" (p. 239). Thus, as seen through Leverett's eyes, the tragedy which occurs in Sambuco observes the unities of time, place, and action; it constitutes, in fact, a kind of play within the novel.

As a modern version of the tragic hero Cass has not challenged the authority of a god or group of gods, but he has challenged the purposive ordering of the universe in which right action is somehow rewarded and wrong action punished, if only within the confines of the individual conscience. Like Camus himself, Styron avoids commitment on words like "god," but also like Camus he is finally able to maintain that the world, which appears to lack all vestiges of order, is in fact governed by "rational reasons." Camus stated that the absurd does not lead to God because "the absurd is sin without God" (Sisyphus, p. 30). What Camus undoubtedly intended to assert was that the sense of sin must come from within, not from some set of traditional rules handed down from an abstract higher power. Perhaps it is sufficient to say that what Cass violates is Rabbit Angstrom's "something out there that wants me to find it." Important to the creation of the modern tragic hero as it is to the modern saint, is the emphasis that there is, after all, something out there, some convergence of individual consciousness in the formation of transcendent values, even though none of the traditional definitions of that something are acceptable. In terms of Cass's own particular vision we might describe it as the humanistic order of the universe; even so, Cass must discover and shoulder his own sin, for there is no authority dictating punishment--least of all is there a threat of punishment after death. Even at the moment of killing Flagg, Cass is aware of his violation of the humanistic order as he had been aware at the time of the destruction of the Negro cabin:

> Perhaps it was then that he drew back, understanding where
> he was, and what he had done. He does not recall. Perhaps
> it was only the "Doll-baby," echoing belatedly in his mind,
> that caused him to halt and look down and see that the
> pale dead face, which was so soft and boyish, and in
> death as in life so tormented, might be the face of almost
> anything, but was not the face of a killer.
> Children he thought, standing erect over the twitching body.
> Children! My Christ! All of us!
> Then in his last grief and rage he wrestled Mason's body to
> the parapet, and wearily heaved it up in his arms and kept
> it for a moment close to his breast. And then he hurled it
> into the void. (pp. 464-65)

What Cass learns after the murder is that Mason Flagg had not attacked and mutilated Francesca on the path outside the village, but that this atrocity was committed by Saverio, the village idiot who had earlier been apprehended in an almost identical crime. The authorities, however, are convinced that Flagg committed suicide after attacking Francesca; only Cass and his soulmate Luigi know the truth. In desperation Cass, who has had no use for religion, turns to a priest with the words, "Help me." The priest cannot help him any more than Slotkin, the psychiatrist to whom Cass once literally prayed, can help him to resolve this moral dilemma. Only the fundamentally humanistic Luigi can assist Cass by convincing him that he must, in order to achieve knowledge, not wallow in his guilt, but expiate it and eventually defeat it by living. Cass "'had come to the end of the road and had found there nothing at all. There was nothing. There was a nullity in the universe so great as to encompass and drown the universe itself. The value of a man's life was nothing, and his destiny nothingness'" (p. 489). Despite this bitter pronouncement, Cass still feels "that old vast gnawing hunger," a hunger for order and meaning in the face of a meaningless universe. Luigi admonishes Cass to expiate his guilt, refusing him the right to sin in his guilt by cultivating it. He urges that Cass must, like Oedipus, become a penitent in life. Cass's choice is the choice between suicide and life which Camus poses in The Myth of Sisyphus, and Cass chooses life. . . . The author sees Cass possessed of a kind of vision for which he had only groped tentatively before his "fall" . . . . Styron sees Cass as a modern Oedipus, and Camus saw Oedipus as an example of the absurd man:

> Happiness and the absurd are two sons of the same earth. They
> are inseparable. It would be a mistake to say that happiness
> springs from the absurd discovery. It happens as well that the
> feeling of the absurd springs from happiness. "I conclude that
> all is well," says Oedipus," and that remark is sacred. It

echoes in the wild and limited universe of man. It teaches
that all is not, has not been exhausted. It drives out of this
world a god who had come into it with a dissatisfaction and a
preference for futile sufferings. It makes of fate a human
matter, which must be settled among men. (Sisyphus, pp. 90-91)
"Oedipus gives," Camus says, "the recipe for the absurd victory," and
suggesting the link between the classical Oedipus and Oedipus the absurd
hero, he adds, "Ancient wisdom confirms modern heroism" (Sisyphus, p.
90).

If the above speech, in which Cass announces his choice of being,
makes no affirmation of the idea of knowledge, it does suggest hope that
he will eventually achieve something like knowledge. Indeed like
knowledge. Indeed he seems to demonstrate such an acquisition in one of
the two letters appended to the novel, in which he writes, "Who was it in
Lear who said ripeness is all. I forget, but he was right" (STHF, p. 506).
As an artist he has turned social critic out of a desire for reform, and he
thus demonstrates the increasing tendency of the existential hero to return
to society. In triumphing over himself, in defeating his sense of guilt, in
establishing a love for humanity, Cass has achieved a singular victory, and
it is necessary to think of him as Camus intended that we think of
Sisyphus, as "happy."

*From The Absurd Hero in American Fiction: Updike, Styron, Bellow,
Salinger: 66-81. Reprinted by permission.

STYRON'S DISGUISES: A PROVISIONAL REBEL IN CHRISTIAN MASQUERADE*

Samuel Coale

Many of William Styron's strengths as a writer come from those that we associate with Southern fiction. Baroque rhetoric powers his narratives; Faulkner's ghost lingers in his language. He evokes the kind of doomed, guilt-ridden landscapes we associate with the Southern vision of the world. The problem of evil haunts him at all levels--social, psychological, metaphysical--and spawns the moral quest, the search for values of his heroes amid the stark realities of pain and suffering. Manichean conflicts ravage his prose, his outlook, his characters, as if an ultimate nihilism or irrevocable Greek fate savaged the vestiges of his own Christian faith or background. Such a war-torn spirit leads to certain death, to spiritual paralysis. He stalks the riddles of personality like the best romancers and sets up extraordinary events and persons: Culver to Mannix, Peter Leverett to Cass Kinsolving, Stingo to Sophie Zawistowska and Nathan Landau. A kind of existential, finally unexorcised sense of guilt relentlessly hounds him.

Styron writes in the tradition of the Southern gothic romance, moving from revelation to revelation, surprise to surprise, pacing his fiction as a series of building climaxes, each more shattering than the preceding one. He has written in this manner from the very first, as in <u>Lie Down in Darkness</u>: "it finally occurred to me to use separate moments in time, four or five long dramatic scenes revolving around the daughter, Peyton, at different stages in her life. The business of the progression of time seems to me one of the most difficult problems a novelist has to cope with."(1) The secret remains "a sense of architecture--a symmetry, perhaps unobtrusive but always there, without which a novel sprawls, becomes a self-indulged octopus. It was a matter of form."(2)

Styron's gothic architecture comes complete with its aura of damnation and doom, a dusky cathedral filled with omens and auguries, nightmares and demonic shadows. And at the end of labyrinthine corridors appear the inevitable horrors: Peyton's suicide, Cass's murder of Mason Flagg, Nat's murder of Margaret Whitehead, Sophie's surrendering her daughter Eva to the gas ovens of Birkenau, Sambuco, "aloof upon its precipice, remote and beautifully difficult of access,"(3) the enclosed white temple of Nat Turner's dreams, "those days"(4) of the 1940s in Sophie's Choice: here are the removed, withdrawn settings for dark romances. Nathan Landau wonders, however, if such a structure for fiction could be "a worn-out tradition," (p. 115), and John Gardner, reviewing Sophie's Choice, considered the ambiguous relationship between the evil of Auschwitz and "the helpless groaning and self-flagellation of the Southern Gothic novel." The suggestion is raised by both Styron and Gardner whether or not this kind of romance has outlived its usefulness, however passionately and grippingly re-created.

The ambiguous nature of Styron's vision may serve to undermine his gothic structures. For one thing, he often relies too heavily upon psychological explanations, a kind of rational reductionism that reduces metaphysical to Freudian solutions. In Lie Down in Darkness, Styron deals with what his character, Albert Berger, calls, "this South with its cancerous religiosity, its exhausting need to put manners before morals, to negate all ethos . . . a husk of culture,"(6) in the new suburban middle-class South, a world hung up on its own narcissistic corruptions. These may be the result of the Old South gone dead, but a stronger case can be made for Oedipal tensions and familial dislocations along a purely psychological grid: nostalgia and self-indulgence, however alcoholic, however wounding, seem almost disconnected from any Southern past, or for that matter any past at all.

The trouble with the elegantly rendered and moving The Confessions of Nat Turner is that the religious fanatic cum prophet tells his own tale. All explanations and suggestions-psychological, tragic, Christian, heroic--tend to look like mere self-justifications. Nat as both interpreter and actor may see himself moving from Old Testament vengeance to New Testament charity and contrition, but within its own psychological maneuverings and suggestions, even this broadly mythic and religious design dissolves. The tidy psychology of the case study threatens to undermine the realities of any political action, any historical commitment. Manichean conflict--black vs. white, good vs. evil, master vs. slave-produces a kind of paralysis, a deeply felt and exquisitely written blank like the smooth white sides of that dreamed windowless enclosure.

Styron once suggested "that all my work is predicated on revolt in one way or another. And of course there's something about Nat Turner that's the ultimate fulfillment of all this. It's a strange revelation."(7) As he once described himself, he remains a "provisional rebel"(8): his sufferers are witnessed at a distance, Mannix's "revolt" by Culver, Cass's angst by Leverett, Sophie's by Stingo. It is as if he has his cake--the rebellion, the guilt--and eats it, too--the "resurrection" and increased awareness of his witnesses. If many of Styron's rebels participate in a kind of self-mutilation or self-flagellation, his witnesses experience this as well, but at a distance. As we shall see in both Set This House on Fire and Sophie's Choice--for me his most passionate and fierce romances--violence and revenge are just barely, if at all, transmuted into Christian symbols; at times, the Christian imagery seems itself "provisional," a literary laying on of uncertain hands. We get finally not tragedies but melodramas, exorcisms rendered "safe" by the remarkably unscathed witnesses.

The whole question of Styron's notion of evil remains ambiguous. In Lie Down in Darkness Styron writes: "Too powerful a consciousness of evil was often the result of infantile emotions. The cowardly Puritan . . ., unwilling to partake of free religious inquiry, uses the devil as a scapegoat to rid himself of the need for positive action" (p. 113). Evil becomes a dodge, an excuse for inaction, paralysis, as if Manichean polarities produced only stalemate, fashioned in a fierce baroque prose style. And Styron adds: "Perhaps the miseries of our century will be recalled only as the work of a race of strange and troublous children, by the wise old men in the aeons which come after us."(9) Infantile emotions: troublous children: a hint of adolescent angst sounded in a void? Evil as howling self? Is there something to Mailer's indictment of Set This House on Fire as the "magnum Opus of a fat spoiled rich boy who could write like an angel about landscape and like an adolescent about people"?(10) Does gothic doom become, then, rhetorical, a literary attitude, a Faulknerian mannerism laced with a fatal Fitzgerald-like glamour, overwrought in a gothic style?

Jonathan Baumbach suggests that Set This House on Fire "attempts the improbable: the alchemical transformation of impotent rage into tragic experience. Styron's rage is the hell-fire heat of the idealist faced by an unredeemably corrupt world for which he as fallen man feels obsessively and hopelessly guilty."(11) This suggests also Gardner's assessment of Styron's writing as "a piece of anguished Protestant soul-searching, an attempt to seize all the evil in the world--in his own heart first--crush it, and create a planet fit for God and man."(12) The Manichean battles in this book reveal the passionate intensity of this alchemical urge.

The sacred and the profane, the prudish and the prurient, God and nothingness, being and nihilism, doom and nostalgia, Anglo-Saxon and Italian honesty battle it out in Set This House on Fire. Peter Leverett, the moderate realistic lawyer, confronts Cass Kinsolving, the guilt-ridden visionary artist. Each has been attracted and played sycophant to the "gorgeous   silver fish . . . a creature so strange, so new" (p. 454) that is Mason Flagg. Flagg represents a Manichean vision in his "dual role of daytime squire and nighttime nihilism" (p. 161), a distinctively American

Jekyll and Hyde, "able in a time of hideous surfeit, and Togetherness's lurid mist, to revolt from conventional values, to plunge into a chic vortex of sensation, dope, and fabricated sin, though all the while retaining a strong grip on his two million dollars" (p. 161). Is this Styron's "provisional rebel"? He celebrates the new frontier of sexual adventure as a gnostic libertine, corrupt in his faith, would and reveals "that slick, arrogant, sensual, impenitently youthful, American and vainglorious face" (p. 194): the spoiled, self-indulgent American child, filled with unfulfilled desire, itself desirous of further increase. He suggests Styron's America in the Fifties, "a general wasting away of quality, a kind of sleazy common prostration of the human spirit" (p. 118), in times "like these when men go whoring off after false gods" in a realm of "moral and spiritual anarchy" (p. 13). Is there any wonder that Peter Leverett's father cries out for "something ferocious and tragic, like what happened to Jericho or the cities of the plain" (p. 15), a promise to "bring back tragedy to the land of the Pepsi-cola" (p. 121)?

The Manichean vision acquires metaphysical proportions in Cass's mind. He "dreamed wild Manichean dreams, dreams that told him that God . . . was weaker even than the evil He created and allowed to reside in the soul of man" (p. 282). Dreams "of women with burdens, and dogs being beaten, and these somehow all seemed inextricably and mysteriously connected, and monstrously, intolerably so" (p. 351) haunt him, the dog beaten to death but refusing to die, "which suffered all the more because even He in His mighty belated compassion could not deliver His creatures from their living pain" (p. 365).

Peter Leverett suffers a recurring nightmare of a shadow beyond the window in the dark, a friend bent on betrayal and murder but for no apparent reason. It is Cass who suggests "that whosoever it is that rises in a dream with a look on his face of eternal damnation is just one's own self, wearing a mask, and that's the fact of the matter" (p. 371). Evil becomes the self-trapped in itself, a spirit at war with itself, a narcissistic and ineradicable sense of guilt that despite Cass's explanations of exile, orphanhood, ignorance, the war, his wife's Catholicism, his own "puddle of self" (p. 260) at the base of his artistic nature, his Anglo-Saxon background, his terror, his Americanness, his actions toward blacks, will not be overcome. "To triumph over self is to triumph over Death," Cass declares. "It is to triumph over that beast which one's self interposes between one's soul and one's God" (p. 260). Between that soul and God lurks the beast of the self, the solipsistic psychological center around which Styron's metaphysical and socio-cultural explanations of Manicheism pale. At one point Cass discusses "the business about evil--what it is, where it is, whether it's a reality, or just a figment of the mind," a cancer in the body or something "to stomp on like you would a flea carrying bubonic plague" (p. 130). He decides that "both of these theories are as evil as the evil they are intended to destroy and cure" (p. 131). Evil thus remains "the puddle of self," which Styron belabors in the book, or the mystery of endless pain that knows no justification, a cruel beating down of the human spirit that in the end, like that puddle, suggests a perpetual entrapment, an imprisonment both of mind and matter, a Manichean mystery that can know release only in the worship of a demonic God or the furtive celebration of sex and sensation.

Both Leverett and Kinsolving press on to make their personal night-mares make sense. "Passionately he tried to make the dream give up its meaning" (p. 320), Styron writes of Cass. He might just as well be writing about his use of the gothic romance to surrender up the significance of his own dark dreams of perpetual conflict and combat. "Each detail was as clear in his mind as something which happened only yesterday, yet when he tried to put them all together he ended up with blank ambiguous chaos" (p. 320). The details refuse to conjure up the overall design: we have reached a standstill, an impasse. "These various horrors and sweats you have when you're asleep add up to something," Cass maintains, "even if these horrors are masked and these sweats are symbols. What you've got to do is get behind the mask and the symbol" (p. 375). Kinsolving suggests Melville's Ahab who, in penetrating the mask, reduces ambiguity to palpable design and submits willfully to the Manichean fire-worshippers at his side. He becomes his own devil. Cass cannot. . . .

Kinsolving and Leverett meet years later to talk in a fishing boat on the Southern river of their childhoods. If at first both seem like opposites, they in fact blend into one Southern sensibility: bewitched and entranced by Flagg, they succumb to a rampant unanchored nostalgia that swallows everything before it, an omnivorous sentimentality, "the sad nostalgic glamor" (p. 268), the Southern mind's ravenous appetite for "a hundred gentle memories, purely summer, purely southern, which swarmed instantly through his mind, though one huge memory encompassed all" (p. 378). Nostalgia begets narcissism or vice-versa: intensity of feeling replaces knowledge as the keystone to awareness. This nostalgia is not seen as tragic, as a flight from adulthood: it survives "pure" in its sweeping intensities, its rhetorical sweep--and is the ominous flip-side of Cass's dread, of Styron's gothic plot and structure. Catastrophe, doom, guilt, phantoms, and diabolical enchantment draw Leverett to Flagg, Cass to Flagg, Leverett to Cass, but a rampant childhood nostalgia surmounts and floods them all, feeding upon itself.

As Flannery O'Connor suggested, "When tenderness is detached from the source of tenderness, its logical outcome is terror."(13) That nostalgic tenderness cancels spiritual stalemate. As Joyce Carol Oates suggests in reference to Mailer, "He has constructed an entire body of work around a Manichean existentialism [with] a firm belief in the absolute existence of Evil [and] a belief in a limited God, a God Who is a warring element in a divided universe. . . . His energetic Manichaeanism forbids a higher art. Initiation . . . brings the protagonist not to newer visions . . . but to a dead end, a full stop."(14) Melodrama deflates tragedy and for all its passion and power leaves a world split between suffering and sentimentality, a dark design of untransmuted spiritual impotence, mesmerized by a Manichean reality but unable or unwilling to succumb to its fatal power and terrifyingly realized inevitability. Perhaps "ultimate" rebellion would insist on such a vision. "Provisional" rebellion can only disguise it in Christian images and psychological explanations. The void which surrounds Cass's tirades, that outer world which dissolves in the wake of his internal cries, may reflect only his own narcissism, suggesting that Styron is intent upon withdrawing from the very Manichean vision he's so fiercely created into a safer hollow.

The Manichean vision of <u>Sophie's Choice</u> is announced in Styron's opening quotation from Andre Malraux's <u>Lazare</u>: "I seek that essential region of the soul where absolute evil confronts brotherhood." Nathan is both Sophie's savior and destroyer; love battles death; Calvinist Southerners are mesmerized by New York Jews; North and South fight over virtue or the lack of it; black and white, slave and master become both victims and accomplices of one another; out of the adversity Poland has suffered comes not compassion and charity but sustained anti-Semitic cruelty; sex in Stingo's 1940s at the age of twenty-two breeds both liberation and guilt; Sophie "could not bear the contrast between the abstract yet immeasurable beauty of music and the almost touchable dimensions of her own aching despair" (p. 94); every choice is fraught with disaster; survival itself produces the ineradicable "toxin of guilt." Poland reflects a defeated South with "her indwelling ravaged and melancholy heart," the sense of inestimable loss, a legacy of "cruelty and compassion" (p. 247). Opposites attract, become entangled, lead to suicide as ultimate paralysis. Steiner's "two orders of simultaneous experience are so different, so irreconcilable to any common norm of human values, their coexistence is so hideous a paradox" that they like "Gnostic speculation imply, different species of time in the same world" (p. 216). Evil itself becomes the banality of duty and obedience, the belief in the "absolute <u>expendability</u> of human life" (p. 235), the reality of Auschwitz that cannot be finally understood.

The most "common norm of human values" Styron undermines is Christianity, at the same time he uses Christian imagery, apparently without irony, to describe the scope and mythic archetypes of his material: "I mean it when I say that no chaste and famished grail-tormented Christian knight could have gazed with more slack-jawed admiration at the object of his quest than I did at my first glimpse of Sophie's bouncing behind" (p. 358). A good line, but the Christian quest motif sticks to the entire form of Styron's use of the gothic romance: it is supposed to lead, however disastrously, to understanding, [to] significance in ultimately religious terms. Stingo's own "Protestant moderation" (p. 299) invests sex with guilt and his "residual Calvinism" (p. 495) sparks his imagination with visions of doom and desecration. On the train, however, with the "dark priestess" toward the end of the book, the black woman, he "went into a bizarre religious convulsion, brief in duration but intense" and reads the Bible aloud with her, not the Sermon on the Mount, but "the grand old Hebrew woe seemed more cathartic, so we went back to Job" (p. 506), the archetypal victim, but one of residual faith, a kind the agnostic Stingo does not share. He disguises himself as the Reverend Entwhistle to get a room with Sophie and admits that "the Scriptures were always largely a literary convenience, supplying me with allusions and tag lines for the characters in my novel" (p. 505), but what are we to make of Stingo's impression of Dr. Jemand von Niemand, the man who forces on Sophie her most chilling choice? He must have done so, Stingo speculates, because he thirsted for faith, and to restore God he first must commit a great sin: "All of his depravity had been enacted in a vacuum of sinless and businesslike godliness, while his soul thirsted for beatitude" (p. 486). The great sin will shadow forth a greater faith "to restore his belief in God" (p. 486).

At the conclusion of the book, Stingo reads lines from Dickinson at the graves of Sophie and Nathan: "Ample make this bed. / Make this bed with awe; / In it wait till judgment break / Excellent and fair" (p. 512). After a night on the beach of Poesque dreams, being buried alive and awaking to find himself buried in sand like "a living cadaver being prepared for burial in the sands of Egypt," he welcomes the morning, blesses "my resurrection," and explains: "This was not my judgment day--only morning. Morning: excellent and fair" (p. 515). The ironies are apparent, but so is the stab at symbolic resurrection, waking from the gothic nightmare, returned to the land of the living. It is as if Stingo/Styron wants it both ways again, provisionally damned, provisionally saved. Auschwitz disregarded "Christian constraint" (p. 235); Stingo will not, despite the revelations of Sophie. He clings to his genteel moderation despite the "Sophiemania" (p. 307) that engulfs him. . . .

Gothic romance usually demands the waking from the nightmare, a return to normalcy after the exorcism. But Stingo, like Peter Leverett and Cass Kinsolving before him, will not surrender to being exorcized; he clings to the very fallacious and out-moded Christian doctrines the narrative of the romance undermines. Perhaps the gothic romance cannot embrace absolute evil; the term itself curdles the narrator's will to embrace it. Others will die; they will survive because of the very harried faith they have been "taught" during the romance to outgrow. Stingo's attraction to a certain morbidity is not the same thing as being "called the 'tragic sense'" (p. 110). It is too guarded, too self-protected, too distanced from the real Manichean vision of things by splendid baroque rhetoric and vocabularies of doom and dark auguries. He loves the doom as he loves a nostalgic South; it is a feeling in his bones, shiveringly enjoyable, a frisson of the spirit. . . .

Yet <u>Sophie's Choice</u> works with its escalating confessions, its ominous rhetoric, its sheer dramatic scope and power, as we learn of the real nature of Sophie's father, the many lovers from the murderer Jozef to the lesbian Wanda, the incredible choice of surrendering her daughter to the ovens. Stingo's climax literally occurs in bed--at last--with the pale, radiant Sophie; hers occurs with her suicide pact with Nathan: sex and death, twin dark towers of Manichean castles: semen and cyanide brutally inter-mingled. Everyone's a victim. The Jews are also the victims of victims, that's the main difference (p. 474). There is the frightening core of <u>So-phie's Choice,</u> evaded or at least displaced by Stingo's awakening from premature burial to the possibility of morning and of resurrection. Sophie weaves tale after tale before her "patient confessor" (p. 355), each until the end "a fabrication, a wretched lie, another fantasy served up to provide a frail barrier, a hopeless and crumbly line of defense between those she cared for, like myself, and her smothering guilt" (p. 237). But the Christian fabrications, the literary allusions, are themselves frail barriers and should crumble completely before the overwhelming presence of guilt, even as small in comparison to Sophie's as is Stingo's in relation to his mother's death, his native region, the money he inherited from the slave sold down river, Artiste (appropriately named). Gothic romance, aligned to Christian images of demonic nightmare, the dark night of the soul, and resurrection, itself crumbles as it did in Hawthorne's <u>The Marble Faun,</u> undone by the pit of Rome, or in Hawthorne's <u>The Blithedale Romance,</u> overwhelmed by the harsh reality of power, of masters and slaves beneath the veils. In Stingo's narrative, it does seem a "worn-out tradition."

Perhaps Styron writes at the end of Southern romance, or perhaps he has stretched the form to include a vision of the world that it cannot contain, that murky spurious mixture of Christian archetype and Maniche-an vision. Rational psychological explanations and Christian archetypes cannot encompass such a fierce conjuring up of guilt; they can only reduce and confine it. Styron's guilt will not be confined in any rational, religious scheme or design: it overwhelms every attempt to comprehend it, existing as some great Manichean black hole that can result only in ultimate with-drawal--the ascetics of suicide--or in sexual revelry--the libertinism of Mason Flagg, of Stingo's starving lust. Rhetoric, however intense and poetic, cannot transmute it into anything finally significant other than its own dark irrevocable existence, men and women entombed for life. As Rilke suggests in Styron's opening quote, death, the whole of earth,--even before life's begun . . . this is beyond description!"

In Styron's world, we are really in Poe country. Faulkner transcended it by his genius, the depth of his complexity of vision; Flannery O'Connor surmounted it through an ultimate religious faith garbed in grotesque disguises, in the grim visages of serious clowns. Carson McCullers and Styron seem trapped within it, McCullers more certain of the Manichean shadows of her vision, setting it up as dark fable, as inevitable as death itself. Styron cautiously moves around it, hanging on to Christian images, archetypes, symbols despite the splendid proofs that they do not apply. Perhaps this is where the Southern tradition in American fiction ends, grappling with absolute evil outside its borders, serving up horrors as it would serve up childhood fantasies. Styron excels at it. His fiction drives itself toward a revelation he cannot or will not accept. All the magnificent rhetoric in the world will not gloss over the provisional nature of his vision, not mere ambiguity but at last evasion. The line between paradox and paralysis is a thin one. Styron's marvelous conjurings up of the former leads finally to the latter, and perhaps this is the absolute evil in contemporary society that haunts him most.

Notes

(1) Interview with William Styron, in Writers at Work: The Paris Review Interviews, ed. Malcolm Cowley (New York: Viking Press, 1958), p. 275.

(2) William Styron, "Recollections of a Once Timid Novelist," The Hartford Courant Magazine, 3 January 1982, 8.

(3) William Styron, Set This House on Fire (New York: Bantam Windstone Books, 1981), p. 3. Subsequent citations are to this edition.

(4) William Styron, Sophie's Choice (New York: Random House, 1979), p. 3. Subsequent citations are to this edition.

(5) John Gardner, "A Novel of Evil," The New York Times Book Review, (27 May 1979), 17.

(6) William Styron, Lie Down in Darkness (New York: New American Library, 1951), p. 346. Subsequent citations are to this edition.

(7) Interview with William Styron by the author, 15 July 1969. Cited below as Interview.

(8) Interview.

(9) William Styron, "The Prevalence of Wonders," Nation, 176 (2 May 1953), 371.

(10) Norman Mailer, "Norman Mailer vs. Nine Writers," Esquire, 60 (July 1963), 64.

(11) Jonathan Baumbach, "Paradise Lost: The Novels of William Styron," South Atlantic Quarterly 63 (Spring 1964), 215.

(12) Gardner, 16.

(13) Flannery O'Connor," Introduction to A Memoir of Mary Ann," in Mystery and Manners, ed. Sally and Robert Fitzgerald (New York: Farrar Straus Giroux, 1962), p. 227.

(14) Joyce Carol Oates, "Norman Mailer: The Teleology of the Unconscious," in New Heaven, New Earth: The Visionary Experience in Literature (New York: Vanguard Press, 1974), pp. 191-92, 200.

*From Critique 26, no. 2 (1985): 57-66. Reprinted by permission.

THE CONFESSIONS OF NAT TURNER

THE FIRE LAST TIME*

George Steiner

As by now almost everyone knows, William Styron's The Confessions of Nat Turner deals with a brief slave revolt that took place in the late summer of 1831 in Southampton County, a remote corner of southeastern Virginia. The uprising was a ragged affair, doomed from the start. It involved seventy-five Negroes and resulted in the killing of fifty-five whites; most of the insurgent slaves were hacked down or executed. The body of Nat Turner, begetter and ringleader, was taken from the gallows, its flesh was boiled into grease, and small leather keepsakes were made of the skin. In Richmond, in 1832, T. R. Gray issued a pamphlet entitled "The Confessions of Nat Turner." Several other accounts of the mutiny were written, among them William Sidney Drewry's The Southampton Insurrection. Though strategically puerile, the revolt of Nat Turner sent a shock of fury and baffled alarm through the South comparable to the one occasioned a generation later by John Brown's raid. It was the only organized rebellion, however short-lived, in the annals of American Negro slavery.

Mr. Styron grew up not far from Southampton County and thought to make of Nat Turner the subject of his first novel. Instead, he produced Lie Down in Darkness, a marvellously dense and vehement statement of what it is to come of age Southern and haunted. This was followed by The Long March and that much criticized but revealing tale of Europe and America in their postwar, post-Thomas Wolfe interaction--Set This House on Fire. After which Mr. Styron embarked on a long silence and the theme that had from the first been ripening in his consciousness. The Confessions of Nat Turner is a return home, a falconlike gyring toward the point of departure which is characteristic of a number of American novelists (among Hemingway's last projects was a novel set in the Michigan of his boyhood). Is it merely fanciful to note how clear and symbolic a design lurks in Mr. Styron's earlier titles? Nat Turner lies in a great darkness, seeks to make the long march to the local and celestial Jerusalem, and leaves houses burning in his wake. But two forces more recent than Mr. Styron's initial impulse have acted on the book. It is difficult to listen to Nat Turner's canny self-baring or impassioned tone without hearing at the same time the voice of Mr. James Baldwin. The other modifier is, of course, recent history--the coming of the storm that now blows across American life. The crisis of civil rights, the new relationships to each other and to their own individual sensibilities that this crisis has forced on both whites and Negroes (as yet, we capitalize one but not the other) give Mr. Styron's fable a special relevance. This is a book about a small fire last time in the light, at once revelatory and magnifying, of the great blaze now.

The narrative is set in a flashback older than Victor Hugo's "Last Days of a Condemned Man," older even than the monitory thieves' pamphlets of the seventeenth century. During the five days preceding his execution Nat Turner reviews the confession he has dictated to T.R. Gray his inquisitor, spokesman before the court and final intimate. Gray is not seeking to rack his doomed client. He is baffled by the fact that Turner has himself killed only one white person--the flower of genteel Virginia girlhood Margaret Whitehead--and that he feels no remorse for the general butchery: "You mean to tell me that now, after all these here months your heart ain't touched by the agony of an event like that?" Seeking to answer these queries not to Mr. Gray so much as to himself, Nat lets his memory play over the past. On the verge of a mean death, he settles accounts inwardly. We eavesdrop on the long dialogue of spirit and self as we do on the actual exchanges--garrulous pungent, broken by long silences--between the white man and the black.

A blackness heavier than the lost African past or the drowsy storm-brooding Virginian nights has gone into the forging of Nat Turner. It is more than the inevitable posture of bondage with its "unspeakable and bootlicking Sambo, all giggles and smirks and oily, snivelling servility." It is more than the shock of seeing a mother acquiescent in partial rape or fellow-slaves chastised in petty or savage ways. It is inner night accepted by both master and slave: to his owners the Negro is by God's definition a creature "who cannot spell cat," whom molasses and the lash keep in a condition just short of humanity. The Negro accepts this devaluation not consciously but because the very words through which he forms his needs and croons his content are borrowed; the image he finds in his mirror has been put there by the white man. To a Negro slave narcissism is subjection. But little Nathaniel is fortunate. Samuel Turner, his master, rejoices in his nascent powers in his learning to read--a wonder of stealth and illumination finely rendered by Mr. Styron. Nat's study of Scripture and reveries of eloquence are fostered. At Turner's Mill the child becomes "a grinning elf in a starched jumper who gazed at himself in mirrors witlessly preoccupied with his own ability to charm. Plans are laid for his further training and, ultimately, for his emancipation. Nat passes into the mulatto zone of the half-free into that sweet and cruel place of special acceptance where white masters have often cajoled and unmanned their more talented colonial subjects. But the South is visited by economic blight and Nat finds himself thrown suddenly into the pit of common hell. First with the Reverend Eppes, who, his homosexual advances thwarted, reduces Nat to a worn chattel; then with Thomas Moore, an illiterate brute of a farmer.

Mr. Styron has set himself the obviously formidable task of representing--no, of finding credible poetic counterpart to--the mentality of an inspired Negro slave who lived briefly and died grimly a hundred and thirty-six years ago. "I have allowed myself the utmost freedom of imagination in reconstructing events," says Mr. Styron. What he means by "events" are necessarily the feelings, surges of memory and introspective musings of Nat Turner. Here the reality available to the novelist, the sole means whereby he can convey his re-creative authority to the reader, is that of style. In few other recent novels has idiom borne so large a weight. We believe in Nat Turner's modes of speech in the world of his words, or we do not believe in him at all. Mr. Styron has not attempted to offer a facsimile of the diction of a Tidewater Negro of the eighteen-thirties, though flashes of dialect and subliterate parlance do come through when minor characters speak. He has tackled the problem that always confronts the serious writer of historical fiction, be he Thackeray or Robert Graves: the working out of a credible linguistic convention of a cadence and turn of phrase remote from yet susceptible to the undertones and pressures of the modern. It is fascinating to watch Mr. Styron at work. Several strands are visible. There is Mr. Styron's ability, salient in everything he writes, to make violent feeling pictorial, to accumulate words toward a graphic crescendo. There is a level of formal Latinity of Miltonic sonorities eroded by time and provincial usage that governed the speech of high feeling in the Old Dominion. Principally we find a constant echo of the Authorized Version and Book of Common Prayer. Nat Turner's conceptions, the timber of which he builds an apocalyptic world inside himself in order to ignite others with something of its visionary flame are Biblical throughout. Job and Ezekiel possess his tongue. This is historically plausible and is, indeed, reflected in what we have of Nat Turner's own speech. But it proves effective at a deeper level as well. It relates the novel to other moments in American consciousness and prose in which the syntax of the Jacobean Bible, compressed by Puritan intensity or loosened and made florid by political rhetoric, served to define the new world. From Cotton Mather to Faulkner and James Baldwin, Biblical speech has set a core of vision and public ornament inside the American language.

One of the subtlest things in the book is Nat's feverish recollection of a buggy ride through the countryside with young Margaret Whitehead. She is brimming with unrealized, teasing sensuality. Nat Turner's nerves are tautened to near madness:

> On she prattled in her whispery voice, love-obsessed,
> Christ-crazed, babbling away in an echo of all the self-
> serving platitudes and stale insipid unfelt blather uttered
> by every pious capon and priestly spinster she had listened
> to since she was able to sit upright, misty-eyed and rapt
> and with her little pantalettes damp with devotion, in a
> pew of her brother's church. She filled me with boredom
> and lust--and now, to still at least the latter emotion, once
> and for all, I let her constant rush of words float uncaptured
> through my mind, and with my eyes on the horse's bright
> undulating rump, concentrated on a minor but thorny
> problem that was facing me at the very outset of my campaign.

His killing of the girl at the climax of the revolt is an enactment both literal and symbolic of the crazed yearnings that assail him in the ferny coolness of the woods. As she leans against him, Nat Turner feels the electric passage across his cheek of Margaret's chestnut-colored hair: "During that moment I heard her breathing and our eyes met in a wayward glint of light that seemed to last much longer than any mere glance exchanged between two strangers journeying of a summer afternoon to some drowsy dwelling far off in the country." The whole episode recalls a nocturnal dog-cart ride, tense with unfulfilled desire and stifled sensuality, in Parade's End. The echo of Ford Madox Ford is probably relevant. The ceremonious intensity of Ford's style seems to have influenced both William Styron and Allen Tate. And it is precisely beside Tate's great novel of the broken South, The Fathers, that we can most fairly set The Confessions of Nat Turner.

The question now is this: Would a Negro recognize Nat Turner for one of his own, would he find Mr. Styron's fiction authentic to his own experience? The literate Negro of today, one gathers, finds little save embarrassment and mauvaise foi in the masks devised for him by Faulkner. Whatever the answer, the question does not infirm the intelligence, the imaginative generosity of Mr. Styron's novel. He has every artistic right to make of his Nat Turner less an anatomy of the Negro mind than a fiction of complex relationship, of the relationship between a presentday white man of deep Southern roots and the Negro in today's whirlwind. The essential imaginative need in this beautiful, honest book arises from a white sensibility exploring its own social, racial future of dramatizing, necessarily in its own terms, the Negro past. It is something like this Styron may have in mind when he says that he wished "to produce a work that is less an 'historical novel' in conventional terms than a "meditation on history."

Nevertheless, the question nags. Nor would a review by Mr. Baldwin give a representative reply (a great gift is like leprosy; it isolates a man or makes him a member of a special community). How many Negro common readers, in Virginia Woolf's positive sense of the phrase, will this novel reach, how many will tell us of their response? What will they make of Mr. Styron's use of a white man--the brilliantly drawn Jeremiah Cobb--as the agent of Nat's awakening, as the goad to Nat Turner's vision of a possible revolt? Or of Mr. Styron's insistence, tactful and ironic as it is, on the role played by loyal Negro slaves in the crushing of Turner's insurrection? ("I had caught sight for the first time of Negroes in great numbers with rifles and muskets at the barricaded veranda, firing back at us with as much passion and fury and even skill as their white owners and overseers who had gathered there to block our passage into Jerusalem.") As one asks them, such questions seem to carry their own charge of relevant sadness. A few years ago, the hope of a natural dialogue between white and Negro, engaging such values as are implicit in Mr. Styron's narrative, seemed in closer reach than it does today. Now, at moments, the intimation of a gap across which sudden violence or hysterical intimacy offers the only bridge is as vivid as it was to Nat Turner. Nat's decision to root out of his mind forever the one white man to whom he stood in a relationship of love is all too suggestive of those spirits of harsh mockery or curtains of silence that so many Negroes now interpose between themselves and those who would be friends, allies, travellers down the same long road. "1831," writes Mr. Styron, "was, simultaneously, a long time ago and only yesterday." Or only tomorrow.

*From The New Yorker (November 25, 1967): 236-43. Reprinted by permission.

THROUGH THE MIDST OF JERUSALEM*

Philip Rahv

This is a first-rate novel, the best that William Styron has written and the best by an American writer that has appeared in some years. One reason at least for its creative success is that its author has got hold of a significant theme central to the national experience. Moreover, he has been able to adapt it to his imaginative purposes without political or sectional bluster. It is a theme that relates mainly to the past but surely to the present as well, for it is obvious that we have by no means seen the last of the consequences of chattel slavery.

In the novel there is no substitute for a real theme, as important works of American fiction demonstrate--from The Scarlet Letter to The Great Gatsby and Light in August. (This is, of course, true of fiction generally). The reason for the relative sterility of the American novel in this decade has not been lack of talent, but a failure on the part of the practitioners of the genre to identify meaningful themes and to work out the proper novelistic method in relation to them. All of this leads one to think that in some significant sense our literature has lately lost contact with its society, perhaps because of the immense confusion that at present prevails in it. I say this in spite of the frenzied, hyperbolic mystique of America, whether blandly positive or perversely negative, by which our literature is now dominated. Styron is one of the very few writers who has not succumbed to this mystique which regularly confounds universal human traits and behavior with "unique" expression of "the American character." In recent fiction this American mystique has been twisted to accord with an exhibitionistic, empty, posturing, "avant-garde" subjectivism, manically expressed, as well as with the "new" pornography, which pretends to be "literary" and "audacious" and which instead of converting its sexual subject matter to aesthetic and social uses, actually exploits it in a flagrant drive for popular success.

Matthew Arnold once wrote that "for the creation of a masterwork of literature two powers must concur, the power of the man and the power of the moment." Styron's novel illustrates the truth of this dictum. The political and intellectual climate of the Sixties has surely provided the appropriate moment (not to be confused with ephemeral fashion or mere topicality). Moreover, Styron, a native Virginian born and raised not far from Southampton County, the locale of Nat Turner's rebellion--the only sustained action of its kind in the history of American slavery--convinces us in this work that he is pre-eminently equipped to deal with the theme. I think that only a white Southern writer could have brought it off. A Northerner would have been too much "outside" the experience to manage it effectively; and a Negro writer, because of a very complex anxiety not only personal but social and political, would have probably stacked the cards, producing in a mood of unnerving rage and indignation, a melodrama of saints and sinners. Styron, however, by an act that at once seizes upon his own background and transcends it, maintains throughout his narrative a consistent and highly imaginative realism not only on the objective plane (the economics of Virginia in the 1820s, the social relationships, the ideological defense-mechanisms), but also by recreating the intimate psychology of his characters, the black slaves and the white owners.

This narrative is something more than a novelistic counterpart of scholarly studies of slavery in America; it incarnates its theme, bringing home to us the monstrous reality of slavery in a psychodynamic manner that at the same time does not in the least neglect the social or economic aspects. In The American Scene Henry James records his visit to Richmond, where for a moment "the Spirit of the South" revealed itself to him as "a figure somehow blighted and stricken discomfortably, impossibly seated in an invalid chair, and yet facing one with strange eyes that were half a defiance and half a depreciation of one's noticing, and much more of one's referring to, any abnormal sign." In this great and difficult sentence many things are hinted at that for a long time our literature could not afford to know or tell about. It is only now that a writer of Southern extraction has proved himself finally capable of grappling with that "figure somehow blighted and stricken," forcing it at long last to speak without equivocation of its "abnormal" condition.

He has gained greatly from his ability to empathize with his Negro figures--with the protagonist, Nat, as well as with some of his followers-- to live in them, as it were, in a way inconceivable even for Faulkner, Styron's prose-master. Whereas Faulkner's Negroes are still to some extent the white man's Negroes, Styron's are starkly themselves. As he himself wrote some years ago in a remarkable article in Harper's:

Most Southern white people cannot know or touch black

people and this is because of the deadly intimidation
of a universal law [universal in the South, that is].
Certainly one feels the presence of this gulf even in a
writer as supremely knowledgeable as William Faulkner,
who confessed a hesitancy about attempting to "think
Negro," and whose Negro characters, as marvelously
portrayed as most of them are, seem nevertheless to be
meticulously observed rather than lived. Thus, in The
Sound and the Fury, Faulkner's magnificent Dilsey comes
richly alive, yet in retrospect one feels this is a result
of countless mornings, hours, days Faulkner had spent
watching and listening to old Negro servants, and not
because Dilsey herself is being created from a sense of
withinness: at the last moment Faulkner draws back, and
it is no mere happenstance that Dilsey, alone among the
four central figures from whose point of view the story is
told, is seen from the outside rather than from that intensely
"inner" vantage point, the interior monologue.

Styron has achieved this "inner" vantage point, this "withinness," in
creating Nat Turner, whose thoughts and memories as he sits chained
down in jail awaiting execution comprise a kind of interior monologue.
This represents a radical departure from past writing about Negroes, even
a breakthrough. The achievement is to no small extent a consequence of
Styron's conviction, as he phrases it in the same essay, that "to break
down the old law, to come to know the Negro, has become the moral
imperative of every white Southerner."

The structural properties of the novel are very fine: no wastage and no
digressions. The language, though faintly echoing the courtly tones of
Southern English in the early nineteenth century, is unmistakably Styron's,
except for the dialogue, which is vigorously and unabashedly naturalistic;
but the set of mind, the emotions, and the pathos are entirely Turner's. I
have heard people say that words like "presage," "effulgent," and even
"apprehension" could not have been known to Turner. This objection is
typical of readers unpractical in the recognition of literary conventions-
-and the particular convention adopted by Styron in his prose, that of an
enlarged vocabulary, is essential to his novelistic aim; for to have
attempted to "imitate" Turner's own restricted idiom, whatever it was,
would have sufficed to render the theme only in one dimension. Styron's
strategic decision to employ the rich verbal resources at his command was
the right one, it seems to me. In the same way, Faulkner bypassed in As
I Lay Dying Darl's native speech in favor of his own, which alone was
capable of adequately representing that character's clairvoyance and
singularity of consciousness.

Styron fully enters into the ideology permitting Nat Turner to organize
his bloody mission--that of exterminating all the whites within his

reach--an ideology which is necessarily religious, absorbed from constant Bible-reading. No other source of ideas justifying his scheme was historically available to him. The prophet Ezekiel declared: "Go through the midst of Jerusalem, and set a mark upon the foreheads of the men that sigh and cry for all abominations that be done in the midst thereof. . . . Slay utterly old and young, both maids and little children. . . ." Such exhortations are immediately present to him; the historical sense is missing as yet. This half-educated slave, an extreme rarity among the Negroes of that time, whose reputation among the whites is that of "a harmless, runabout, comic nigger minister of the gospel," conceals his purpose for years even as he builds up the image of himself as the "illimitable, devastating instrument of God's wrath." He fails of course in his larger purpose of a break for freedom, but after his small band of rebels has cut a swath by sword and ax and gun through southeastern Virginia, killing about fifty-five whites and terrifying the entire South, he still insists that he feels no pangs of remorse.

Styron, who is not essentially a political writer, is admirably faithful here to revolutionary psychology. A lesser novelist might have been tempted to finish expediently with some kind of reconciliation scene, such as one showing Nat, the primitive revolutionary, embracing a phony universalist ideal to ease his plight and calm the apprehensive reader. But far from sounding a note of reconciliation, Styron thoroughly explores the Negro militant's hatred of whites, which grows "like a granite flower with cruel leaves." It is the first time a white writer has faced up to this "pure and obdurate" hatred, which can on no account be perceived by the slave-owners if they are to preserve their self-righteousness or even ordinary equanimity. This hatred, inevitably bound up with the social and emotional heritage of slavery, is perceived even today by the majority of whites in all sections of the country with bafflement at best and at worst with a sense of outrage which betrays a wretched failure of imagination. The consciousness produced by slavery still persists and it can be said of this novel that, by virtue of its insights into this consciousness, its "historicity" does not at all exclude contemporaneity. Indeed, it suggests analogues with the present that are vivid and urgent. After all, the national disposition to violence and hypocritical ideologizing to cover up ruthless practices can in no way be dissociated from the experience of slavery. In the shaping of American culture--and I am using "culture" in an anthropological rather than a literary or philosophical sense--this experience has proven to be far more lasting and significant than the professors of our history and literature, sheltered by a "cloud-canopy of idealism" (the phrase is Van Wyck Brooks's), have ever allowed us to understand. Our literary scholars, with their endless mouselike fussing about the Brahmin culture of Boston and related matters, have been particularly slack in distinguishing between historical actualities and professed ideals.

In 1832, months after the rebellion, a pamphlet of some twenty pages, by a T. R. Gray, was published in Richmond. This document, entitled "The Confessions of Nat Turner," is a bare recital of facts, without elaboration or any effort to understand Nat's mentality. Styron has not only used this document but also has incorporated Gray into his cast of characters. As he visits the prisoner, taking down his testimony and arguing with him, he blurts out his essential atheism, blaming Christianity for the enormities committed: "Nineteen hundred years of Christian teaching plus a black preacher is all it takes--is all it takes to prove that God is a God durned lie!" Gray is only one of many whites on the scene who are sharply individualized. There are, among others, the decent, philanthropic owners, like Marse Samuel who encourages Nat to learn reading and writing, but whom financial need drives to sell his Negroes into bondage in the steaming, dreaded plantations of the lower South; there is the "nigger-breaker" Mr. Francis; the Irish overseer who rapes Nat's mother as the boy watches; and Judge Cobb, the enlightened Virginia gentleman who nonetheless cannot believe that there can arise among the blacks "one single specimen capable of spelling cat." The position of the whites is thoroughly explored, both those deploring the institution of slavery and those upholding it, without rancor or even a hint of parti pris on the author's part. It is Nat who sees them, knows and judges them. The upholders of the system are of course the majority among the whites, and typical of them is a Mr. Benjamin, who is convinced that "a darky is basically as unteachable as a chicken . . . his only value is the work you get out of him by intimidation, cajolery, and threat."

The novel has dramatic coherence: its texture consists of innumerable details, firmly planned, the concreteness of which compels our belief. Some of the scenes are truly arresting, such as the one exhibiting a pair of traveling Episcopal clergymen--"the Bishop's visitants" as they are called--garbed in funereal black, "blinking through square crystal glasses and emitting delicate coughs behind long white fingers as thin and pale as flower stalks." In another we read of a backwoods fundamentalist, the Reverend Eppes, whose skinny face has "a pentecostal, Christ-devoured . . . look of laughterless misery about it," and who tries to bugger Nat behind the woodpile while intoning the question whether "a nigger boy's got an unusual big pecker on him" as he heard people say. Then too the scenes depicting the relation between Nat and the young white girl, Margaret Whitehead, who likes and confides in him, are very affecting. Though respecting and in a sense recognizing his humanity, she still can run around half-exposed, in her undergarments, in front of him, prattling in a giggly, girlish way. She is the only white person he kills with his own two hands during the rebels' rampage through the countryside; for though an inciter of killing, he turns out to be no mass killer in the end. Margaret thoughtlessly provokes his maleness and an overpowering fantasy of rape as, full of sympathy, she sits close beside him on the carriage seat while he drives her to church, "close enough to smell her sweat, pungent and womanly and disturbing." And again: "Her closeness stifled me . . . wafting toward me her odor--a disturbing smell of young-girlsweat mingled with the faint sting of lavender." Even as he wants her he hates her. "It is not hatred," he assures himself, the "sudden rage and confusion arise just from that sympathy irresistible and unwanted." Truly the pangs of life are keenly felt in this tableau of mingled murder and desire.

Very few facts are known about the real Nat Turner, and Styron has mostly invented his early and later experiences, his feelings, and the incrustation of religious fanaticism and revolutionary zeal that propelled him toward his brief triumph and final doom. No doubt Styron has benefitted from the perspective that historical distance provides and the resulting ability to see the system of slavery clear and whole. It is far more difficult to see our contemporary society with the same clarity and to express its tendencies with equal force. Whether he can progress in this direction is a question to which only his future novels can supply the answer.

It will no doubt be said that this book's excellence is the result of its author's splendid talent. To be sure, he is in possession of this talent. But isn't the word "talent" used all too frequently, so much so that it explains everything and nothing? Styron's precipience in handling his difficult theme (never before attempted on a large scale by a modern American writer) and the psychological and linguistic modulation of it are poorly explained by that catchall term. I recall the episode in Anna Karenina, when Anna, Vronsky, and their friend Golonischev visit the painter Mihailov's studio, and on the way back their spirits rise. Tolstoy remarks in this canny way: "They talked of Mihailov and his pictures. The word talent, by which they meant an inborn, almost physical skill, independent of brain and heart, which was their expression for everything an artist gains from life, occurred frequently in their conversation, since they required it to cover something of which they had no conception but wanted to talk about." Technical proficiency is indispensable of course, but in and by itself it cannot yield creative mastery. Tolstoy knew that it is qualities of "brain and heart," rare and unspecifiable at bottom, that distinguish the work of art from the ordinary product.

*From The New York Review of Books (October 26, 1967): 6-10. Reprinted by permission.

YOU'VE TAKEN MY NAT AND GONE*

Vincent Harding

In the course of a <u>Newsweek</u> interview celebrating the publication of his latest novel, William Styron said, "I want the book to exist on its own terms as an American tragedy. . . .   And I certainly don't mean to indiscriminately glorify the figure of the Negro rebel against society to-day." Then he added, "You can see Nat Turner as an archetypal American tragic hero, but this doesn't make Rap Brown an archetypal American hero, nor does it make what he is preaching capable of anything but disaster."

As one ponders these and other words attributed to Styron, as we explore the glossy surfaces and the ambiguous substructure of <u>The Confessions,</u> it becomes painfully clear that this semi-fictional work and its author's gratuitous comments are indeed part of our long rehearsal in tragedy. But it is also evident that Styron--true to one element of the tragic figure--speaks and writes without comprehension of either the meaning of the drama, or the profound and bitter depths through which America continually moves towards the creation of a thousand Nat Turners more real than his could ever be. For he is obviously convinced that he has discriminately "glorified" the Nat Turner of history, that he has built this strange black mystic into a true hero, and that he has thereby attained the right to judge other dark rebels and their role in America today.

This set of dangerous misapprehensions is only the beginning of our sorrows, for they are compounded by the host of critics who have joyously proclaimed that Styron has finally done the impossible--entered starkly white into a black man's skin and mind--and has in the course of his impossible feat created a major work of American fiction. (That <u>they</u> should be called upon by journals and reviews to decide when successful penetration of blackness has been accomplished is another parable of our pain).

How shall one speak of such things in any sense other than the tragic, especially if we attribute some scintilla of well-meaning beneficence to William Styron and his noncritics? For as I sat, black and increasingly anguished, experiencing Styron's audacious attempt to recreate his own Nat Turner out of the sparse materials of history and out of the strangeness of his creative dreams, I could not escape one terrible, constant impression--the overwhelming presence of failure. Or was it something worse than failure? Perhaps so, for the subtitles which came most regularly to my mind were "the Annihilation of Nat Turner" and "The Emasculation of Prophet Nat" (that last being intended in its most obvious sense and more).

No other conclusion seems sensible if one takes the basic historical document (Turner's own dictated Confessions) with the seriousness claimed by Styron. There, although the context is limited, Turner leaps forth as a religious mystic, a single-minded black believer with a powerful sense of messianic vocation. He fits well into the apocalypticism of much antebellum religious thought in America, and he is an impressive leader of men. Almost against his own will, Thomas Gray, the white Virginia lawyer who took down the original Confessions, ends the transcription of Nat's words with his own remarkable testimony. He says he sees in Turner, "The calm, deliberate composure with which he spoke of his late deeds and intentions, the expression of his fiend-like face when excited by enthusiasm, still bearing the stains of the blood of helpless innocence about him; clothed with rags and covered with chains: yet daring to raise his manacled hands to heaven, with a spirit soaring above the attributes of man . . ." In response, Gray wrote, "I looked on him and my blood curdled in my veins."

The man reported by Gray far overshadows the character created by Styron. Indeed, it appears that the twentieth-century white Virginian was no less overwhelmed by black Nat Turner than was his nineteenth-century counterpart, but he was evidently not so honest. Instead of admitting to the curdling of blood and letting things stand, William Styron's novel becomes an exercise in domestication, assimilation, and finally destruction. At every crucial point it is almost embarrassingly obvious that Styron is unable to comprehend Nat Turner's real stature and meaning, that he does not perceive Turner's role as a tragic-triumphant hero in the biblical genre.

It is Styron's very attempt to enter the biblical world of the rebel slave which most fully provides a symbol for his total betrayal of the historical Turner. Near the beginning of the work, Styron-Turner says, "Of all the prophets it was Ezekiel with his divine fury to whom I felt closest by kinship . . . ." Any careful reading of Turner's own Confessions indicates that there is certainly ground for such a conclusion, for Turner surely lived in the world of those divinely obsessed spokesmen, including one

Jesus of Nazareth. But Styron's particular choice of Ezekiel is of great significance as an illustration, for it was this prophet above all others in the Old Testament who was driven to enter personally and without reserve into the very words and judgment he spoke. It was Ezekiel who was forced to eat the scroll with the Lord's words, to fill his stomach with the terrible oracles of God until they became "sweet as honey." It was he who had to give up his own wife to death as a sign to the people of Israel.

Now this is precisely what William Styron fails to do with the world and words of Nat Turner. He has been unable to eat and digest the blackness, the fierce religious conviction, the power of the man. He has been kept apart from these realities while attempting to tell the inner tale. As a result of such peculiar self-deception, as a result of his separation from Nat's power and drivenness, William Styron has distorted and broken each major truth of Old Prophet Nat. And he has done it to the strange accompaniment of critical applause for his "total" integration" into Turner's world. Thus the whitened appropriation of our history by those who have neither eaten nor mourned goes on, tragic because it is not recognized for what it is: a total negation of our power and our truth, indeed an ultimate betrayal of all creative power and liberating truth.

We see the difficulty emerging early in Styron's handling of Nat Turner's secular and religious education in childhood. While Turner, in his Confessions to Gray, attributes almost all of his early religious inspiration and teaching to his parents and, especially, his grandmother, Styron totally eliminates this source in his novel. In the fictional work Turner's grandmother dies before the boy's birth, and his mother and father are relegated to negligible roles in the matter of instruction. A white family--particularly the young women in that family--replace them as Turner's major teachers. Why such a change--one which immediately wrenches Turner out of the unique environment of black religion? Whatever the reason, from that point on Styron-Turner's religious experiences continue to produce a feeling of falseness and lack of power. His life, robbed by Styron of its roots, is somehow neither black nor white, and suffers from the loss of particularity as well as power.

Even more important as a symbol of Styron's degradation of Nat and his messianic vision is the novelist's handling of one of the major religious rituals--baptism. According to the book, Nat's first experience of self-baptism along with the baptism of another person comes when he is in his late teens, and brings with it his initial sense of calling as a special messenger of God. But the startling development by Styron is that this crucial baptism takes place immediately after Nat has been engaged in homosexual mutual stimulation with a young black friend, Willis, and it is obviously his sense of guilt over the act which drives Nat into the river for baptism. Thus Styron-Turner can say,

"Lord," I said in a loud voice, "witness these two sinners who have sinned have been unclean in Thy sight and stand in need to be baptized."

"Das right Lawd," I heard Willis say.

In his own <u>Confessions,</u> Nat Turner referred to only one joint baptism, one involving himself and a white convert named Brantley. Styron has used this event too, but in such a way as to continue the demeaning of Nat Turner. For in the novel Brantley is not only a social outcast among whites he is a mentally retarded, personally repulsive homosexual whose specialty seems to be the molesting of young boys. Again we see the driving force of his search for baptism not in the power of Nat's religious message or personal charisma, but in Brantley's own sense of futility, fear, and sexually confused guilt. Since there was very little description of Brantley in the historical records, Styron alone chose to create such a pariah-like personality for the one white man who is drawn to Nat Turner's religious teaching. How else can this be read except as an act of diminishing the power of William Styron's black "hero"?

Styron does no better with Turner's blackness than he does with his religious vision, especially in relationship to women. For one of the major destructive continuities in <u>The Confessions of Nat Turner</u> is Nat's fascination with white women--a fascination entirely of the novelist's own making. Perhaps the insidious nature of Styron's distortion becomes most apparent when one notes that his Nat Turner is able to offer clear and often tender descriptions only of white women, not of blacks. In the realm of sexual desire black women become mere shadows in relationship to the many evocations of silken hair, pale, smooth skin, and white, white lives. In his almost overwhelming erotic fantasies--from adolescence to his death--only one black woman appears to Nat Turner as an object of desire, and she is finally pierced only by his tongue.

On the other hand (and every black admirer of Styron's work must speak to this set of contrivances), two white women are introduced into the novel's structure for no other evident purpose than to become the objects of Nat's fierce sexual longing. Even beyond all of this there exists one of the most significant distortions of the historical Nat Turner: Styron's creation of Nat's strange love affair with a teen-age white girl. What manner of black commander is this, whose major heterosexual activities--even in fantasy--are with white women? Is this a heroic black leader who finally helps to destroy his movement because of his weakness for white flesh? Since this major theme and its supporting scenes are entirely of Styron's creation, the questions belong to him alone. Whose mind has he entered save his own?

Nor do any of the other black men in the novel fare much better . . . . Perhaps most obvious and suggestive is Styron's insistence that Will, the slave who kills more regularly than any other, must be a demented, lecherous wild man. Is it only sex and insanity which can motivate a black man to such a large-scale assault on white lives? Is this an attempt to deny the present as well as the past?

But it is the loss of religious center with which I am most concerned, for religion was evidently the focus of Turner's own life. There is in Styron's work no black messiah, no true lover of Ezekiel, not even a superior religious exhorter. For though William Styron-Turner talks about religion a great deal and though he quotes biblical passages in excellent style, the "divine fury" of Old Testament experience is almost totally absent. Though Nat Turner is a preacher, only one major attempt at a sermon is made in The Confessions, and it fails to catch any of the peculiar rhythmic and thematic strengths of this black folk art form. Equally striking is the fact that the religious music of Afro-Americans never enters as a major structural element of the novel as one would expect if such a work had been done by an Ellison, a Baldwin, a Wright.

No, black Prophet Nat has failed to make this scene. The Old Testament is present only as a collection of words in The Confessions. There is no wrestling with angels, no anguished groping after God. There is nothing in any way equal to the terse power found in Robert Hayden's poem, "Ballad of Nat Turner." The only wrestling we see in Styron-Turner is with the ephemeral bodies of white women, with the very real penis of a black man, and with his own confused and confusing fears. If any of these is sincerely meant to contribute to the glorification or clarification of the portrait of Nat Turner, then we are surely in the realm of tragedy (almost tragi-comedy). For they only contribute to our picture of a wretched precursor of the Moynihan report; and that is a Nat Turner who is simply not to be found in the astringent report of Lawyer Gray, or in the living traditions of black America.

Perhaps we must now say with charity that it is likely too much to expect a white, twentieth-century American novelist to be able to conceive of the world of a black, Old Testament-type messiah (William Faulkner, Flannery O'Connor and Robert Penn Warren might have made more interesting attempts, I suspect). The power of belief, the power of righteous anger, the dynamism emanating from a sense of divinely or-dained vocation, the power of blackness--none of these is a hallmark of the major section of current American fiction. Erotic fantasy in the world of unreal women, aborted black-white assimilation, confused and ambiguous sexual organs--these may be the best we can do. And if there is any power in Styron's book it is the power of unfulfilled desire, the power of substance wasted in the dust, of weakness and fear, the power of insanity and the murder of God. As such, the novel has snatched Nat Turner out of the nineteenth century, out of the community of black religious rebels, and placed him totally into our own age of nothingness and fear. Is there any salvation from this, from the insensitive arrogance which raises the applause?

It is when we speak of salvation and arrogance that the most profound and final degradation of black Nat Turner is revealed. The issue of his salvation is broached in a negative way at the outset of the novel. In his cell shortly after capture Nat confesses a sense of separation from God and says, "There seemed no way at all to bridge the gulf between myself and God." Soon it becomes clear that we are dealing not simply with a sense of separation, but more. For Styron-Turner says, "The sense of His absence was like a profound and awful silence in my brain. Nor was it His absence alone which caused me this . . . feeling of despair . . . instead it was a sense of repudiation I felt, of denial, as if He had turned His back on me all. . . ."

This theme appears repeatedly throughout the novel until it builds to a place of dominating significance at the end. What is it that has caused this God-driven man to endure these days of separation and repudiation? Why would his God hide His shining face? Finally, the answer comes clear. Nat's God has turned His back because this black leader of rebellion has not admitted his remorse for someone's death. So He waits on Nat to repent. But the repentance demanded is not for the death of helpless, guiltless white children, not even for the destruction of more than one hundred innocent blacks who were killed in reprisal for his rebellion. No, Styron-Turner's God does not deal in such trivialities. He does not shut the door of heaven for those things. Instead, at the end of the novel it becomes clear that this God will not return until Nat repents for the death of one white girl, the same adolescent who has sexually aroused Styron-Turner and supposedly opened in him deep wells of desire and love. This is the girl who becomes his only victim, his sacrifice; and after he has pierced her body with his sword and bludgeoned her head, he circles her lifeless frame like a faithful black dog (all this in the midst of a rebellion he is leading).

This young woman becomes the object of Nat's final fantasy in jail, and once more he sends out his life-giving fluid into the nothingness of delusion. Nevertheless, Styron (is it maudlin ineptitude or sheer mockery?) can have his antihero say, "with tender stroking motions I pour out my love within her; pulsing flood; she arches against me, cries out, and the twain--black and white--are one." In the midst of this love of emptiness, this integration into a dream, Nat is able to repent, and with his repentance his God immediately returns and calls him home. (So baptism and extreme unction are devoured by inverted sexuality). Little Miss Margaret Whitehead, the pure virgin, yet not virgin, the dead recipient of black seed, has become Nat Turner's mediator-mistress. Her arched white body becomes Styron-Turner's pathway to their white, white God.

If this is not tragedy, nothing is. It begins with Styron's belief that such a caricature is really Nat Turner. It is deepened by America's eager acceptance of this uninspired offering of homosexuality, pseudo-religion, and dreams (so wonderfully safe!) of black-white grapplings in the dust as an authentic view from under the black skin. Nevertheless, as will all tragedy, the deepest level is to be found within us--black us. And it was perhaps symbolized by one of our most important artists, James Baldwin. For it was Baldwin who praised his friend's work highly, Baldwin who saw himself in Styron's Turner, and Baldwin who dared to say, "This is the beginning of our common history."

Surely it is nothing of the kind. In spite of Baldwin's largest, kindest hopes, Styron has done nothing less (and nothing more) than create another chapter in our long and common agony. He has done it because we have allowed it, and we who are black must be men enough to admit that bitter fact. There can be no common history until we have first fleshed out the lineaments of our own, for no one else can speak out of the bittersweet bowels of our blackness. On the way to that achievement a crucial direction must surely be found in the words of our so recently departed brother, Langston Hughes. For he spoke to our present condition when he wrote:

> You've taken my blues and gone
> And you fixed 'em
> So they don't sound like me . . .
> But someday somebody'll
> And write about me,
> Black and beautiful--
> And sing about me,
> And put on plays about me!
> I reckon it'll be
> Me myself!
> Yes, it'll be me.

Only then will we capture Nat Turner from the hands of those who seem to think that entrance into black skin is achieved as easily as Styron-Turner's penetration of invisible while flesh. Only then may it be possible to transform the powerful suggestions of Robert Hayden's marvelous poem about Nat Turner into a full-orbed and faithful encounter with this compelling but mysterious black man. Then we shall judge him for ourselves, and brother Rap will be free to draw his own conclusions--if he is still interested. Then even the Styrons may sense some solid intimation of our darkly glowing, tragic depths. At that moment, as possessors of our own past, we shall have claimed the right to go on with fear and the trembling of joy into whatever divine fury lies ahead on these white and maddening shores.   Only then shall common history--and common destiny--begin.

---

*From <u>William Styron's Nat Turner: Ten Black Writers Respond</u>: 23-33. Reprinted by permission.

THE CONFESSIONS OF NAT TURNER: HISTORY AND IMAGINATION*

Floyd C. Watkins

The Confessions of Nat Turner . . . begins with Nat's view of a "barren, sandy cape where the river joins the sea"--a landscape that provides for the reader an image of the teeming life of the sea, which Nat had experienced only through the bars of his prison and in his imagination. He knows that there is a river estuary below a cliff, but he is physically and mentally locked within a totality of physical, spiritual, and civil imprisonments as well as within chattel slavery. He does not know which river estuary, the name of the river, or the appearance of any landscape where the land joins the sea. William Styron says that he intended the landscape to be vague, in congruity with the enforced blindness of Nat's prison cell.(1) Nat had never been "allowed the opportunity of a trip to Norfolk and the ocean."(2)

The other gaps in the mind of the protagonist in this section of the novel are appalling. He can see that the day is clear, but this is a vision of a sky without a world. Time is so out of joint with him that he does not know whether it is the beginning of spring or the end of summer. The world to him, as prisoner and slave, is essentially a vacuum--"benign and neutral, windless, devoid of heat or cold" (p. 3). His helplessness is envisioned as an approach to the place in a boat merely adrift: "I do not row" (p. 3). That he is at the mercy of his world is shown by the boat's "moving obediently" to the currents of the river. The shores of Nat's world are peculiarly devoid of life and habitation, "unpeopled, silent." There are "no deer," no gulls, only "great silence and . . . even greater solitude" (p. 3).

As Nat drifts in his imagination on the river he sees one building, and so far as he can tell it does not even have an aperture, "neither doors nor windows" (p. 4). He does not venture an interpretation but envisions only a "profound mystery which to explore would yield only a profusion of darker and perhaps more troubling mysteries, as in a maze" (p. 4). The reader can understand Nat's impenetrable mystery: physically it is a complete enclosure, so far as we can see without the exit or egress even of air. It is the structure, the box, the tomb, even the pyramid of slavery. Nat does not himself know its meaning. Its enclosure is emphasized by Nat's ignorance of the sea (the world), which he has not seen but only heard about from "a few Negroes of Southampton" (p. 5). But slavery has its extraordinary hungers, intensified so much that Nat's imagination is "inflamed." Slavery, of which all this is symbol or image, provides Nat no release, and he has to content himself with "recurring phantasm" (p. 5).

Styron has been accused of not describing the real places of Nat's life.(3) In reading or writing there are different kinds of associations between the place of fiction and that of the source. When I read about Faulkner's Compsons, for example, I see one of my grandfather's old farm homes the barn and the pasture. Styron's places seem to be much more inventions of the mind. He built his own homes and established his own terrain. Thus those charges that he looked at the wrong Whitehead home when he made a short visit in Virginia seem irrelevant as long as the home is true to the kinds of homes some families lived in during the time of Turner's rebellion (interview). It is, Styron says, just a combination of all the old country homes in Virginia of this style, but not a thing of grandeur in the manner of Westover.

History leaves gaps about the feelings and the things of slavery--such as, for example, what a slave took with him when he was sold to another owner. Fiction must fill in. When Samuel Turner sold Nat to the Reverend Eppes, "My Bible was the only possession I had to take away from Turner's Mill save for these things: a single change of denim pants, two cotton shirts, an extra pair of what are elegantly known as nigger brogans, some little bone crosses I had carved, a needle and some thread, a pewter cup left to me by my mother, and a ten-dollar gold piece which Marse Samuel had given me" (p. 229). Compared to the traded slaves, Steinbeck's migrant Joads were wealthy. What Nat takes with him defines slavery. These are the images and things of human chattel. History does not provide a list of the objects, and consequently the symbolic meanings of the objects are lost except to the imagination. This is not merely to say that history is limited but that it is circumscribed by the stated conjecture and the absolutely known. Here is fiction's virtue. It does not have to be minutely accurate, but if it contradicts too many facts or the spirit of the times it can be historically flawed.

Of course any item of the life of white or black is subject to a racial, a historical, or a social interpretation. Styron's very selection is subjective. The cultural data of the everyday world, for one thing, show how much the slave is acted upon, how little he may do for himself, how passive he is. Objects which revealed many independent actions of the slave and thus freedom would depict a false culture, erroneous history. Readers may judge (as I do) that Styron's view of the liberty of action allowed the slave is about right, but no kind of critical or social study can furnish a measurement of this accuracy.

The beginning of The Confessions of Nat Turner, then, provides a set of images designed entirely to show the state of mind of one who is both civil and criminal and chattel slave--at least in the mind of the dominant class. The succeeding pattern reveals the physical abasement of the slave. In prison Nat has a cedar plank for a bed, leg irons to limit movement and prevent escape, no heat to relieve the "wintry touch about the morning" (p. 6), and no warm breakfast on arousal. The glimpses of life Nat may see from his open barred window reveal a world only somewhat less miserable than the cell. He sees a moving candle, a woman emptying the accumulations of the night's chamber pot, and the privy. The first real activity of the morning comes when "a distant drumming noise, a plunging of hoofbeats" (p. 7), signals the arrival of fresh soldiers and the changing of the guard to prevent the escape of this least free of all mortals. Slowly the life of the prison begins to stir.

This is an extensive account of the imagery of Nat's pitiful world at the beginning of the novel. Styron has chosen a wretched circumstance for the beginning. It is the time of all the despair as well as the dullness of life in prison and in chattel slavery--which is worse one might question without answer. Hope is gone; all the action but confession and execution is over; and the intensity and trauma of the final emotional moments have not begun. There is a particular reason for this point of departure. In a sense every single aspect of The Confessions of Nat Turner is a revelation of slavery, its objects, and, most importantly, the states of mind created by the condition. Nat's mind in the beginning is a metaphor for the most abject slavery, yet every other slave and indeed the mind of every white man in the book is to be seen somehow in its relationship with slavery. Schematically and in structure the novel starts with the darkest hour of the rebellious and revolutionary slave at the physical and psychological mercy of his oppressors.

Knowing that it is still impossible to cut through all the rumors and records and lies about Nat and even slavery itself, Styron attempts what he has been so defamed for, "a meditation on history." Styron made some efforts to get at previous subjective impressions of the facts of the case: He read Frederick Law Olmsted, Stanley Elkins, the Grimke sisters, Malcolm Cowley and Danille Pratt Mannix's Black Cargoes, B. A. Botkin's folklore, excerpts from slave narratives, Fanny Kemble, and others. And he had lived in Virginia. Necessarily, he did not read Henry Irving Tragle's The Southampton Slave Revolt of 1831: A Compilation of Source Material--it had not been written. He might have learned some more facts from Tragle, but rumors and errors are so great in that work that one would not expect greater accuracy on the whole from it than from the novel. History is generality, social fact, a violent but impersonal episode as it is written. Slaves and their masters in history, for example, seldom speak in direct quotation. Journalistic accounts collected from the time seem to possess less truth than the rumors of war and battle in The Red Badge of Courage.

A good novelist must create a living man. Even the supposedly factual slave narratives are different from life; a diary is an interpretation. Slaves and ex-slaves have written narratives, but they admittedly are colored by the slaves' memories as well as by the propagandistic intent of the slaves' amanuenses and editors. Thus even an account of a slave by the slave himself is revealed as he remembers his past and meditates on it at the present moment.

This is a flaw of any history, of course, but it is much more so a flaw in the remembered works of folk history and an illiterate people. Slave narratives strove for truth and effect, but The Confessions, I believe, is the only significant novel by a white man which attempts to re-create the immediacy and intensity in its presentation of the moment-to-moment events and thoughts of a slave.

In the twentieth century the oppression of slavery has not existed except in isolated primitivistic situations and criminal circumstances. Parallels to slavery may exist in folklore, printed history, and racism. Analogies to slavery exist in any oppression--in the family, military service, prisons, and concentration camps. But in no situation in the twentieth century does a man legally own the body as well as the services of another man. A great chasm must be leaped when one attempts to get back to the ways a slave and his master spoke and thought. The paucity of objects in a slave's world must reveal his oppression; and the objects and ways of the life of the master must reveal the effect on him of being the oppressor, willing or not. These objects are not vast social issues, but they are the furniture of daily life, things like the cradle that the slave "flang" down on John Hartwell Cocke's plantation when he became disgusted at work not for his own gain,(4) the food and the toilet, the hoe and the musical instrument. This was the task William Styron set himself. History has not preserved what Styron wanted except as some well-sanded and polished and painted or varnished curio on the wall of an antique shop. Some things have not survived at all. Coffles have been endured and witnessed, but any modern narrator's mind must imagine them at a great distance. At the moment of its existence Styron's coffle is experienced from the perspective of a pampered black man living in the abjectness and deprivations of a coffle's food, sanitation, and toiletry. Nat Turner thinks a story that no living person has ever seen, recounts it, and recounts the reactions of the other characters.

So long as fiction re-creates rather than violates the spirit of the times and the mysteries of human nature, it may be superior to or truer than history. Fiction must be fuller, more personal, more dramatic. As the historian follows his method and creates the lifeblood of a man, he cannot say what he does not know. The novelist must present and enact scenes whether he knows them factually or not. History may have to accept gaps in the Watergate tapes: fiction must create material to fill them. The historian may conjecture what happened; the novelist has to know. There is a small body of facts agreed on by many of Nat's contemporaries and the historians, but they do not get at the lifeblood of the man and his times. Styron's Nat is a meditation, and not enough is known about the real Nat to make him anything else. The Nats of Styron's critics and historians are also meditations, but there is not enough characterization of him to make him a person. Their syllogism runs that all rebellious Negro slaves of some success were heroes; Nat was a slave and a rebel; therefore Nat was heroic and without blemish. In general Styron invents in a way different from that of the presumed historian. He creates details from daily living, sexual episodes for example, which are unknown to the historian. But ideologically what he does is not more far-fetched than the writings of pseudohistorians, no more so than Thomas Wentworth Higginson's or the writings of the crusader William Wells Brown. Styron had to extend the range of his imagination beyond the ken of many historical novelists. He had to find what he could about slavery in history, imagine the rest of it in human terms, and draw analogues from autocratic authority in relationships outside slavery. His task was difficult because the life of the slave, like that of the yeoman white, had been recorded only in folklore and in the writings of others about black and yeoman white.

Practices of fiction do not demand that Styron follow true history in relating what happened to Nat in the places where he lived and with the families who owned him. Fiction must conform only to the possibility of life at the time and in the place and according to human nature. Cultural and daily facts of life in a historical novel may derive from sources besides known events in the life of the subject. A credible historical character must conform to the novelist's experience of people. Manners may derive from the recorded facts of personal history, but such detail varies from person to person and from farm to farm. One who knows rural life in one age may with some success transfer folklore and culture to another time. A washpan in one time is like a washpan in another, even if one is of tin and another is of china. To the extent that an attitude is valid in general human terms, it may be transferred to another era.

The totality of the world of The Confessions, then, is known in our time only by limited analogues. Styron assumes the incredible obligation of creating a world which is unknown to us but which must seem as real to us as our own kitchen stove. Every image, every object, is related to the world of slavery, and besides having its own reality it must impinge on the mind of the reader and that of the character as being routinely real.

On the whole, with some exceptions, authors do not choose from the humanly imagined so much as from the factually known or historically researched. Obviously, Styron has failed for some readers from an ideological perspective; from the human and cultural perspectives, however, I believe that he has succeeded in terms of what men might have been in that remote world.

Not a single character in the book has an entirely correct view of the relationships between the races. Even Nat's condemnations of whites are not always to be trusted. Although he recognizes that there is "a kind of love" felt for him by his owner, he maintains that his education "began as surely an experiment as a lesson in pig-breeding or the broadcasting of a new type of manure" (p. 155). Nat's prejudice is understandable, but the statement is unfair to his white owner. In a time when many believed that the "darky is an animal with the brain of a human child" (p. 162), when Negroes did not read, any change could be unfairly called an experiment no matter what the personal feelings of the master. Nat first hears himself called a slave when he is old enough for Samuel Turner to plan to teach him to read. Then "a wicked chill like cold water filled the hollow of my gut as the thought crashed in upon me: "Yes, I am a slave" (p. 164). Thus the idea of slavery first invades the consciousness of a child. But Nat's view is not the whole truth. He lived in such a kindly situation that he remained ignorant of his chattel status for a long time. The phenomenon was not unusual. The historian John W. Blassingame has shown that "many young blacks had no ideas they were slaves."(5) Nat's insurrection is not attributable to the physical horrors of slavery but to his spiritual and psychological rebellion despite the comforts of his own situation. Provided education, training, and opportunity, Nat revolts because his owner did not give him promised freedom and because he lived a life soft enough to enable him to plan and lead a revolt. Styron has thus depicted primarily not the physical horrors of slavery so much as the moral and psychological aspects of it, which are especially demeaning.

No one can defend slavery now. Because slavery is indefensible, slave-owners in Nat Turner's time were wrong. From this point, it is easy to proceed and to maintain that the white was inhumane, monstrous, absolutely evil. The defenders and justifiers of Nat, similarly, demand almost absolute heroism. Any flaw in the character is an attack on a George Washington of the Negro race, an emasculation of the black race by the novelist. But fiction cannot be created about perfect heroes. Extremism denies humanity, and humanness is the first principle of art.

Styron, I believe, is less bigoted than any significant novelist who has extensively treated the race question in recent decades. Black and white are credibly human. One relationship in the novel, for example, attributes great humanity to white and black, to the Judge and to his prisoner whom he condemns to death. Nat and the Judge are human as well as racist. Judge Cobb, who has suffered greatly, lives in physical pain. He has lost stables, horses, and a Negro groom in a fire; his wife and two daughters have died of typhoid. At first Nat takes joy in Judge Cobb's disasters. He mutters to himself, "Feel sorry for a white man and you wastin' your sorrow" (p. 58). Cobb overhears him and still condemns slavery in a vehement rhetorical tirade. "Oh, Virginia, woe betide thee! Woe, thrice woe, and ever damned in memory be the day when poor black men in chains first trod upon thy sacred strand." When two whites drive the lovable Hark up a tree to punish him by his fear of heights, Cobb pities him (p. 83). Then Nat does precisely what he had said the Negro should not do--he feels "sorry for a white man." When his mission comes to pass "and Jerusalem is destroyed," he says, "this man Cobb will be among those few spared the sword" (p. 75). The humanity of Nat and Cobb encloses the inhumanity of the punishers of Hark. More than that, Nat can feel sorrow for Cobb even as the judge passes out the death sentence. Seeing Cobb's eyes "sunk deep within their sockets," Nat realizes "that he too was close to death, very close, almost as close as I myself, and I felt a curious pang of pity and regret" (p. 105). Nat Turner is a fanatic, but not only that: he is compassionately human too. Again there is a general source rather than a particular one. Styron derived the compassions of the two from a mere hint, he says, in the original confessions (interview).

The purpose of The Confessions is not to take us back to history. All the searchings and researchings seem to indicate that the story of Nat Turner can be known only in rumors and small and fragmentary parts. One purpose is to get back to a social and cultural world. So far as I can tell, Styron is culturally correct except in one instance. He erred, I think, in regard to cemetery customs. Lucy Skipworth, the "black Ma" on the John Hartwell Cocke plantation, was buried in the family cemetery, and "others of their caste received similar respect."(6) Similarly, Nat's mother, "alone among all the Negroes at Turner's Mill, had been laid honorably to rest in the family plot among white folks" (p. 185). But the graves of the other Negroes rest idle for a brief respite, then are returned to agriculture. As one cemetery is plowed up at the Turner place, one Negro man observes, "Dem old dead peoples is sho gwine grow a nice passel of yams!" (p. 132). The incident is one of moment in Nat's understanding of slavery. To me this is Styron's worst misrepresentation of culture of black or white. Slaves in many family cemeteries in north Georgia were buried in the same graveyard with whites--though only the latter might have tombstones. Southern respect for the dead prevented abuse of all cemeteries both black and white. (I have compared my views with those of Bell I. Wiley and others). At most churches black and white cemeteries were adjacent rather than integrated. There may be, however, a direct source for the plowing up of the cemetery on the Cocke plantation. There was a Cemetery Field on the plantation, but whether it was named that because it had been a cemetery or a field close to a cemetery is now an imponderable. Styron defends himself: "Anything that was possible," he says, he "could use. If that places fiction above history, I am willing to do so if it does no disservice to the spirit of the time. An out and out lie is not acceptable. If plowing up the cemetery is wrong, it was an honest mistake" (interview).

Perhaps the final question about The Confessions is whether the system of slavery as Styron presents it allows for the "great variety of personality types in the quarters,"(7) whether there are characters other than some rebellious Jack, a fawning Sambo, or a decorous house butler--and whether there are whites other than blessed white Massahs, Simon Legrees, poor whites, and cruel overseers. Precisely here, I think, Styron has been fairest to black and white of any novelist writing primarily about a race question in the history of the American novel. Even slavery per se does not altogether govern the character of a man, does not determine his goodness and badness by his blackness and whiteness. Styron has said that he was not consciously aware of attributing good or evil to any character on racial grounds (interview). The pattern was human nature, which tends to survive any system with some modifications. Indeed, slavery, Styron says, was a human situation in which people reacted very much as they do now (interview). That is, they are true to their natures in any racial or human situation.

Nat's own failings and accomplishments are seen basically in human terms. Styron has bestowed on him the mixed blessings of humanity and complexity. He is in twentieth-century terms a visionary and even a meditative intellectual. He thinks and thinks and meditates more than he acts. Faced with a confrontation, he is as impotent physically and spiritually as Faulkner's Gail Hightower or the man before the gate in Allen Tate's "Ode to the Confederate Dead." To the modern militant black his failure to kill whites (except for the beautiful Margaret) is a cop-out by Nat Turner and a blatant example of white racism by William Styron.

In a work where virtually everything relates to race, the difficulty lies in making everything also human and credible. One critic has charged that Styron is "overly schematic" in showing the variety of relationships which exist between master and slave.(8) Nat himself describes the categories of whites: "I think it may have been seen by now how greatly various were the moral attributes of white men who possessed slaves, how different each owner might be by way of severity or benevolence. They ranged down from the saintly (Samuel Turner) to the all right (Moore) to the barely tolerable (Reverend Eppes) to a few who were unconditionally monstrous" (p. 299).

Nat's statement reveals Styron's determination to be human and artistic rather than racial, not to allow color of skin to determine goodness of character. Race and personage are of course inseparable. Some may believe that they can look at others with absolutely no regard for color. But as some black militants have discovered, culture and race are not clearly distinguishable. In complex interrelationships it is often extremely difficult to tell what is racist and what is not. In the best fiction the racism of a thing may be ultimately undefinable.

One statement, depending on the speaker, the perspective, and the context may be antiwhite or antiblack or not racist at all. Sometimes Nat himself seems antiblack. Negroes, he says, are "a people not notably sweet-natured around domestic animals." And he knows why: "what else but a poor dumb beast could a Negro mistreat and by mistreating feel superior to?" (p. 293). The possibilities of interpretations here are numerous. A sociological field investigation might discover that the statement about the black man's mistreatment of animals is a factual error. That hostile critic to slavery, Fanny Kemble, the English actress who resided for a time in the South, agreed with Nat. She saw no gentleness in the manner of Negro to animals. "I was constantly struck with the insolent tyranny of their demeanor toward each other. . . . They are diabolically cruel to animals too. . . . These detestable qualities, which I constantly heard attributed to them as innate and inherent in their race appear to me the direct result of their condition."(9) But who is to say after so long a time that it was almost a universal characteristic and who is to define the cause? One can only stumble through the blind corridors of history wondering whether there is any conclusion at all. Indeed, Negro slaves could have been kinder to animals than whites because their bondage induced them to be sympathetic to chattel beasts. See, for example, the love of the old Negro for the dog in "Marse Chan," Thomas Nelson Page's sentimental story. Here Styron's fiction is as complex as race and life. There is no clearly correct attitude. This again is what Styron aimed to write--a kind of meditation in which the historical novelist gives no precise clues as to how it is to be interpreted. Only in this way can fiction allow the human truth to prevail over a bias.

Even praise of the black by the white may be biased racism. T. R. Gray is a gross and callous white racist whether he condemns or praises. Negroes who attempt to carry out an "insurgent action" are cowardly. They are weak men marked by "irresolution, instability" (p. 88). But the blacks who defend their masters on the contrary are heroes who can fight as bravely as any man (p. 86). Gray's bigotry decides whether he will praise or damn the black.

Styron obtains balance by refusing to measure a character by the system, by setting one event against another, one character against another. A black extremist offsets a white one. A good white man is a counterweight to a good black in the novel. The moral system balances almost like balancing scales. A black sells his racial brother for his own material and returns the runaway Hark to his master and slavery. Benjamin Turner who is more hostile to Negroes than his brother Samuel is also a gross and callous alcoholic. Styron's design makes the racist bad in other ways. Those whites unmarked by the system of slavery, those "reared outside the tradition of slavery often made the most callous taskmasters" (p. 343), at least according to Nat. A white mob casts stones at Nat and Ethelred Brantley when Nat baptizes the white man. This mob is a counterweight to Nat's own insurrection. And the white uprising after the insurrection kills more Negroes than the blacks had killed whites. Styron does not portray heroism as much as violence among the revolting Negroes, but even here slavery may be responsible for the Negroes' hatred.

The necessity and the extent of imagination is a baffling aspect of The Confessions. There are two slave coffles which Nat sees close by, and both of them had to be cut from the cloth of invention. On one occasion Nat rides back home from Richmond in joy and exultancy (p. 195) because he has been given the chance to work his way to freedom in Richmond by the time he is twenty-five. At this moment of penultimate hope of the higher-caste slave he sees a coffle of some forty men "skimpily clad; linked to each other by chains . . . and manacled with double cuffs of iron" (p. 196). They do not talk while one pisses in the ditch and a small boy weeps. After elaborate accounts of their drovers and of the slaves, who derive from the rider plantation, they pass on.

But Nat is not one of them. He is a house slave, and with inhuman lack of compassion he tells the poor devils in the coffle that his master is going to set him free in Richmond (p. 200). But even slaves are human. One from the coffle speaks and tells Nat, "Yo' shit stink too, sugah. Yo' ass black jess like mine, honey chile" (p. 201). The story is from the offal of history. Indeed, it may be excessive in the descriptions of the slaves, their drovers, their destitutions, and their methods of travel. The intimate details of the coffle could be precisely based on a first-hand documented witness of the coffle, but so far as Styron knows the whole scene came to him in a flash and at a single second and with no particular recollections that he could recall separately (interview). When he was a little boozed up, as he says, the scene came to him in its entirety as if it were already written. With no research and no correction, he says, it came to him as if he had been a witness.

Fiction must see a slave coffle personally. Despite its small part in the action of The Confessions, it is filled with living detail: a weeping child, an anxious father, a leader of slaves, drovers, a plantation owner grieved by another owner's need to sell his slaves, and, most important of all, the consciousness of an arrogant house nigger vain of himself and contemptuous of the shitty shepherds of his time. On the whole Styron's mind seems to have worked (this is a guess on my part) from a very broad and general social situation to render it in such particularity that it is a representation of the utter inhumanness of slavery.

Just after the creation of the mass coffle and its representation of the life of the slave, Styron turns to a different condition and situation in an extended account of Nat's relationship with his friend Willis. Nat leads him to an acceptance of the light of Christianity, fishes with him, joins in a sort of homosexual masturbation with him, prays with him for forgiveness, and finally baptizes him. He plans eventually to help free Willis and immediately to go with him to a Baptist camp meeting. Abe is supposed to carry four boys to be sold to a coffle at night. But Abe gets sick, and Nat has to carry them. Instead of carrying Willis to the camp meeting, Nat finds himself carrying him off to be sold into slavery clandestinely in the night. Not only does this episode magnify the evils of selling slaves, but it shows the inhumane separation of friend and friend. Yet even this, Styron argues, is carried out in somewhat human terms (interview). The white felt a tremendous reluctance to sell off slaves, and when he was compelled to do so, he sold the slaves--like Willis--who had no family ties. Willis was an orphan and was therefore least vulnerable to a profound grief (p. 219; interview). Once John Cocke sold some of his brother-in-law's slaves at low prices rather than sell them to traders, and the brother-in-law was distressed. Cocke sold his own slaves to the Deep South only after they had committed a crime.

Almost without exception in The Confessions Styron has had to build structures with scarce materials. Usually the detailed and personal life of Negroes has had to be imagined more than that of most slave-owning whites, many of whom kept journals, diaries, ledgers, account books, and records of plantings and harvests. When the Negro improved a tool or a toy, he left no record. Owners left extensive diagrams of wooden wheels and lengthy records of the quantities and kinds of food they gave to their slaves. The library, clothing, hiring out of Nat to an architect, the newly invented Carey plow, the cleanliness (or filth) of the Negro quarters, Negro songs and sayings and wisdom, the transporting of slaves to America in inhumanly crowded circumstances (see the account of Nat's fierce Coromantee grandmother)--the world exists in historical fullness in The Confessions.

The manners and everyday events and personal relationships of white culture are revealed in elaborate detail and always carefully from the perspective of a slave narrator with the character of Nat Turner. He overhears white secrets, as when he hears Miss Emmeline Turner making love during an assemblage. Styron and Nat present social customs as fully as the earlier writers of Old Southwest humor did. There are revivals of fundamentalist whites, a camp meeting, a church service, allusions to Negro songs ("Sweet Woman Gone," "Old Zip Coon"), a Christmas on a plantation, and all the details involved in the knowledge of complicated occupations like carpentry and blacksmithing. There are unusual musical instruments, a Jew's harp, and a banjo made of fence wire and pine strips. Study, research, culture, history, fact, characters, imagination--all of these and much more must come together to create the life of an older time.

In some fashion all the materials of The Confessions are in Nat's original confessions, Coyner, Fanny Kemble, Olmsted, and other sources.

But the novel itself is not there at all. Styron could have taken the appearance of John Hartwell Cocke (whose plantation and life he knew extensively), for example, and with a little transmogrification have made it his Samuel Turner, but despite Styron's admission that Turner derives from Cocke, they bear little physical resemblance. Cocke is a sterner man than Turner even though he is more radical as an opponent to slavery. Cocke is tall and weather-worn:

"tall commanding"
"rough-hewn"
"pleasant blend of sternness and kindliness"
"dark haired"
"large featured "(10)

but Turner is softer, perhaps, more kindly to slaves but less effectual in his dealings with the system:

"a curious, abiding sweetness"
"kindly, shrewd, luminous strength in his face"
"patriarchal and venerable grandeur"
"cheek whiskers . . . which end in small tufts whiter
   than a cotton tail's butt"
"wrinkles around his mouth . . . lines"
"singular face too long and horselike"
"ugly as a mushrat"
"the nose too prominent beaked"
"Lawd didn't leave Marse Sam a whole lot of jawbone."
            (p. 26)

The two men are not the same. Not only has fiction filled out the portrait more fully, but it has made the man more contradictory complex enough even to be hard to visualize. Cocke may be even harder to see because his features have been taken from an historian's facts rather than an artist's conception of the appearance of a whole man.

Again and again it is in this fashion that the critic and the source-hunter proceed from whatever source to the novel. The generalities of the novel appear in history over and over; the particulars never. The particulars are invented as are necessarily the meditations. In almost tabular fashion one can see the difference between Cocke's life as reported by Coyner and life on the Turner plantation as reported by Styron. Often to a flaw historians fail to speculate and interpret.

Anything belongs to the province of the novelist, Styron believes, as long as it is in the interest of his fiction. He does not name Coyner or Cocke or the source of quotations from them with footnotes. A footnote even to a plagiarized passage in a novel, if that is what it should be called, is in a sense a betrayal of fiction. It would make fiction history and when the novelist finds exactly what he wishes somewhere else he may use it as Styron did here . . . without any regret or respect for property rights.

I have long and do still steadfastly believe that
Slavery is the great Cause of all the chief evils
of our Land--individual as well as national . . .
eating upon the vitals of the Commonwealth.(11)

I have long and do still steadfastly believe that
slavery is the great cause of all the chief evils of
our land. It is a cancer eating at our bowels . . . .

(p. 159)

"The novelist," Styron says, "has a right to appropriate anything"
(interview). In a way also it is curious what Styron chose to use. The only
direct quotation is an unspecifiable passage chosen from a general letter
about a rather commonplace opinion and cast in a rather commonplace
vocabulary. Strange are the vagaries of novelists.

The sources of fiction not found in history may be stranger than those
that are. Indeed, if one were to read somewhat cursorily the long
dissertation of Martin Coyner, Jr., he might not be at all aware that it is
a source of The Confessions. This historical source and the art derived in
part from it are a world apart, as perhaps they should be. In general
Styron takes an episode or principle and has his Turner talk about it. The
drama and the talk come from the principle and indeed the historian may
have no obligation at all to entertain as the novelist has. As the fiction is
more human and particular and heightened than the source, so it may also
in many instances be much more heightened than life itself. The artist
may choose from all the things he has known in order to create. As he
often chooses the most colorful so also he may leave out the dull. Finding
a source may be a disappointing experience for the scholar. And he must
turn, not to the source for the mysteries of the work of art, but to the
totality of the author's experience as well as the associative cerebrations
of his mind in putting a work together. The deep well of the author's
mind from which the creation springs may exist in monumental
proportions, but it may also be picked from tiny debris and filaments
which have no connection at all except in the final product.

What is not in any source for a work of fiction may show ultimately
more about the work and the mind of the author than about factual
history. The bare fact of history takes on flesh and blood and drama in
art. A couple of instances may prove the extensive difference between the
bland world of academic history and that of the flesh, indeed the carrion,
of actual history. Styron does not recall reading about a communal slave
privy, seeing the picture of one, or ever seeing an actual privy once used
by slaves on a southern plantation before the Civil War. No plantation
privy has been preserved in the twentieth century in all its fecal
abundance. If there is a modern analogue it would be the line of
commodes or outdoor latrine holes used as depositories in the modern
army. The sad but comic account of the scorching of Nat's private parts

when someone pours oil in the latrine and sets it afire during a moment of Nat's solitary cogitation after the morning rush (p. 137) has its analogues in stories of at least hundreds of episodes of latrine humor during World War II.

The novelist's cleverness in inventing sociological and antiquarian phenomena out of whole cloth so to speak is not a mark of artistry; his ability to use such inventions to illuminate personality, however, is artistry. Negroes had to use the woods or go to some kind of structure. Visual and odoriferous as the latrine may be, it conveys vividly the lack of privacy in the rural South, especially among gangs of Negroes in the morning rush. "Hit's a shame in dis world," Nat's mother complains: "Us folks in de house is quality. And we ain't got no outhouse for our own selfs, hit's a cryin' shame!" (p. 136). That is a general condition portrayed in the fiction but the ultimate aim must be personal: how does our protagonist react to the filth and the stench? With all the sensibility and finickiness of one reared with indoor plumbing, black or white. Nat avoids "the morning rush, training my bowels [obviously with discomfort] to obey a later call when I can enjoy some privacy if not dry sanitation" (p. 136). From a little experience and much imagination Styron has created a situation and a character indeed remote from any facts that he may have ever learned from historical sources.

Other situations in The Confessions concern strictly the private life of the slave. No man in the twentieth century--no child like Nat--has witnessed the rape of a mother house-slave cook in a plantation kitchen. Doubtless there have been numerous analogues but ultimately the entire scene must come solely from the imagination of William Styron. The journalist or the historian of the nineteenth century would be interested in the general effect of master or overseer-slave sexual relationships in their extent and in the social and moral economic effects. Except in very general terms, however, he would not provide a full account of the inter-course of one person with another. Search as he would through history, the source-hunting novelist would find few such incidents or none. In Coyner's dissertation, for example, the episode of overseer-black sexual relationships is but a detail under the assertion that "Cocke's luck with Alabama overseers [that is, on the plantation of which he was absentee owner] was more uneven." Elam Tanner was an outstanding problem. He was "a little hare brained" but smart. Cocke thought his plantation problems were due "to Tanner's contrariness and failure to attend to his business." And "in the end, charges against Tanner of cohabiting with several slave women became substantial enough for the overseer to confess in part." He refused to marry and therefore find sexual solace in one woman, so he "was released."(12)

That is history, history of the entirely respectable kind, perhaps history of the most common sort. But it does not furnish the materials of the situation in its intimate details. Fiction in most of its usual modern forms enacts the episodes on stage. After a stark warning by the black driver Abraham Nat's mother Lou-Ann refuses to leave her kitchen. She sings a song of her desire for protection:

> Bow low, Mary, bow low, Martha,
> For Jesus come and lock de do',
> An carry de keys away. (p. 145)

Jesus does not lock the door for Lou-Ann. Styron enacts the scene of her rape by the white overseer McBride. In an antique kitchen which would delight the heart of an antiquarian, a brutal white man rapes a gentle black mother while he holds the splinters of a broken brandy bottle to her throat. The small son of the woman watches the force the denial and the sexual experience itself. The humanness of the scene is apparent in Nat's Mother's ultimate relinquishment. The scene begins as rape and ends in acquiescence: "her brown legs go up swiftly to embrace his waist, the two of them joined and moving in that . . . strange and brutal rhythm" (p. 148). The complexity of the scene is not that it ends merely in the semirape and oppression and miscegenation, but that it ends with the impingement of this experience on the mind of a sensitive young Negro boy. The rape is not itself so spectacular to him as its ultimate meanings. With his mother involved he sees "that same strange and brutal rhythm I have witnessed . . . through the cracks of half a dozen cabins and which in the madness of complete innocence I had thought was the pastime or habit or something of Negroes alone" (p. 148). Despite the enactment of a scene which reveals a knotty entanglement of many of the situations of slavery, the supreme accomplishment of Styron here has been the creation of the effect of the mystery of a small boy who knows not where he came from what he is and what he is to be. And there was no specific source for this. It is an enactment of all of history selected from tiny shards of experience derived from biography, history, the daily newspapers, and the witnessing of many trivial acts of violence. The jagged bottle, Styron says, for example, leaped into his mind from he knew not where (interview).

All the analogies do not enable the historian or even the novelist to turn back the clock to the facts of slavery. Whether The Confessions is a success or a failure, it is to the everlasting credit of Styron's fortitude that he was willing to attempt to create the mind of a black man living in a system that does not now exist and one that was not accurately or fully recorded when it did exist. Few records provided what Styron had to tell about Nat Turner. Some of the physical realities existed, but the records of observers were unreliable much more so than usual in history. Not only is The Confessions more fiction than most, but also the resolution of the debate about its accuracy is more difficult than in most instances. The final decisions about the authenticity of the novel are personal, racial, historical, subjective. . . .

Notes

(1) Interview with William Styron, June 18, 1974. Hereafter cited in text as "interview."

(2) William Styron, The Confessions of Nat Turner (New York, 1967). All parenthetical references in the text are to this edition.

(3) Henry Irving Tragle, The Southampton Slave Revolt of 1831: A Compilation of Source Material (Amherst, Mass., 1971), p. 6.

(4) Martin Boyd Coyner, Jr., "John Hartwell Cocke of Bremo: Agriculture and Slavery in the Ante-Bellum South" (Ph.D. dissertation, University of Virginia, 1961), p. 397.

(5) John W. Blassingame, The Slave Community: Plantation Life in the Antebellum South (New York, 1972), pp. 95-96.

(6) Coyner, p. 89.

(7) Blassingame, p. 153.

(8) Quoted by Alan Holder, "Styron's Slave: The Confessions of Nat Turner," South Atlantic Quarterly 68 (Spring 1969): 169.

(9) Frances Anne Kemble, Journal of a Residence on a Georgian Plantation in 1838-39, ed. by John A. Scott (New York, 1970), p. 305.

(10) Coyner, p. 16

(11) Ibid., p. 305.

(12) Ibid., pp. 394-96.

*From In Time and Place: Some Origins of American Fiction: 51-70. Reprinted by permission.

THIS UNQUIET DUST: THE PROBLEM OF HISTORY IN STYRON'S THE CONFESSIONS OF NAT TURNER*

James M. Mellard

Once upon a time novels achieved validation as a form by identifying themselves as history. In recent years, however, it has been argued that history has taken its primary forms from fiction. To the epistemologically naive, according to the view, histories are accounts of "reality" and "truth" but to the sophisticated modernist no history, however meaningful, can exist apart from the shapes conferred by fiction's narrative archetypes.(1) In reducing the gap between the kinds of knowledge generated by history on the one hand, and by fictions such as novels on the other, modern philosophers of history have uncovered a crisis of another sort than has usually undercut the value of either history or the novel. That crisis lies in the apparent dissolution of historical knowledge of any kind in "proper" history and in "realistic" novels. For one sort of historian, historical narratives today are "verbal fictions the contents of which are as much invented as found and the forms of which have more in common with their counterparts in literature than they have with those in the sciences."(2) But such a view of history does not legitimize fiction since for many literary critics influenced by modernism novels have lost now whatever legitimate historical and cognitive value they once were thought to have. Thus, between a fictionalized history and a dehistoricized fiction, little valid knowledge in our historical narratives would seem to remain. The problem of history now endemic to both the novel and proper history is especially acute in a work such as William Styron's The Confessions of Nat Turner. There the claims of history and the claims of fiction are made together, but both claims are rejected alike by historians and literary critics, thus leaving one to wonder what cognitive purpose is served by this or any other historical fiction.

Styron has called The Confessions of Nat Turner a "meditation on history." He did so because he wished to avoid the more pejorative associations of a label such as "historical novel." The historical novel, Georg Lukacs notwithstanding, is usually thought of as "merely" a popular form, one often employing the flimsiest of factual details simply to give an interesting place for an author's created hero to stand: its connection to real history is usually tenuous and its ability to deepen our historical understanding negligible. But Styron does not provide his label to evade a critique of his novel's connection to actual history. He makes this and other concerns very plain in his "Author's Note" to the novel: "During the narrative that follows," he says," I have rarely departed from the known facts about Nat Turner and the revolt of which he was the leader."(3) Still, he insists, his main concern is for his role as a novelist, not as a historian. ". . . in those areas where there is little knowledge in regard to Nat, his early life, and the motivations for the revolt (and such knowledge is lacking most of the time), he says, "I have allowed myself the utmost freedom of imagination in reconstructing events--yet I trust remaining within the bounds of what meager enlightenment history has left us about the institution of slavery." Then he speaks of his primary insight and purpose: "The relativity of time allows us elastic definitions: the year 1831 was, simultaneously, a long time ago and only yesterday. Perhaps the reader will wish to draw a moral from this narrative, but it has been my own intention to try to re-create a man and his era and to produce a work that is less an 'historical novel' in conventional terms than a meditation on history."

The Confessions of Nat Turner, then, is not meant primarily to be an objective "historical novel," but an expressive artifact in which Styron gets inside history in the only ways open to either the novelist or the historian: through the representation of the historical consciousness of a subject. Thus, the novel is in one sense "psychohistorical," but it is also "metahistorical"--a work that is deliberately, even self-consciously concerned with concepts of history, of history as history. Above all the novel addresses (and causes readers to address) the problem of history. I shall take up the metahistorical aspects first showing the ways in which two major characters--Thomas Gray and Nat Turner--present competing notions of history. In the essay's last section, I shall consider certain psychohistorical(4) dimensions of both the novel and the criticism it has elicited. In the end The Confessions suggests, not so much what historical knowledge is, but what its social function might be.

I

The opening section of The Confessions, "Judgment Day," is crucial to any consideration of the novel's portrayal of historical consciousness, for it dramatizes several opposed conceptualizations of history. The section, first off, is virtually a forum for the view of Thomas R. Gray, the lawyer who recorded and published Turner's confession as history. But history, as Styron demonstrates, is always someone's history. Consequently, we must recognize that when we look at Gray's version of Nat Turner's rebellion we are interpreting an interpretation. Contrary to the unusually naive, premodernist assumptions of too many of the novel's early critics (black and white alike), Gray was never a transparent lens, never an objective, disinterested recorder of Turner's narrative. Gray's "history" is open to all sorts of interpretation--not only of the sort Styron provides, but also of the sorts provided by different critics and historians. In a remark in one of the most important essays on Nat Turner and Styron's novel, Seymour Gross and Eileen Bender summarize the problem Gray represents: "Our impression," they write, "is that he was anything but a blank-faced scrivener; . . . he was, on the contrary, a very shrewd man who knew precisely what he was doing and why; and . . . his pamphlet is a political document in the most basic sense of the word."(5)

Two reasons this novel after early popular success has fallen into critical disrepute are quite contradictory. On the one hand, Styron takes his documents too seriously; on the other, he doesn't take them seriously enough. Both are given credence by Styron. The most damaging critique today would be the claim that Styron too easily accepted Gray's report as the "history" claimed by the lawyer. But in fact Styron insinuates a critique of Gray's document within The Confessions of Nat Turner. Styron's actual presentation is not nearly as naive as the reviewers and later readers have sometimes insisted for the novel actually dramatizes some of the same issues Gross and Bender considered early on. There is, for example, the whole question of the "origin and progress" of the insurrection and the public's curiosity to know details. While Styron's Gray has some ironic fun with Nat's repeating the Biblical phrase, "'Confess, that all nations may know'," Styron the novelist makes plain the public's need of an adequate "history":

"So the Lord told you: Confess, that all nations may know?
Reverend, I don't think you realize what divine justice lies
in that phrase. For near about onto ten weeks now there's been
a mighty clamor to know, not only in the Virginia region but
all over America. For ten weeks, while you were a-hidin' out and
a-scamperin' around Southampton like a fox, the American people
have been in a sweat to know how come you started a calamity
like you done. All over America, the North as well as the South,
the people have asked theirselves: How could the darkies get
organized like that, how could they ever evolve and promulgate
not to say coordinate and carry out such a plan? But the
people didn't know, the truth was not available to them. They
were in the profoundest dark." (pp. 16-17)

But all irony aside, Styron's Gray is quite serious in his attempt to promulgate at least one version of Turner's "history of the motives." The people have to know something and either that something must be acceptable to them or an entire cultural and economic system may well collapse around them. Unless Gray and the court can determine the identity of the organizer or organizers of the insurrection they are faced with the possibility first that it was spontaneous--and thus could occur again at any time--and second that every participant in it is equally guilty and therefore subject to a sentence of death. Thus, one purpose of the trials of the slaves is as Nat puts it, "to separate the wheat from the chaff" (p. 19).

If Nat Turner remains as virtually the only worthless chaff "amongst the wheat" (p. 24), the court can be justified in returning alive the majority of the slaves to their owners. The issue here as Styron's Gray recognizes is less that of justice than of economics: ". . . you might say it was to protect the rights of property," Gray says to Turner (p. 19). Yet Gray must also claim justice for the trials; hence, when Nat implies that the only thing proven by the trials is the "rights of property," Gray angrily exclaims:

> "Sixty-odd culprits in all. . . . Out of sixty, a couple dozen
> acquitted or discharged another fifteen or so convicted by
> transported. Only seventeen hung in all. In other words, out of
> this whole catastrophic ruction only round one-fourth gets the
> rope. Dad-burned mealy-mouthed abolitionists say we don't show
> justice. Well, we do. Justice! That's how come nigger slavery's
> going to last a thousand years." (p. 25)

The ploys behind this version of the judicial history, as Styron's Gray interprets it, catch liberals in a double bind: on the one hand, slave owners are permitted to retain their "animate chattel," and on the other to claim that their protection of a valuable property is actually an exercise in "justice." It is a neat "history," but one that remains concealed. Styron puts it into Gray's speech to Nat Turner in private, but it cannot be uttered in the public event of the trial itself. Although it may bear a premise that lay behind Gray's actual historical documents, it was to remain only implicit, for the real Gray was a crafty rhetorician who never gave his best ploys away.

Styron further dramatizes the issue of the historical authenticity of the original confession though he has contradicted himself elsewhere. In his essay "This Quiet Dust" Styron clearly agrees with those critics and historians who perhaps for want of any other data would naively accept the document's validity. "There are several discrepancies in Gray's transcript," he writes, "but it was taken down in haste and in all major respects it seems completely honest and reliable" (p. 15). But in the novel Styron, like any historian dealing with documents, quickly runs into problems--for instance, the problem of language--when he handles Gray's version of the confession: how does Nat talk; how many dialects can he command; can his thoughts legitimately be cast into a biblico-literary mold; how do other characters talk? These are some of the questions various readers of the novel have asked,(6) but Styron himself shows acute awareness of one particular problem, the fact that Nat Turner's words in the confession may only be Gray's. The novel contains an interestingly ambivalent passage on the subject of words, language, and even details at a point where Gray begins to read his transcript back to Turner:

> Gray had begun to read slowly and with deliberation, as if
> relishing the sound of each word, and already he interrupted
> himself, glancing up at me to say:
> "Of course, Nat, this ain't supposed to represent your
> exact words as you said them to me. Naturally, in a court
> confession there's got to be a kind of, uh, dignity of style,
> so this here's more or less a reconstitution and <u>recomposition</u>
> of the relative crudity of manner in which all of our various
> discourses since last Tuesday went. The essence--that is, all
> the quiddities of detail are the same--or at least I hope they
> are the same." (p. 30)

As Styron portrays Gray, the lawyer is a man in love with words, with rhetorical ploys, and Nat's remarking upon the relish with which Gray reads the statement suggests Gray's sense of possession, of creative literary pride. Styron again, in a later passage, makes clear he understands the problematical authenticity of the confession, for he depicts Turner's thoughts while Gray shuffles pages and reads to him: "His words (mine? ours?) came back in my brain like a somber and doleful verse from Scripture itself (p. 37). And as one further indication that the language of the document is not necessarily attributed to Turner, Styron does not permit Nat to repeat or meditate upon the words of the original confession until after they have been read to him by Gray. To have allowed Turner to think them in detail before this point would "authenticate" them as the slave's own, as a part of his being. Styron thus achieves a distinct irony as a result of Nat's discomfort at hearing words he no longer can claim as his alone. Like his acts, his words have moved out of himself and into history, much as the prosecutor Trezevant's reciting a list of the villains of the past prompts Turner to think how those words, also, propelled me thus into history" (p. 81).

II

Nat Turner also presents (indeed, even embodies) a version of history. But he must defend his version against the conflicting claims of other versions, or else renounce his. Nat suffers under the interpretation of Biblical history by one such as the Reverend Richard Whitehead, yet Nat's own conception of history can hardly be other than Biblical, either. The only book easily available to Turner was the King James Bible, so perhaps the only view of history he can arrive at--other than the ones the slave owners and preachers try to impose upon him--is one also found there.(7) But in the novel Turner's historical consciousness is slow in developing along any lines. As Styron presents the issue, the reason is simple enough: there can be no historical sense without a consciousness of a past and a future both potentially different from the present. As William E. Akin says, political resistance "required a vision of the future,"(8) and that had to grow within Nat. A consciousness of the future first dawns upon Nat when Marse Samuel Turner speaks of "grander plans for this young darky" (p. 171). Nat reports that he had been unable to answer Marse Samuel's question about the "fruitless lifetime" spent by other slaves because

> I do not believe that I had ever thought of the future; it is
> not in the mood of a Negro, once aware of the irrecoverable fact
> of his bondage, to dwell on the future at all, and even I in my
> state of relative good fortune must have simply assumed without
> thought that the days and years which stretched out before me
> would present only the familiar repetitious and interminable
> clutter of dirty dishes, chimney ashes, muddy boots, tarnished
> doorknobs, chamber pots, mops and brooms. That something different
> might befall my lot had never occurred to me. (pp. 170-71)

Samuel Turner's phrase, "grander plans," registers considerable irony with readers, for it must inevitably be connected with those "grand plans" for political resistance which the older Nat later will speak of and eventually carry out. But for the moment all that these plans entail is Nat's becoming--in the way a savior figure ought--an apprentice carpenter, apprenticed appropriately enough to a man whose name is both Godt and Goat, suggesting, perhaps, "God" and "scapegoat." Connected as well to a somewhat grander plan to give Nat his freedom at age twenty-five, this grand plan ultimately has its greatest impact upon Nat Turner by creating in him a consciousness of history and time, of "Old Times Past" and of the future symbolized in the "Judgment Day" of "Revelations." In his mind he is thus irrevocably separated from the bulk of his race, who, he believes, "Like animals . . . relinquished the past with as much dumb composure as they accepted the present, and were unaware of any future at all" (p. 224).

Nat Turner's sense of history goes along with a developing sense of self, of his own individuality, importance, and destiny. Both history and self are brought together when he is left by Samuel Turner to the care of the Reverend Eppes. The Turner family had been forced by a severe depression affecting the Tidewater to abandon Turner's Mill; there, just at his twenty-first birthdate and the time when he was (according to Marse Samuel's grander plan) to go to Richmond, at twenty-five to become a free man, the young Nat is left to await the arrival of Eppes. Alone at the Mill, Nat thinks of himself "adrift between that which was past and those things yet to come" (p. 228). And though he feels "abandonment and loss," he feels "at the same time obscurely excited by the promise of a new world, liberty, the fruition of all those dreams I had entertained in the recent past of myself a freedman . . ." (p. 229). But Nat's dreams of freedom, of course, are not to come to fruition: the Reverend Eppes is not the honorable man for whom Marse Samuel had taken him and after Eppes works Nat "like an animal" through a long winter he sells him into bondage--to Thomas Moore--for $460.(9) Consequently, Nat's dreams must take on a new form. His future is not going to be what he had expected. Cast "adrift" again on an imponderable ocean of time--as he imagines it at all crucial moments (for instance, here and in the dream-vision beginning the novel)--Nat must find a new vision and a new means for attaining his goals. Sold to Thomas Moore, clutching his Bible, having felt for the first time what it is to be whipped and to have to say "Master," riding in a wagon "heaving and rocking like a rudderless ship amid a sea of frozen glass" (p. 253), Nat hears at this moment the voice of the Lord "booming in the trees: 'I abide.'"

As long as Nat Turner imagines his history in the terms the Biblical theology of the South gives him, I abide is the only message the Lord can speak to him. He really has no earthly future other than abiding until the great plan, the divine mission he eventually carries out is revealed to him. He then must give up the New Testament view of himself taught him by the Turners, especially by Miss Nell. But Nat still does not escape a Biblical historical consciousness, for he turns to the Old Testament and to the Prophets--"mainly Ezekiel, Daniel, Isaiah, and Jeremiah," Nat says, "whose relevance to my own self and future I had only commenced to divine" (p. 259). Thus, he abandons a simple diachronic, linear view of his own history, in which he would move from bondage to freedom in an unbroken line. He comes to accept in its place a somewhat more complex, though still linear and teleological, vision of time and history in which bondage and freedom, like sin and salvation, shall be able to exist synchronically in the same time and place.

Essentially, Styron's Turner, though he could not have known it, comes to visualize something like the historical philosophy of St. Augustine.(10) Augustine imagined a City of God and a City of Man existing in the same place, and in the same time; he illustrated the concept with Christ's parable of the wheat and the tares (Matthew 13); though both exist together, only the wheat, Christ suggests, shall be gathered into the Lord's barn at the end of the harvest. Nat Turner also envisions around him human wheat among tares of good people, even among his enemies: such is his acceptance of Jeremiah Cobb as one who shall bear the mark that shall save him from destruction. Even as he had begun studying the works of the prophets, Nat had been "toying with the notion of slaughter" (p. 259). But as he accepts God's words through the Prophet Ezekiel, he accepts the charge to

Go through the midst of Jerusalem and set a mark upon the foreheads of the men that sigh and that cry for all the

abominations that be done in the midst thereof . . . [sic].
Slay utterly old and young, both maids and little children,
and women; but come not near any upon whom is the mark . . .
(pp. 52, 75; italics eliminated)

He eventually comes to see Jeremiah Cobb, therefore, along with his "convert" Brantley, as one who shall be spared the sword (p. 75). Nat's own life begins to take on something of this wheat and tares aspect (we recall, of course, his comment to Gray about the court separating the wheat from the chaff). He is able during his nearly ten years at Moore's to set up his own private "cathedral" in the nearby woods where he can go into retreat for fasting, meditation, and the visions by which his "grand mission, divinely ordained," will be revealed to him.

Even the great plan for changing history he hits upon is touched by this Biblical aspect of the wheat and tares. Nat realizes that, though he gather together "a majestic black army of the Lord" (p. 361), he can never conquer more than the immediate vicinity of Jerusalem--that Jerusalem, in Nat's imagination, which is closely akin to the "O Jerusalem" so frequently blessed and cursed, loved and hated by the Prophets. What he must do, Nat decides, is to fight his way into the Dismal Swamp, and there his small band might indefinitely hold off forces of far superior size. There he would set up a colony within the former colony itself, wheat amidst chaff, as the tribes of Israel created their nation among other nations. But in the end, Nat abandoned that Old Testament, Prophetic, political vision of history, and, in effect, Styron also abandoned the most rigorous historical vision underlying The Confessions of Nat Turner.

III

Having arrived at his own powerful view of history, Nat Turner would seem compelled to think of himself as a political savior, just as Old Testament prophets speak less of individual or personal than of a collective, national redemption. Believing their words, Nat must share their vision. As long as Styron's Turner maintains that historical vision, in fact, there are no problems with his self-confidence, nor, for that matter, for Styron himself with the structure of the novel. But when Styron's Nat relinquishes that vision and resumes a New Testament vision of personal rather than political salvation, his confidence abandons him--as he imagines God to have done. Unfortunately, the novel, too, begins to break down at this point. The problem seems to be this: the Dismal Swamp, though it be no place for man or beast to flourish, is a real place and one could indeed escape it, in the way, for example, that Twain's Huck Finn lights out for "the territory." Faulkner's Ike McCaslin escapes to the woods, and Joseph Heller's Yossarian paddles off toward Sweden like his friend Orr. Moreover, the Jeremiah Cobb of the Southampton court is also real, a metaphor, perhaps, of a powerfully brooding God-the-Father, yet one to whom Nat can relate concretely. But the heaven to which a repentant Nat would escape, a heaven vaguely imagined at the end of his life in the dream passage that opens the novel, is not at all concrete. Nor is the God who speaks to Nat-as-Christ, saying now, not I abide, but I come quickly.

The problem, in short, seems to be that a man concerned with history must work with existences, not essences, realities, not idealities. A Christian view of history is meaningful only when God, as Christ, descends into historical time; it is considerably less meaningful in the novel when through Christ, Nat Turner hopes to rise above his historical being. At the moment he attempts to fly beyond time and destiny, not to achieve a collective, "national," racial redemption for himself and other slaves, but merely a personal salvation, his whole vision begins to look distressingly like a failure of nerve in the face of death, his vision an incarnation of history, perhaps, but history become neurosis. The neurosis Styron's Turner reflects, however, is much more pervasive than one might think, if any conclusions regarding Styron and his critics are valid.

The Confessions of Nat Turner has become more than just a novel; it has become a cultural Rorschach test. Thus responses to it reveal to us some important psychological insights into black and white attitudes toward American history. It seems clear enough from what Styron has said in "This Quiet Dust" that the novel represents for him a kind of penance. It is an act of contrition by a writer who, indeed, is what his critics contend--white, Anglo-Saxon, Protestant, and a Southerner as well. As a penitential act the novel epitomizes the main thrust of WASP speculations on history as they are seen, for example, in Absalom, Absalom!, All the King's Men, Little Big Man, and Rabbit Redux. The goal of WASP revisionism in these novels seems to be the redemption of a national guilt for the oppression of blacks and the attempted genocide of Native Americans. The revision, however, should not achieve this goal by deleting ugly facts from American history, but by bringing them clearly into the analytic light of historical consciousness.

That seems to be what, on at least one level, Styron hopes to achieve in The Confessions of Nat Turner. Nat Turner was made in America by Americans, so Styron wants to restore him to all of us--black and white alike--in order to make us fully aware of our responsibility and Nat Turner's human grandeur. In "This Quiet Dust," Styron speaks of his interest in terms that have a broad cultural basis. He says that "to break down the old law, to come to know the Negro, has become the moral imperative of every white Southerner" (p. 14). And he adds: "my search for Nat Turner, my own private attempt as a novelist to re-create and bring alive that dim and prodigious black man has been at least a partial fulfillment of this mandate" (p. 14) to know the black American. But he connects the redemptive historical revisionism to other terms so personal that we must realize that not even Styron himself fully understands some psychological dimensions of the book. If the remarks from "This Quiet Dust" are not conclusive enough on this point, surely his answer in an interview to a question by R. W. B. Lewis is: "I wanted . . . to explore in some kind of depth this whole area of American life and history, to take on the lineaments as well as I could of a slave and, using that persona, walk myself through a time and a place in a manner of self-discovery."(11) As a consequence of this connection we must conclude that when Styron speaks of Nat Turner's redemption, he speaks of William Styron's; when he speaks of the book as redemptive, he must recognize it as redeeming both Nat Turner and all those who, taking on Turner's lineaments, identify with him. The novel is, then, a most problematical projection of Styron's--and perhaps, his white audience's--need for exculpation as much as it is a confession of Nat Turner.

The critics, especially the black critics, have recognized the personal redemptive project of Styron's "meditation." The essays in <u>William Styron's Nat Turner: Ten Black Writers Respond</u> show this recognition clearly: John Oliver Killens, for example, entitles his contribution to the book "The Confessions of Willie Styron," and Lerone Bennett, Jr., says, simply,

> The voice in this confession is the voice of
> William Styron.
> The images are the images of William Styron.
> The confession is the confession of William Styron.(12)

But as a rule the black critics, with powerful social reasons behind them, do not accept Styron's confession at all as an expression of personal and national <u>mea culpa</u>; instead, they are inclined to see it as a racist attack on Turner, black history, and 1960s black militancy, whenever it is not just another expression of WASP imperialism, of a white writer's expropriating property that rightfully belongs to black people.(13) They speak of all the ways in which Styron has subtly or blatantly deprecated black people through his portrayal of Nat Turner: his cutting Nat off from a family life (especially a relation to his father), eliminating a wife and giving him sexual fantasies that focus upon white women and suggesting that the failure of the insurrection was a result of a vacillating leadership growing out of a suspect masculinity. Most of all the black critics attack what they consider Styron's retrenchment of a philosophy of Southern history. As Bennett puts it: "Styron is playing the 'new history' game of reviving Big Black Sambo. . . . [H]e is trying to prove that U. B. Phillips, the classic apologist for slavery, and Stanley Elkins, the sophisticated modern apologist, were right when they projected Sambo--the bootlicking, head-scratching child-man--as a dominant plantation type" (p. 7). In its place these critics would rather see another "history," one such as that propounded by Herbert Aptheker, who writes, "The Turner rebellion cannot be understood unless it is seen as the culminating blow of a particular period of rising slave unrest. This was never absent in the South for long; it appeared and reappeared in waves and the Turner cataclysm was the highlight of one such wave which commenced about 1827 and played itself out in 1832."(14) Thus, instead of Sambo, the black critics would see in every slave an H. Rap Brown or a Stokely Carmichael, a Malcolm or a Cleaver.(15)

Black readers of the novel are not wrong to react as many have. There are indeed very troubling aspects to Styron's creation, apart from any apparent or actual distortion of historical facts. Alan Holder, in The Imagined Past, has pointed out some of these. Since Nat's attitude toward the morality of his fellow slaves, as Styron depicts it, is marked by feelings of contempt and disgust (p. 177), one is led to wonder why Nat would ever have embarked upon a mission to free them from their servitude. The recognition of a bond with them, says Holder, "does not jibe with the intense disgust for them he shows throughout, right up to the end" (p. 179). The repugnance Styron portrays in Nat is not merely of the moral weakness of slaves; it embraces a powerful physical distaste of appearance, hygiene, and odor as well. Styron's Nat certainly reflects the stereotypical attitudes of white people toward blacks. But one ought not conclude that it is derived from an acceptance of racist stereotypes. As Holder points out, Styron is no more charitable in his depiction of whites than of blacks as seen through Nat Turner's eyes. "The physical descriptions of people in the novel, taken as a whole, do not add up to a white or black bigot's view. Rather, they operate without prejudice to establish a democracy of repulsiveness in which man, white and black, are created equally ugly" (p. 180). Holder finally suggests that the utter unattractiveness of all people in the novel must be attributed to Styron, not simply to his characterization of Nat Turner: "The world of the book is aesthetically fallen," says Holder: "it is stained with Original Ugliness" (p. 180).

This witty reduction of Nat Turner's world to "Original Ugliness" allows us to get at another important issue underlying Styron's view of history. Holder's phrase suggests that Styron's vision of existence--and thus his vision of history, too--is erected upon a very negative foundation. Judging from the endings of other novels--Lie Down in Darkness and Sophie's Choice, for example--one must conclude that Styron sees no real resolution for troubled humanity within the material world, though that world decidedly provides grounds for one's wanting to escape it. It is not accidental at all that the sacrificial deaths of characters such as Peyton Loftis, Sophie Zawistowska, and Nat Turner appeal to Styron's imagination. Their frustrated eschatological impulses, their unconsummated efforts toward earthly transcendence, are necessitated by the tragic mode in which Styron seems inevitably to prefigure the historical world. His narrative rendering of Nat Turner's life can no more escape Styron's habitual modality of prefiguration than we might escape the law of gravity. This conclusion, finally, is the most important residue of the problem of history: no history can escape a very personal form of prefiguration, regardless of whether the prefigurative impulses are positive or negative, whether productive of a heroic or a tragic emplotment.

As human beings, our ways of looking at the world are psychologically and culturally determined. As readers, then, we too look at or interpret texts in terms of our own modes of prefiguration, which no doubt, as the psychologists would say, will encompass both our psychic needs and defenses. It seems plain, therefore, that the critics' reactions to The Confessions of Nat Turner are perhaps as much an outgrowth of our collective American psychic heritage as are Styron's explanations of the novel's form. Both the critics' denigrations and Styron's rationalizations inevitably must have underlying psychological causes associated with national, not merely personal, complexes. Richard Gilman has partially explained the psycho-social conflict. Much of it indeed has to do with the continuing interface between history and literature:

> the prestige of literature has been used to get around history's obduracy, its refusal to allow its facts to constitute meaning; but the imagination, which only respects facts as grist, remains insouciant. In this way the historical Nat Turner can be used by whites, as the protagonist of a new drama, which may or may not be patronizing to Negroes or subversive of their truth but is in any case comforting to us. At the same time, because literature's prestige is felt by Negroes, too, it becomes the instigation for a violent effort to repudiate Styron's newly shaped myth and put another in its place: that of Nat Turner's nobility, grandeur, his representative existence as spearhead of Negro consciousness, as exemplar of clear, clean, undeviating urgency towards liberation.(16)

If, therefore, we look at The Confessions of Nat Turner as an aesthetic expression born into an environment of historically determined cultural neurosis, we can begin to get beyond the critics' psychologically defensive objections to the novel at the same time we begin to get around the author's psychologically defensive justifications of its "redemptive" conclusion,(17) the novel's really major structural (not moral) fault. The novel Styron actually wrote is flawed because of his projecting into it a need he has himself, but which is in no way necessarily a need of the character he created. In the same way, the critical readings of the facts in Styron's novel are too often flawed because the critics are also projecting into it a need not necessarily implicit in Styron's or history's Nat Turner.

But, by way of conclusion one may finally ask: if the novel and the responses to it have been so problematical, what of possible value can it have achieved? The one value that cannot ultimately be disputed is the new knowledge of our history and our selves the novel has generated. At a crucial time in American civil history it dramatized conclusively that there were indeed important gaps in America's case history that could prevent its understanding of itself. "The purpose of historical knowledge,"

John Lukacs has said, "is not so much accuracy as a certain kind of understanding, one that provides a pragmatic but unsystematic knowledge of humans about other humans."(18)   Though Hayden White has been associated with a movement thought to deny any but the most relative truths to history, he does not deny the human value of history. He has written, at a point where he is exploring the analogy between psychotherapy and historiography, "Historians seek to refamiliarize us with events which have been forgotten through either accident, neglect, or repression. Moreover, the greatest historians have always dealt with those events in the histories of their cultures which are 'traumatic' in nature and the meaning of which is either problematical or overdetermined in the significance that they still have for current life. . . . (19)

It must now seem that this function of the historian is precisely what Styron and his novel have performed. They have dealt with traumatic, problematical, even repressed material and made an entire nation become aware of it. They have made possible a goal Norman O. Brown has enunciated: "if historical consciousness is finally transformed into psychoanalytical consciousness, the grip of the dead hand of the past on life in the present would be loosened, and man would be ready to live instead of making history, to enjoy instead of paying back old scores and debts, and to enter that state of Being which was the goal of his Becoming.(20) Thus, the essential value of Styron's novel, which many would still repress,(21) is that it has led us toward a better historical understanding, a human knowledge of other human beings that might help lead us a little way out of the nightmare of the American neurosis known as history.

Notes

(1) See especially Hayden White, "The Historical Text as Literary Artifact," in Tropics of Discourse: Essays in Cultural Criticism (Baltimore and London: Johns Hopkins University Press, 1978). Most of the dozen essays in this collection deal, in one way or another, with the problem of history, and particularly with the relationship between literature and history, a relationship also underscored in White's Metahistory: The Historical Imagination in Nineteenth-Century Europe (Baltimore and London: Johns Hopkins University Press, 1973).

(2) White, "The Historical Text as Literary Artifact," p. 82.

(3) William Styron, The Confessions of Nat Turner (New York: Random House, 1967), p. ix, unnumbered. Further references to the novel will be given within parentheses. . . . Styron's ambivalence about having taken his fiction writer's license with the facts surfaces again in the "Introduction" to the section of essays called "South" in the volume This Quiet Dust and Other Writings (New York: Random House, 1982); see p. 7 especially. On the subject of Styron's historical accuracy, one might consult Henry Irving

Tragle, "Styron and His Sources," <u>Massachusetts Review</u>, 11 (Winter 1970), 135-53; Henry Irving Tragle, <u>The Southampton Slave Revolt of 1831: A Compilation of Sources</u> (Amherst: University of Massachusetts Press, 1971); John White, "The Novelist as Historian: William Styron and American Negro Slavery," <u>American Studies</u>, 4 (1971), 233-45; Seymour Gross and Eileen Bender, "History, Politics and Literature: The Myth of Nat Turner," <u>American Quarterly</u>, 23 (October 1971), 487-518; and <u>William Styron's Nat Turner: Ten Black Writers Respond</u>, ed. John Henrik Clarke (Boston: Beacon Press, 1968). Three excellent essays concerning the problem of history--by George Core, Ardner R. Cheshire, Jr., and Mary S. Strine--appear in <u>The Achievement of William Styron</u>. Revised Ed., ed. Robert K. Morris, with Irving Malin (Athens: University of Georgia Press, 1981), which also includes a useful bibliography by Jackson Bryer. As one might guess, Styron's motives are questioned as often as his facts. Black critics and Marxists have often attributed Styron's changes or omissions to his overt or unconscious racism. Two essays by non-black, non-Marxist writers who saliently address the motives (as well as the aesthetics) of Styron's portrait are, negatively, Alan Holder, <u>The Imagined Past: Portrayals of Our History in Modern American Literature</u> (Lewisburg, Pa.: Bucknell University Press, 1980), pp. 172-89, and, positively, Richard Gray, <u>The Literature of Memory: Modern Writers of the American South</u> (London: Edward Arnold, 1977), pp. 290-305.

(4) My use of the term <u>psychohistorical</u> is, of course, figurative: Styron's novel remains a fiction, and while there are many parallels between the crafts of historian and novelist, a novel remains something other than history . . . the methods of the psychohistorian . . . are remarkably similar to those of any literary exegesis. [I do not] claim that Styron is a psychohistorian, though the psychogenesis he provides for Nat Turner is at least as plausible as that historians have provided for the behavior of other real persons. The essays by Holder and Gray are especially useful because of their antithetical points of view on the psychogenesis of Nat Turner's personality as Styron represents it.

(5) "History, Politics and Literature: The Myth of Nat Turner," p. 492. Early in the Styron/Nat Turner controversy, Gross and Bender make an important point concerning the rhetorical impress of Gray on the confession: Gray's pamphlet is an exercise in reassurance. . . (p. 493); as curious as this claim at first appears, I quite agree with the case they make for it.

(6) Mike Thelwell, in "Back with the Wind: Mr. Styron and the Reverend Turner," <u>William Styron's Nat Turner: Ten Black Writers Respond</u>, pp. 79-91, points out one of the major problems of the novel's language: "the voice that we hear in this novel as Turner's is that of a nineteenth-century plantation owner" (p. 81). Styron, however, can account adequately for Turner's style and vocabulary, and one of the interesting features of the book is the way Styron forces Turner to be ironic in his

perceptions of his ("their") language. Richard Gilman, in "Nat Turner Revisited," The New Republic, April 27, 1968, pp. 23-28, is especially hard and often very perceptive on the literary flaws in the style of the novel. For an interesting account by another novelist of the problems of language and imagination in a historical novel, see George Garrett, "Dreaming with Adam: Notes on Imaginary History," in Ralph Cohen, ed., New Directions in Literary History (Baltimore: Johns Hopkins, 1974), pp. 249-63; Garrett deprecates Styron's Confessions, but his premises surely defend Styron's practice as much as Garrett's own in Death of the Fox (on Sir Walter Raleigh). The best sympathetic essay on the novel's style/language is that by Richard Gray, The Literature of Memory, esp. pp. 293-95.

(7) In an interview with George Plimpton, Styron says, "If there is a focus to Nat Turner's vision, it is surely that of the Bible": George Plimpton, "A Shared Ordeal: Interview with William Styron, New York Times (October 8,1967); reprinted in William Styron's The Confessions of Nat Turner: A Critical Handbook, ed. Melvin J. Friedman and Irving Malin (Belmont, Ca: Wadsworth, 1970), pp. 36-42, 41.

(8) "Toward an Impressionistic History: Pitfalls and Possibilities in William Styron's Meditation on History," American Quarterly, 21 (Winter 1969), 805-812, 810. This essay, I must add, is perhaps the best available on the relationship between fiction and history as it might generate art history--or history-as-art.

(9) Tragle, in "Styron and His Sources" (p. 138), tells us that Nat Turner's value at execution was listed at $375.

(10) In Versions of the Past: The Historical Imagination in American Fiction (New York: Oxford University Press, 1974), pp. 273-77, Harry E. Henderson III suggests that The Confessions represents the tensions between two dominant modes of historical interpretation now current: the "holist" and the "progressive," associated respectively with a conservative and a radical social ideology, one content to work within a society to save it, the other bent upon total revolution. Henderson further suggests that the black critics and the Marxists attacked Styron because he treated the revolt in too holistic a fashion (p. 276), as evidenced by his turning the black hero into the psychologically warped victim of a racist society (p. 277), rather than a militant revolutionary who will overcome it by violence.

(11) R. W. B. Lewis and C. Vann Woodward, "Slavery in the First Person: Interview with William Styron," in William Styron's The Confessions of Nat Turner: A Critical Handbook, p. 52.

(12) Ten Black Writers Respond, p. 4. Note that Bennett seems uncritically to assume that Gray's account truly represents the real Nat Turner.

(13) Styron has discussed this issue directly in an interview with Ray Ownby, "Discussions with William Styron," Mississippi Quarterly, 30 (Spring 1977), 283-95; esp. 287. Styron insists, with some justice, that

while he could not enter the consciousness of a contemporary black man, he can do so with a black slave in the early nineteenth century just as readily as any black writer today; neither author can have experienced slave life in old Virginia.

(14) "A Note on the History," in William Styron's The Confessions of Nat Turner: A Critical Handbook, p. 90.

(15) This is a point Seymour Gross and Eileen Bender make very vigorously in "History, Politics and Literature: The Myth of Nat Turner, p. 489.

(16) "Nat Turner Revisited," in William Styron's The Confessions of Nat Turner: A Critical Handbook, p. 106.

(17) In The Literature of Memory, Richard Gray provides an excellent analysis of the way in which Styron attempts to redeem Nat Turner through an interiorized journey of self-emancipation (p. 303).

(18) John Lukacs, Historical Consciousness (New York, Evanston, and London: Harper & Row, 1968), p. 7. Lukacs' study is, in part, a response to what has been called the crisis of history, a crisis resulting from the undercutting of both historiography and philosophy of history by the intense irony of the modernist era. Perhaps the most remarkable study of this crisis available is Hayden White's Metahistory . . . which combines various models from Northrop Frye, Stephen C. Pepper, Karl Mannheim, and Roman Jakobson in order to show that history can only be written out of the forms of pre-figuration consciousness provides in plots, root metaphors, ideologies, and tropes. One should point out that White does not believe his tropological theory destroys the cognitive value of history.

(19) Hayden White, "The Historical Text as Literary Artifact," p. 87.

(20) Norman O. Brown, Life Against Death: The Psychoanalytic Meaning of History (New York: Vintage, n.d.), p. 19.

(21) In the Mississippi Quarterly interview with Ray Ownby, Styron has discussed the successful efforts to block the book's being made into a film. Quite properly, Styron regards these efforts as a form of censorship whose motives are understandable, but whose aims are incongruent with American ideals of literary freedom.

*From Mississippi Quarterly 36 (1983): 525-43. Reprinted by permission.

SOPHIE'S CHOICE

A NOVEL OF EVIL*

John Gardner

Early in William Styron's new novel a character named Nathan Landau
tells the narrator, an aspiring young Southern writer, "I admire your
courage, kid . . . setting out to write something else about the South." And
Landau adds a moment later, "you're at the end of a tradition." The
aspiring writer is a virtually undisguised William Styron at 22 (we get
allusions, from the now mature narrator, to his earlier fiction, easily
recognizable as Lie Down in Darkness, The Long March, Set This House
on Fire, and The Confessions of Nat Turner), and what Landau says to the
young Styron is clearly very much on the mature Styron's mind as he
works out the immense Gothic labyrinth that is the weighty, passionate
novel we are reading now.

Sophie's Choice is a courageous, in some ways masterly book, a book
very hard to review for the simple reason that the plot--even the double
entendre in the title--cannot be given away. Certain things can be said
without too much harming the novel's considerable effect: The story
treats two doomed lovers, Nathan Landau, a brilliant, tragically mad New
York Jew, and Sophie Zawistowska, a beautiful Polish survivor of
Auschwitz, and their intellectual and emotional entrapment, for better or
worse, of the novelist-narrator.

Thematically, the novel treats the familiar (which is not to say trivial)
Styron subject, the nature of evil in the individual and in all of humanity.
Brooding guilt is everywhere: in the narrator's story of how, when his
mother was dying of cancer and could not take care of herself, he once
went on a joy ride with a friend, failed to stoke the fire in his mother's
room and, when he returned, found her half-frozen, teeth chattering,
shortly after which catastrophe--whether or not as a result of it--she died;
in the narrator's awareness that the money he lives on as he writes his first

novel comes directly from the sale of a 16-year-old slave, a boy who, having been falsely accused of accosting a Southern young lady, was sent into a kind of slavery few survive; in the memories of the novel's wonderful complex heroine, Sophie, a Catholic turned atheist and a woman who, for love of her son, made inept attempts at collaborating with the German S.S.; in the drug addiction and occasional fiendish violence of the gentle, humorous, intelligent and humane--but also mad--Nathan Landau. In the stories of Sophie's Resistance friends, and so on.

The novel's courage lies partly in this: After all the attacks on Styron, especially after The Confessions of Nat Turner, which some blacks and liberals (including myself) found offensive here and there, we get in Sophie's Choice the same old Styron, boldly and unmercifully setting down his occasional lapses (or his narrator's) into anti-Semitism, anti-feminism, and so forth, bearing his chest to whatever knives it may possibly deserve, even begging for it. Those who wish to can easily prove him anti-black, anti-white, anti-Southern, anti-Yankee, anti-Polish, anti-Semitic, anti-Christian, anti-German, anti-American, anti-Irish--the list could go on and on. No bigotry escapes him; the worst that can be said of humanity Styron claims for himself, wringing his hands, tearing his hair, wailing to all the congregation, Mea culpa! (Only in their taste in music are he and his favored characters faultless).

Such all-inclusive, self-confessed sinfulness should absolve a man, and in a way, of course, it does; no reader of Sophie's Choice can doubt that Styron has put immense energy into trying to understand and deal justly with the evils in American history and the European holocaust, to say nothing of the evil (as well as the good), in his characters. Yet for all the civilized and, in the best sense, Christian decency of Styron's emotions when he's watching himself, the rabid streak is always ready to leap out and take command.

One example must suffice: After the double suicide of Nathan and Sophie at the end of the novel, the narrator, trying to get to their bodies, finds himself blocked by a police cordon. Styron's observation is that "everywhere stoods clots of thuggish policemen chewing gum and negligently swatting their thick behinds." He adds: "I argued with one of these cops--a choleric ugly Irishman--asserting my right to enter. . . ." The scene is crowded with these piggish policemen, also "a cluster of wormy-looking police reporters"; not one of them is portrayed as timidly decent; none of them can be seen as, merely, confused children in grown-up bodies. Styron is far more just in his treatment of the Southern racial bigot Senator Bilbo, or Sophie's viciously anti-Semitic, woman-enslaving father, Prof. Zbigniew Bieganski, or even the master of Auschwitz, Rudolf Hoss.

My point--and I labor it because it seems to me important--is this: Styron's justice and compassion, the desperate struggle to get to the bottom of even the most terrible, most baffling evils--the holocaust, above all--and to come back a just and loving man are impressive, almost awesome, precisely because we know by his slips that they are not natural to him but earned. When he forgets the ideal he sets for himself, as he does with the cops, with a Unitarian minister we meet later, with the McGraw-Hill organization men we meet in the first chapter, and as he does in numerous other places, he shows us how serious this novel is as not merely a story of other people's troubles, but a piece of anguished Protestant soul-searching, an attempt to seize all the evil in the world--in his own heart first--crush it, and create a planet fit for God and man.

In a moving passage near the end of the novel, Styron admits that he has not succeeded, quite, in doing what he set out to do. He writes (recalling his earlier dream): "Someday I will understand Auschwitz. This was a brave statement, but innocently absurd. No one will ever understand Auschwitz. What I might have set down with more accuracy would have been: Someday I will write about Sophie's life and death, and thereby help demonstrate how absolute evil is never extinguished from the world." Though no one will deny that writing about the holocaust and its aftermath in personal terms--"Sophie's life and death"--may be the best thing one can do to wring at least some fragmentary sense out of those numbing times, I wonder if Styron's scaled-down goal is not as innocently absurd as the earlier goal. "Absolute evil." What a chaos of medieval phantoms nestles in those words! Like absolute good, a conceit abandoned in Styron's vision as in much of modern Christianity, absolute evil is the stuff of which cults, country sermons and Gothic tales are made.

As I said at the outset, Styron is very conscious of being one of the last to work a dying literary tradition--in effect, the Southern Gothic, the vein mined by, among many others, Walker Percy, Robert Penn Warren and, possibly, William Faulkner. (In my opinion, Faulkner has too much humor, even joy, to belong). Styron makes a point, in Sophie's Choice, of naming his influences--Thomas Wolfe, Faulkner, Robert Penn Warren, etc.--and claims, in Nathan Landau's voice, that he has surmounted them. In Sophie's Choice he does far more than that: He transfers, down to the last detail, the conventions and implicit metaphysic of the Southern Gothic--especially as it was handled by Robert Penn Warren--to the world at large. It is no longer just the South that is grandly decayed, morally tortured, ridden with madmen, idiots and weaklings, socially enfeebled by incest and other perversions: it is the world.

The requisite madman is Nathan Landau; the requisite webs of guilt reach out toward the present from Auschwitz and the American North and South. For slavery and the necessary racial-taint theme, Styron chooses (besides America) Poland, occupied for centuries first by one cruel master, then another, pitifully devoted to both German culture and Nazi-style anti-Semitism, and genetically so mixed that blond Polish children can be saved from the death camps by being slipped into the Aryan Lebensborn, or New Youth Program. The Southern Gothic must have vaguely symbolic weather--if possible, murderously hot and muggy (Brooklyn in the summer

will do fine)--and some crazy old house--Styron chooses Yetta Zimmerman's huge old apartment house, entirely painted, from end to end, in
Army-surplus pink. Doom must hang over everything, ominously, mysteriously forewarned throughout the novel; and of course there are special
requirements of style and plot.

Styron is, of course, a master stylist; but notice the precisely Gothic
quality of the following passage, which I've chosen by opening at random.
Note the intricacy of the sentences, the ironic use of jarring images, sly
biblical hints (the Professor's hiss), the inclination to choose objects that
are old, "authentic" and likely to spell doom; note the fondness for
suspense and rhythms that seem to pant. Sophie's father, the Professor, I
ought to explain, having long ago written a Polish tract arguing that Jews
should be exterminated, is now trying to get an audience with some--any--
bureaucrat among the occupying German forces, hoping to curry favor.
Styron writes:

> Loathing her father now, loathing his lackey--her husband--
> almost as much, Sophie would slip by their murmuring shapes in
> the house hallway as the Professor, suavely tailored in his frock
> coat, his glamorous graying locks beautifully barbered and fragrant
> of Kolnischwasser, prepared to sally forth on his morning
> supplicatory rounds. But he must not have washed his scalp. She
> recalled dandruff on his splendid shoulders. His murmurings
> combined forgetfulness and hope. His voice had an odd hiss.
> Surely today, even though the Governor General had refused to
> see him the day before--surely today (especially with his
> exquisite command of German) he would be greeted cordially by
> the head of the Einsatzgruppe der Sicherheitzpolizei, with whom
> he had an entree in the form of a letter from a mutual friend
> in Erfurt (a sociologist, a leading Nazi theoretician on the
> Jewish problem), and who could not fail to be further impressed
> by the credentials, these honorary degrees (on authentic
> parchment) from Heidelberg and Leipzig, this bound volume of
> collected essays published in Mainz, Die Polnische Judenfrage,
> etc. and so on. Surely today. . . . (The ellipsis is Styron's)

The hothouse quality of the style--the scent of overripe black orchids--
seems to be throughout appropriate, as suited to rotting Europe as to the
decaying Old South. The only question I would raise is Heisenberg's:
Does the instrument of vision--in this case, the transferred Southern Gothic
form--seriously alter the thing seen?

But even more than style and setting, the glory of the Southern Gothic
is plot. We must get surprise after surprise, revelation after revelation,
each more shocking and astonishing than the last. (Unavoidably, but
nonetheless to my great annoyance, I have already given away one
surprise: We do not know till near the end of the novel that our beloved
Nathan Landau is a maniac). Insofar as plot is concerned, Sophie's Choice

is a thriller of the highest order, all the more thrilling for the fact that the dark, gloomy secrets we are unearthing one by one--sorting through lies and terrible misunderstandings like groping for a golden nugget in a rattle-snake's nest--are not just the secrets of some crazy Southern family but may be authentic secrets of history and our own human nature: why people did what they did at Auschwitz--people on every side--why often the Polish underground hated the Jewish underground on which they sometimes depended; how the Catholic, Protestant, and Jewish souls intertangle in love and hate, and can, under just the right conditions, kill.

Sophie's Choice, as I hope I have already made clear, is a splendidly written, thrilling book, a philosophical novel on the most important subject of the 20th century. If it is not, for me, a hands down literary masterpiece, the reason is that, in transferring the form of the Southern Gothic to this vastly larger subject, Styron has been unable to get rid of or even notice-ably tone down those qualities--some superficial, some deep--in the Southern Gothic that have always made Yankees squirm.

Judging at least by its literary tradition, the South has always been an intensely emotional and, in a queer way, idealistic place--emotional and idealistic in ways not very common in, say, Vermont or New York State, or, anyway, up-state. I would never claim that Yankees are more just and reasonable than Southerners. I would say we hide our evil in a different style. Though we may secretly cry our hearts out at a poem like, say, James Dickey's "Celebration," we wince at novels in which the characters are always groaning, always listening in painful joy to classical music, always talking poetry--much of it having to do with terminal disease. And we blush at passages like the following:

> "I don't recall precisely when, during Sophie's description of
> those happenings [I] began to hear [myself] whisper, 'Oh God, oh
> my God.' But I did seem to be aware, during the time of the
> telling of her story . . . that those words which had commenced
> in pious Presbyterian entreaty became finally meaningless. By
> which I mean that the 'Oh God' or 'Oh my God' or even 'Jesus
> Christ' that were whispered again and again were as empty as
> any idiot's dream of God, or the idea that there could be such
> a thing."

Which is not to deny that the story that follows this Gothic introduction is not terribly moving and shocking.

In short, though I am profoundly moved by Sophie's Choice and consider the novel an immensely important work, I am not persuaded by it. Styron's vision may have humor in it--he tells us about Nathan's hilarious jokes, none of which turn out to be funny on the page--but if so, not an ounce of that humor is in the novel. Perhaps it may be argued that, in a book about American guilt and the holocaust, humor would be out of place. But it seems to me that humor is central to our humanity, even our decency. It cannot be replaced, as it is in Sophie's Choice, by great classical music or (a major concern in the novel) sex. If anything, classical music leads in exactly the wrong direction: it points to that ideal Edenic world that those master musicians, the Poles and the Germans, thought in their insanity they might create here on earth by getting rid of a few million "defectives." I'm not, God knows, against Bach and Beethoven, but they need to be taken with a grain of salt, expressing, as they do, a set of standards unobtainable (except in music) for poor silly, grotesque humanity; they point our hearts toward an inevitable failure that may lead us to murder, suicide, or the helpless groaning and self-flagellation of the Southern Gothic novel.

*From The New York Times Book Review (May 27, 1979): 1, 16-17. Reprinted by permission.

EVIL AND WILLIAM STYRON*

Pearl K. Bell

In an introductory note to <u>The Confessions of Nat Turner,</u> his brooding story of the Negro preacher who led the only significant slave revolt in American history, William Styron wrote that he had tried "to produce a work that is less an 'historical novel' in conventional terms than a meditation on history." His new novel, <u>Sophie's Choice,</u> is also, in part, a meditation on history, a gravely ambitious attempt to confront the truth of the Nazi death camps and to define the moral legacy of the Holocaust not only for the Jews but for all of humanity.

. . .

<u>Sophie's Choice,</u> more frankly autobiographical than the earlier novels, provides a memoir of the summer of 1947. Styron has recently come to New York from Virginia, "a lean and lonesome young Southerner wandering in the Kingdom of the Jews." Living in a rooming house in Flatbush, he has just embarked on the Faulknerian tale of family damnation that will become <u>Lie Down in Darkness,</u> and we are told a great deal about the genesis and composition of the book. Yet as a lifelong captive of historical memory, he is also haunted by the stories of the Turner revolt he has heard since boyhood, and Stingo, as young Styron is called in <u>Sophie's Choice,</u> frequently declares that someday he will "write about slavery . . . make slavery give up its most deeply buried and tormented secrets."

Here Styron displays the two sides of his literary imagination in high relief. In the course of his career, he has been strongly attracted to the flamboyant melodrama peculiar to Southern romance, a regional genre awash in the morbidity of ruin, guilt, and decay. He has also been deeply engaged with the actualities of history. The lure of Gothic sensationalism was responsible for his worst book, <u>Set This House on Fire,</u> a synthetic

Sturm and Drang about American expatriates in Italy; but this was followed by The Confessions of Nat Turner, whose poignant exploration of the humiliations of slavery and densely textured rendering of the antebellum landscape and of plantation life made it his most powerful piece of work. (What infuriated the black nationalists who excoriated Nat Turner as a "vile racist myth" was no so much the liberties Styron took with the known facts about the slave leader, but the presumption that any white man could understand the soul of a black slave.) Caught between the inconstant seductions of Gothic romance and the realities of history, Styron has now tried to resolve this creative dilemma by plunging into the actuality of the death camps.

. . .

The ravaged [Sophie] remains a prisoner of her past. As with many survivors, guilt at being alive has reduced her to a victim yearning for punishment, and this she finds in masochistic abundance through her Jewish lover, Nathan Landau, a brilliant but violently mercurial intellectual who enters her life as a savior only to become her doom. A Harvard-educated research biologist who claims to be within sight of cures for cancer and polio, Nathan is a polymath who can range with miraculous ease over the world's body of knowledge, "as brilliant of Dreiser as he was on Whitehead's philosophy." To the bedazzled Stingo he is "the embodiment of everything I deemed attractive and even envied in a human being."

Styron the novelist is enthralled by men like Landau--glittering charmers who cast a rapturous spell--and there is a decadent version of the same sinister enchanter, Mason Flagg, in Set This House on Fire. But Nathan, at one moment generous, loving, high-spirited, erudite, funny (this last we must take on faith; Styron tells us about the comic genius but fails to show it), can without warning turn into a snarling fiend, raging at Sophie for imagined infidelities and at Stingo for his incurable Southern racism. Only toward the end do we learn that Nathan's bewildering fluctuations of mood are in fact psychotic, that his beguiling facade is a crazy pack of lies--he has never been to Harvard, he is not a research biologist--and that he has been in and out of mental hospitals most of his life. Despite this explanation, however, Nathan never develops into a credible human being, for Styron paints him in such garish shades of genius and bestiality that, mad though he may be, he is deprived of plausibility. No matter, for his role in the story is primarily instrumental. It is not Nathan's operatic madness but Sophie's slavish devotion that absorbs us, and she is the passionate heart of the book.

With a sure instinct, Styron has written Sophie's story in the grand manner of 19th-century fiction--she is, indeed, one of the very few women in contemporary American fiction to possess something of the tragic stature and self-defeating complexity of such classic heroines as Tolstoy's Anna Karenina and Hardy's Sue Bridehead. A victim of absolute evil, she is not simply a pathetic survivor trembling before the lash of fate. She is lover, liar, masochist, drunk--a martyr, but not a saint. Despite the cowardice and deception she divulges to Stingo, it is impossible not to be touched by the nobility of this lovable woman devoured by self-loathing. Even when she summons up the courage to tell her young friend, with self-flagellating candor, about her pretense of anti-Semitism when making a futile attempt to seduce Rudolf Hoss, the Commandant of Auschwitz, while working as his secretary, we cannot bring ourselves to condemn Sophie. The cruel secret hidden in the title is withheld until almost the last, and it is the darkest reason of all for Sophie's suppurating guilt. In Sophie Zawistowska, Styron has achieved an intensity of feeling and pain that is admirably sentimental, and he forces us to see that her sins deserve, beyond pity, the generosity of forgiveness.

Sophie's Choice, however, deals not only with this fragile survivor of Nazi barbarism. It is also an account of William Styron's young manhood, and clearly one of his motives for placing Sophie's life in the context of his own, though they are so disparate, is to play on that recurrent theme of American fiction, the contrast of New World innocence and European experience. If in Henry James this encounter brings about alterations of manners and morals, in Sophie's Choice it acquires the extremity of nightmare. Listening to Sophie, Stingo is shattered by the realization that while millions were being massacred in Europe, the rest of the world, oblivious, went on with its ordinary business. Stingo feels he can never come to terms with the fact that on the very day Sophie arrived in Auschwitz, he was stuffing himself with bananas in North Carolina to meet the weight requirement of the Marine Corps.

But it is a question whether the collision of innocence and experience requires the profuse indulgence of Styron's portrait of the artist as a young man. There is too much in this novel about Stingo's frustrated efforts to unburden himself of his pent-up virginity. Except for the lyrical celebration of Prospect Park in high summer and a funny account of his failure to conquer an impregnable fortress named Leslie Lapidus, Stingo's horny preoccupations are prolix and faintly embarrassing.

At the end of the novel, Stingo vows that "Someday I will write about Sophie's life and death, and thereby help demonstrated how absolute evil is never extinguished from the world," and Styron has tried to honor this vow in Sophie's Choice. On one level it is an extraordinary act of the novelist's imagination, which recreates Sophie's ordeal in Auschwitz and beyond through a wealth of immediate, dramatic detail. We see the "bluish veil of burning human flesh" that darkened the sunlight in the camp; we see and are repelled by Hoss taking a break from his murderous duties to gaze lovingly out the window at his Arabian horse. Or, in an appalling episode, Sophie, haggard and defenseless, during her first weeks in New York, is crushed in a rush-hour subway train and, when the lights go out, raped by an anonymous marauding finger.

But Styron does not limit his scrutiny of evil to these devastating obscenities. He has read widely and conscientiously in the literature of the Holocaust--not only such detailed chronicles as those of David Rousset, Tadeusz Borowski, Eugen Kogon, Andre Schwarz-Bart, but also the theoretical efforts of Hannah Arendt, George Steiner, and the Jewish theologian Richard Rubenstein--and he means to wrest some lesson from the slaughter. Styron has been particularly impressed by Rubenstein's thesis, in The Cunning of History, that the concentration camps were not only "places of execution" but a new kind of slave society--"a world of the living dead"--based on ruthless domination and "the absolute expendability of human life." Midway through Sophie's Choice, then, Styron abruptly and for a long moment exchanges the voice of the novelist for that of the moralist. What especially troubles him is the fact that the world is, to this day, largely unmindful of the millions of non-Jewish Russians, Serbs, Gypsies, Slovenes, and Poles like Sophie who died alongside the Jews. It disturbs him that "it is surpassingly difficult for many Jews to see beyond the consecrated nature of the Nazis's genocidal fury." Though Styron allows that such parochialism is understandable, in his view it reveals a deficiency of moral responsibility and a dangerous insensitivity to those forces in contemporary life that might spawn new Holocausts. In a recent interview, he has even questioned the validity of the word Holocaust, as Jews have defined it for more than a decade, and argues that the French terms l'univers concentrationnaire more accurately describes "the significance of this intolerable crime."

In one sense, given his revulsion at the radical evil of the Nazis, Styron may be right. But what he misses is that, precisely as an expression of radical evil, the Holocaust gained its significance because its first purpose was the total eradication of one people, the Jews--not for anything they had done but only for being who they were. It is this that distinguishes the Jewish victims in the death camps from all others.

Styron also neglects the historical fact that the word Holocaust acquired importance for Jews only twenty years after the defeat of Nazi Germany. What happened between 1940 and 1945 became fully manifest to Jewish consciousness not in the decade after World War II but with the Arab-Israeli war of 1967, the third time that the Israelis had to defend their lives, when it became evident that the symbolic and actual history of the people was again being threatened. It was then that the theological meaning of the Holocaust became clear: that, as Emil Fackenheim put it, Hitler should not achieve in death what he failed to do in life.

Styron's insistence on seeing the Holocaust as an example of slavery--if a particularly horrible one--is perhaps to be expected in a Southerner who has devoted a good deal of his mature life to contemplating that institution. Yet by emphasizing not the end goal of the Nazi plan--mass murder-- but rather the means of domination and enslavement which they settled on to effectuate that goal, Styron loses a sense of the full enormity of the

Holocaust. He is, in any case, too prone to highly charged but dubious generalization: "And were not all of us, white and Negro, still enslaved? I knew that in the fever of my mind and in the most unquiet regions of my heart I would be shackled by slavery as long as I remained a writer." Sentiments like these, intended to enlarge the didactic range of his novel, have, rather, the effect of undermining its dramatic power.

Yet it should be stressed that Styron's "philosophy" is, in every way that counts, external to Sophie's Choice. Philosophers analyze, classify, and make distinctions of language, but a novel like this one cuts across distinctions because human beings embody within themselves endlessly various motives. The art of the novel is necessarily dramatic, concrete, and idiosyncratic, and it can reveal complex truths about individuals, and their dissonant impulses, in devious and untidy ways. Styron may not be persuasive as a philosophic mind meditating on history, but that does not diminish his genuine strength. So powerfully does the novelist bring Sophie to life that she seems less imagined than remembered. As we read her story, we bear witness to her fatality, and it is the world made flesh that remains with us in the end.

*From Commentary (August 1979): 57-59. Reprinted by permission.

SPEAKABLE AND UNSPEAKABLE IN STYRON'S SOPHIE'S CHOICE*

Michael Kreyling

William Styron brings [the Biblical character struck dead for touching the Ark of the Covenant] Uzzah back in the character of Stingo, hero-narrator of Sophie's Choice, but the world sanctioned by the certainty of the central word of Yahweh is so corrupted that Stingo's Uzzah's touch of Auschwitz aims to resuscitate the human community, the body of mankind. Styron's call to this prophetic office is no less dramatic than that of [the Biblical author] Samuel himself. Farrell, the failed priest, tells Stingo, "'Son, write your guts out,'" and from that moment the young writer's mission is clear: he must abolish l'univers concentrationnaire by reconnecting the character of the word to the human community. Auschwitz, which Styron often considers as a human condition beyond its limits in actual time--the logos or continuing character of a lifeless void--is the great unspeakable that fattens on man's silence. This Uzzah's touch will bring back life.

Language, then, is the medium and subject of Sophie's Choice. The danger, as Stingo sees it, lies in the very silence that critics such as George Steiner suggest as the fitting response to the enormity of the evil of Auschwitz. Stingo would rather have language, even with its myriad thorns of irony and double meaning, tone and connotation, suggestion and play, than the ominous silence in which and because of which Auschwitz robs man of humanity in robbing him of his speech. As writer, more pertinently as southerner and writer, Stingo is convinced that telling his story of becoming a writer is also telling the story of how the Holocaust came about. Denying the unspeakable any ground, Styron aims to drag Auschwitz back into the public forum of the speakable. To accord it the sanctuary of the unspeakable is, in Styron's verbal universe, to surrender to it the power to haunt, to kill, to blight the human community that survives by speaking.

Steiner's admonition, taken up by Styron near the midpoint of <u>Sophie's Choice</u>, operates by implication from the beginning of the novel. Robert Towers, reviewing the novel in the <u>New York Review of Books</u>, thought enough of the aside on Steiner to place it at the crux of his review. Here is Styron's passage:

> Yet I cannot accept Steiner's suggestion that <u>silence</u> is the answer, that it is best "not to add the trivia of literary, sociological debate to the unspeakable." Nor do I agree with the idea that "in the presence of certain realities art is trivial or impertinent." I find a touch of piety in this, especially inasmuch as Steiner has not remained silent. And surely, almost cosmic in its incomprehensibility as it may appear, the embodiment of evil which Auschwitz has become remains impenetrable only so long as we shrink from trying to penetrate it, however inadequately; and Steiner himself adds immediately that the <u>next</u> best is "to try and understand." I have thought that it might be possible to make a stab at understanding Auschwitz by trying to understand Sophie, who to say the least was a cluster of contradictions.

Styron's use of Steiner's language eventually gives way to his own usage, a sort of serious play, alternately clownish and pregnant, admitting the radicals, associations, and double meanings of the very weapon he brandishes in the face of the incomprehensible.

Styron seems unconcerned that the handle is very slippery. According to Kevin Sack (<u>Duke Alumni Register</u>, May-June 1981), Styron once commented:

> "I've always thought that English was a wonderfully rich and descriptive language. . . . It's wrong not to exploit it to the hilt, even if it courts criticism of overwriting--which I have been accused of. I find the use of extraordinary words valuable. It keeps the mind going. You have to use discrimination. But I would rather err in the usage of more ornate language than with language which has no vitality and color."

Words are close to being living things, with color, movement, and vitality. They are warm, they make noise--Stingo mumbles them to get the prose rhythms right. Using words makes us part of the body of man; allowing words to go unspoken leads that body to atrophy, to Auschwitz.

Styron, in rebutting Steiner, twice uses the word <u>penetrate</u> and once <u>stab</u> to sexually characterize the act of writing by which he hopes to fathom Sophie and Auschwitz in the same act. To <u>shrink</u> from the challenge is unmanly, he implies. From the early pages of the novel describing Stingo's arid life at McGraw-Hill and his frustrated celibacy at the University Residence Club, we are carried along on the double currents of sex as language and language as sex, not immediately certain that the destination is Auschwitz.

Outside Stingo's window is a "ravishing garden"--nicely ambiguous phrase--into which, like a horny Giovanni Guasconti, Stingo gazes with starved libido and the concomitant creative viscosity of molasses in January. Recalling Gertrude Stein on the latter point, Stingo says of himself that he had the syrup but it wouldn't pour. Given the spurts, gushes, and deluges of his later orgasmic achievements, we are alerted to Stingo's idee fixe: luxuriant seminal liquidity means verbal fluency. Stingo's occluded currents of sex and literary creativity are undamned in his verbal conquest of the maid in the ravishing garden. Spying the shapely woman of the house across the way, Stingo transforms his lust into a figure of language, which then aptly slithers into the garden where Stingo, safe in his hermit's cell, "fucked her to a frazzle with stiff, soundless, slow, precise shafts of desire." Or of language, being honed to penetrate and stab no less precisely and slowly (Sophie's Choice unwinds to 515 pages) the unspeakable enigma of Auschwitz.

Stingo confesses that his obsession with words is almost "erotic," and Styron's affection for this type of play runs to raunchy uproar rather than to chaste awe at the ravishing phrase. But the faith in language is of no less crucial importance to Sophie's Choice. Readers may differ on the degree of Styron's "discrimination" in approaching such a subject as Auschwitz armed solely with the English language, with help from phrases from a few others. But that is what he does.

In his youthful hormonal and literary maelstrom Stingo must choose between moving Venus pencils (Tannhauser of the yellow legal pad) across a blank sheet of paper, or masturbating. Masturbation, in fact, is one of the prime distractions from the writing Stingo desperately wishes to complete. Writing his "snotty" manuscript evaluations for McGraw-Hill, he has to fight off the temptation to masturbate; every second he abandons pen for penis is one more second he is delayed from reaching the company of Melville, Dostoyevsky, Faulkner, Warren, or any of the dozen or so literary idols he wants to knock off.

Stingo, for his sins of self-abuse, becomes something of an authority on lingual and manual venery--not that a connoisseur's knowledge brings him a scrap of joy. With Leslie Lapidus and Mary Alice Grimball he learns that sex and speech are contiguous parts of the whole human organism.

Leslie enters Stingo's life first; her sex-talk literally inflames Stingo. But her "totally lingual" sexual performance smothers the flames. "Her [Leslie's] sex life is wholly centered in her tongue. It is not fortuitous therefore that the inflammatory promise she has been able to extend me through the hyperactive organ of hers finds correlation in the equally inflammatory but utterly spurious words she loves to speak." Stingo found no fulfillment with Leslie, but blessed her future. Mary Alice Grimball, whose maddeningly workmanlike services as a "whack-off artist" Stingo endures for a term of three nights, fares less well. Her hand is a clammy and unnatural substitute for the proper organ of copulation; in that, she is not much more foolish than Leslie. Mary Alice's language, however, condemns her more sternly than Leslie's. Only a few years after millions of victims had been incinerated in Nazi furnaces, Mary Alice Grimball, American, complains to Stingo that the reason she will not go all the way is that she "got burnt so badly" when her fiance left her at the altar. Just this trick of vocabulary Styron faces head on by relentlessly maintaining the speakable nature of the universe. The risk is huge, for the medium of his narrative--words--has the power, by an unpredictable double meaning or errant association, to overturn itself. There is something mysterious yet fecund in language that makes the female, Sophie, the end of Stingo's sexual and linguistic yearnings.

With Sophie sex and language are always a different matter, and often the same matter. From the outset Stingo's obsession with Sophie is fraught with muted resonance as he tries to interpret her with an energy second, it seems, only to that he pours into the story of the doomed Maria Hunt. Sophie is her speech, her self-recreation in a new tongue. Characteristically, the first shouting match between Nathan and Sophie dwells upon the appropriate usage of a word, cunt. Nathan belabors Sophie with her erroneous usage of the female epithet for him. More telling, however, is Stingo's reaction to Sophie's language. He too corrects her in the American idiom, all the while maintaining that Sophie's speech carries an elusive essence: "Without overdoing it, I will from time to time have to try to duplicate the delicious inaccuracies of Sophie's English. Her command was certainly more than adequate and--for me, anyway--actually enhanced by her small stumbles in the thickets of syntax. . . ." Sophie's body registers the same "delicious" charm as her speech:

As she went slowly up the stairs I took a good look at her body
in its clinging silk summer dress. While it was a beautiful body,
with all the right prominences, curves, continuities and sym-
metries, there was something a little strange about it--nothing
visibly missing and not so much deficient as reassembled. . . .
Despite past famine, her behind was as perfectly formed as some
fantastic prize-winning pear; it vibrated with magical eloquence. . . .

Sophie's voluptuous, fleshly "eloquence" merges with her "delicious" speech, so that talking or standing still she is an object to be savored on the tongue. Her self-proclamations in skewed syntax, X-rated malaprop-isms (e.g., complimenting Stingo on his handsome appearance in a "cocksucker" suit), or the tortured confessions of her choices in Auschwitz literally embody her, for her flesh is her story, the text in which her sins are recorded. The book of her life shows the heavy patronage of men, too; each use is rudely stamped.

It is essential to see Sophie as created by and netted in language. A series of men appropriate her through the imposition of a superior language. Her father, the minor league fascist Professor Bieganski, imprisons Sophie within the language of his anti-Semitic pamphlet. The word Vernichtung, which he surreptitiously slips into the manuscript that Sophie types, penetrates her mind and memory with more destructive force than the phantom finger that rapes her in the New York subway. This word becomes the vacant center into which her life vanishes.

Her first meeting with Nathan is also commemorated by the special mediation of language. The Brooklyn College librarian literally slams Sophie to her knees with his harsh words for her misapprehension of the name "Emily Dickinson." Nathan soothes Sophie with his own voice, later puts names on all of her maladies and deficiencies, and eventually brings on a semblance of health. When Nathan is not cooing to Sophie, though, he is scourging her with words. His verbal abuse is no less aching than the blows and kicks he lands, for the bruises to the body will heal.

As tortured and melodramatic as the pact between Nathan and Sophie is, Sophie's encounter with Hoss is more laden with meaning for the quest of the novel and Stingo. In Styron's protracted dramatization of the scenes between Sophie and the commandant of Auschwitz, the relevance of language to the unspeakable evil, indications of the origin of a curse beyond the immediate horrors of the camp, and the possible efficacy of silence in the healing body of mankind are central to the theme. Sophie is, first of all, Hoss's amanuensis, as she was her father's, his hands in the drafting of letters and his liaison with the world. Sophie translates the world of local priests and camp suppliers for Hoss, and revises his own verbal presentations to his superiors in Berlin.

Sophie, for example, handles the correspondence when Hoss begs Berlin to relax the pace of mass death in his crematoria. The ovens, Hoss fears, will not hold up under the steadily increasing stream of human victims shipped in for experimentation. Sophie types his unoriginal and awkward prose: "the mechanism for Special Action at Birkenau having become severely taxed beyond all expectation, it is respectfully suggested that, in the specific matter of the Greek Jews, alternative destinations in the occupied territories of the East . . . be considered." Aware of "the reality behind these euphemisms," Sophie automatically strips the official, passive prose of its betrayal: "'The Greek Jews being such a pathetic lot and ready to die anyway, we hope it is all right that they have been assigned to the death commando unit at the crematoriums, where they will handle the corpses and extract the gold from the teeth and feed bodies to the furnaces till they too, exhausted beyond recall, are ready for the gas.'" Sophie "finished [Hoss's] letter without a mistake," typing the official text while the true one spoke in her mind. Language undermined her moral ground, tainted her with complicity, doomed her to a life without hope even in survival. She participated in the act of betrayal by which a word is uttered but its natural bond of meaning in the world is ignored. This is a blasphemy against language, for it negates the human connection of language and relegates it to the sphere of knobs, switches, and keys--the manufactured world that has usurped the human. And it also constitutes a misuse of the tongue--the organ of speech. The sexual handicaps of Mary Alice, Leslie, and others find their more serious cognates here.

Sophie is corrupted by language misused; the agent of her personal Vernichtung is, appropriately, the tongue. Rape by the oafish Wilhelmine is more than graphic: "the brutish muzzle and the bullethead of a tongue probed into what, with some dull distant satisfaction, she realized was her obdurate dryness, as parched and without juice as desert sand." Stingo makes this point with a succession of modifiers, each one reinforcing the same impression: passion and life are wet; death-in-life is parched, arid, dry. Wilhelmine's tongue, brutish as it is, must probe deep into Sophie's psyche as well as her body. As the words Vernichtung, Special Action, Final Solution, even the word Holocaust itself, penetrate or stab at the vast void of Auschwitz, they belittle it with verbal utterance, ignoring the awful assumption that an evil so absolute might not be compassable in a human word. We all are doomed to the usage of language, however; even in our attempts to name the absolute we displace it into the human sphere of language and thereby falsify. To avoid this necessary falsification Steiner counsels silence. Auschwitz is the word that negates the Word, the darkness that finally extinguishes the Light of the World. We can, therefore, understand Sophie's hatred for religion, her truly desperate cry: "'I hate religion. It is for, you know, des analphabetes, imbecile peoples.'" Language is also revealing; Sophie associates religion with those people who have no language. Once we have language, we have Auschwitz.

In this shadowed world, dimmed by the clouds that float out from Birkenau--an atmosphere of despair that Styron had used similarly in Lie Down in Darkness--the wise suspect doom comes with the act of speech. To be a hero, to counter Hoss and his numerous clones in the SS, one must, Styron pleads implicitly, inject meaning back into the womb of silence. Figuratively, then, the male writer's priapic urges and verbal libido are phases or aspects of his foreordained calling to sow the world with meaning.

Perhaps the Southern writer is best positioned to see this facet of the world of words and relations in language. Stingo certainly fields and dodges most of the assumptions about Southern life and writing which have been the pride and bane of generations of Southern writers. But the immersion in the word for the Southern hero-writer is more complex than the mere record of a literary situation in any given time and place, and Styron sees through to its important function in his quest for the return of the speakable world in the aftermath of Auschwitz.

Stingo is the southern man of letters in a radical sense: he is a man whose very character is composed of words. His father, significantly, appears in the novel first in the language of his epistles to his exile son. The first letter to Stingo introduces themes of sex, slavery, and money that reverberate throughout the novel. The father's letters are the distant preparation for the assault on Auschwitz.

The ultimate cause for Stingo's hope in the efficacy of language is the "Southern Lord Chesterfield," his father, whose symmetrical prose is part and parcel of a universe in which all can be named and ordered in a moral as well as a linguistic grammar. What cannot be thought is never said, and therefore does not exist. Stingo's experiences in the world beyond this linguistic and moral arcadia teach him that too much has been repressed or simply excised from the verbal record to support the perfect world of the father. The lynching of Bobby Weed, with which Nathan taxes Stingo, is a gruesomely apt event: "While he was still alive Bobby Weed's cock and balls had been hacked off and thrust into his mouth, . . . and when near death, though reportedly aware of all, had by a flaming blowtorch received the brand on his chest of a serpentine 'L'--representing what? 'Lynch?' 'Lula?' 'Law and Order?' 'Love?'" The white mob conveniently fits into the linguistic-sexual motif of the novel, for their torture of Bobby renders him sexually null and unable to speak with the same act of barbarity.

Preceding and accounting for Stingo, in the person of his father, is a universe of the known, utterable world. The father's world, however, is not portable, does not travel across time and space. His visit to Stingo in New York confirms the limited boundaries of this once and former universe.

The father, from deep in his past, had nursed "an undying hatred for the vicious monopoly capitalism that tramples the little man." He carried his antipathy to the modern city made by that capitalism, New York, and into a cab driven by one Thomas McGuire. McGuire, with the sullen linguistic aggressiveness we all recognize, rejected the father's five-cent tip and called him a "fucking asshole." The father is at first taken aback, then quite carefully requests that McGuire repeat himself, his words. The father then blasts McGuire with words he probably had never heard: "detestable scum," "sewer rat," one who "disgorg[es] . . . disgusting filth" and "spew[s] . . . putrid language upon fellow citizens." At this point McGuire abandons his tenuous footing in the world of verbal discourse and slugs the father.

Stingo takes the episode with a mixture of dazed concern and tired resignation. He is a few sheets to the wind already, deeply depressed over Nathan and Sophie, and unsurprised that his father had virtually sought out the lowest of the lower orders in the Northern Babel. The episode is also Boschian in its richness and fertility for the novel. The father, hating the modern order from the distance of a past and agrarian enclave (although he does work in a shipyard, his antiquarian pursuits and dreams of the Southampton peanut farm are stressed in Stingo's narrative), hurls himself directly at the corruption of the tongue in Babel. McGuire has uttered words that, save by a tortured process of socio-linguistic explication, cannot be said to carry any meaning. They not only carry the force of a sexual insult; by their obscene coupling of antitheses, they negate the erotic act of language itself. The father flies into his tirade, heaping scorn on the unnatural oral and linguistic perversity of McGuire's offense, for he sees that the offense inheres not in the speaking of "dirty words," but in the blasphemy against the human act of speech and the betrayal of the community naturally and lovingly to be engendered by its right use. McGuire is the vulgar apparition of Hoss.

About one hundred pages earlier, Stingo had limped to the defense of Theodore Bilbo, race-baiting Mississippi demagogue, whose mouth cancer seemed, both to Nathan and to Stingo, strikingly apt punishment for a lifetime of name-calling. Stingo's refusal to equate Bilbo and Hitler, however, is weakened by his earlier luke-warm farewell to Bilbo: "Glad to see you go, you evil-spirited old sinner." The father takes a harder line when he recognizes the signs of human corruption in the corruption of the word.

Stingo's fixation with language, the physiology of its formation by the mouth and tongue, and the symbolic and actual links between language and its instruments and sex and the same instruments, fills Sophie's Choice with ornate and vital--if minimally discriminated--associations and images. The echoes and double entendres are never totally escapable; somehow, through a raunchy wisecrack or a solemn pronouncement, language always turns up as the sacramental act in question. If, as Auschwitz seems to prove, the mystery and sacred potency has been filched from man's tongue, then we are indeed in a universal death camp, a totally new form of human society.

The supercharged use of language is nowhere more intensely pressed for meaning than in Styron's ultimate assault on the central signifier of death-in-life: Auschwitz. Auschwitz, in Sophie's Choice, and in the modern Judeo-Christian world that has survived the butchery, is more than a mere word. It is the articulation we use to signify an otherwise inexpressible trip into nullity. The killing, Styron ventures, was a peculiar result of a modern cancer--boring, unimaginative yet efficient, and utterly without symbolic import. The executioners of Bobby Weed had more claim to meaning something. Auschwitz stands at the beginning of a wholly new scripture; when Morris Fink asks Stingo "'What's Owswitch?'" the author of Sophie's Choice makes his central point: American Jews and Gentiles alike operate in a naive dispensation, are in a sense des analphabetes, illiterate in the new covenant of absolute nothing. The new Uzzah enters to topple the evil covenant of silence.

For Americans, Stingo asserts, the names of all concentration camps are "stupid catchwords," the usage of which signifies a shallow, puerile sense of history and morality. The elderly cricket's voice of H.V. Kaltenborn, from whom Sophie and Nathan listen to the news from Nuremberg, seems an appropriately thin voice, with a whiff of Disney, for the degree of reality Americans are capable of mustering to the Nazi horrors. With Auschwitz a new language looms in the world of man--a language now spewed forth, as the novel periodically claims, by a carcinoma on the soul of the technologically efficient society that has replaced the human community. Stingo's father, and Sophie's uncle in the ill-fated Polish cavalry recognize the contagion, but neither is any match for the onslaught.

Styron thrusts at the tremendous evil of Auschwitz in a variety of movements, each one having to do with a crucial lapse, corruption, or betrayal of language. One revolves around the attempt by Sophie to seduce Hoss, after her own ill-defined reasons, away from the stark realm of his sclerotic language and into a living realm where the link between word and thing, speaker and lover, has not been erased. She wants to put them both back into a condition where lips, hands, tongues--and the words they make--are used for eros, not death. Crucially, the utterance that might have drawn Hoss away from the mechanistics of his obsession with death is never given voice. Sophie confesses to Stingo that, after a pause in her stenographic work for Hoss, she tried to compose herself, to make herself look "'as if I wanted to fuck. Looking as if I wanted to be asked to fuck.'" Hoss never says the word; he remains in the cell of disembodied language.

The absolute poverty of Hoss's moral and verbal world is revealed in his reaction to Sophie's request that she be permitted to see her son Jan. Hoss's words cap a tortured chapter (chapter 10) in which Sophie tells Stingo of her attempts to seduce Hoss, the failure, and her pleading for her son. Hoss responds with his own disgust for most sex, and to Sophie's plea turns what he no doubt believes to be a benign and assenting face. Stingo gives Hoss's words in both German and English: "'Glaubst du, dass ich ein Ungeneuer bin? Do you think I am some kind of monster?'"

Hoss is a monster; that he does not suspect this testifies to the thorough inversion of language that enabled Auschwitz. For Styron to put on Hoss's lips the single word, monster, most frequently used to name the Nazi horrors, is a touch of verbal irony. At the base of the problem facing the redeeming writer-hero is the failure of language to hold the natural human community together in a world of reality. Once the Adamic check upon word and thing is lost, the route to the death camps is open. No one in Sophie's Choice, with the possible exception of Stingo, knows a way back.

Nathan is peculiarly doomed, for he is as riddled with the monstrous Nazi contagion as any SS functionary. His excessive worship and fascination for science, and particularly for the pharmaceutical miracles of the Pfizer company, pushed him perilously close to the bloodless horrors he loathes. Stingo gathers from Nathan's boasting that he and his research team are creating life in a test tube, a somewhat boozy conclusion but nevertheless uncomfortably close to the monstrous. Nathan's infatuation with cyanide, the capsule of which bears the conspicuous logo of the Pfizer company, apes Herman Goring's suicide and is the probable source of Nathan's choice for his self-destruction. Nathan is destroyed by his obsession with the Nazi technology; at one of Morty Haber's parties he listens as if transfixed to the news of fresh discoveries of "the Nazi handiwork." God's "Hande Werke," so joyously celebrated in the music that Nathan and Sophie play, has been demolished.

Perhaps more tragically than Sophie, then, Nathan is a victim of Auschwitz. As deranged, imaginary scientist, he manifests the sinister curse of scientific progress that Styron locates in the Nazi enterprise. In One-Dimensional Man: Studies in the Ideology of Advanced Industrial Society, Herbert Marcuse has identified its residue for the world after Auschwitz:

> Auschwitz continues to haunt, not the memory but the accomplish-
> ments of man--the space flights; the rockets and missiles . . .
> the pretty electronic plants, clean, hygienic and with flower
> beds; the poison gas which is not really harmful to people; the
> secrecy in which we all participate. This is the setting in which
> the great human achievements of science, medicine, technology
> take place; the efforts to save and ameliorate life are the sole
> promise in the disaster.

For Marcuse, Auschwitz is the central fact in the post-Holocaust world Western man has made for himself. Not even the atomic bomb supersedes it. Inseparable from the consciousness of his accomplishments is the horror at the ease with which we can and will use our marvels for more heartless killing. And we twist the language to shield us from our handiwork. If Nathan is a paranoid schizophrenic, it is not because of chemical imbalances in the hippocampus of his brain. He carries the post-Holocaust disease: identification with the victim, envy of the evil manipulator.

The world that Styron proposes in order to render Auschwitz speakable and readable in Sophie's Choice is a version of the modern world Marcuse calls "Advanced Industrial Society." Putting severe burdens to his narrative logic, Styron tries to establish this world by first introducing Stingo's father as a capitalist hater and then much later bringing on the character of Walter Durrfeld, boss of I.G. Farben. Styron nearly trivializes the novel by suggesting that the root of evil is in the organization man.

In "Hell Reconsidered," a 1978 essay collected in This Quiet Dust, Styron broaches the argument that light could be shed on the hellish darkness of Auschwitz through attention to the advanced industrial ends to which it and other camps were set up. In the essay Styron tries out many of the theories later advanced by Stingo in the novel. The form of slavery practiced by the Nazis in the camps, for instance, is understandable as existing on a "continuum of slavery which has been engrafted for centuries onto the very body of Western Civilization." A southerner, especially one with the convenient memory of the slave Artiste, is thus ideally situated to decode the ominous monolith of Auschwitz.

The type of slavery the Nazis made, Styron continues in his essay, having been accelerated in degree of harshness, suddenly became different in kind:

> Slaving at the nearby factory of I.G. Farben or at the Farben
> coal mines (or at whatever camp maintenance work the SS
> were able to contrive), the thousands of inmates initially
> spared the gas chambers were doomed to a sick and starving
> death-in-life perhaps more terrible than quick extinction, and
> luck was more often than not the chief factor involved in
> their survival.

That the Nazis, whom Styron glibly describes as "among this century's leading efficiency experts," are squeezed into the position so often reserved for Yankee mill owners in unreconstructed defenses of slave society (in fact, to the detriment of the novel, Stingo gratuitously likens New Jersey factories to the crematoria at Birkenau), places Styron and the novel in jeopardy. By first advancing toward the assertion that the Nazi death camps were a uniquely different kind of slavery, and then resorting to shopworn comparisons between "efficiency experts" and SS officers, Styron undermines his achievement by grasping at the easy answer. Stingo had tried the same disappearing act when he refused to toast Bilbo's death with Nathan. Southerners owned slaves, and lynched some of them: so far the parallel with Hitler that Nathan pushes. But, Stingo insists, the numbers were fewer, and Bilbo pushed some good social legislation. Nathan will not allow him the unearned piety of absolution through the higher average of good. Nathan's madness is not without its flashes of insight, and the numbers trap is one of them.

Another example of this facile maneuver appeared on the editorial page of the New York Times for October 16, 1946--about eight months before time present of Sophie's Choice. In a series of brief editorial commentaries linked by the motif of batting averages, the editorialist moves from baseball to the American record on the Negro to the Nazi horrors. Even though a few American blacks have been lynched, the editorialist admits, the numbers are negligible compared to the millions murdered by the Nazis. Our national moral purity remains, in the terms of the image, unsullied:

> It is a distorted arithmetical sense, a completely atrophied
> sense of proportion, which insists that because of the mote in
> our own eye we are estopped from taking note of the monstrous
> beam in a stranger's eye.

Happily, we as a nation retain our moral right to judge others, especially those "strangers" on trial in Nuremberg, because we have the higher batting average. The word estopped, letting in the slightly musty odor of antique diction reminiscent of Stingo's father, hints back to the father's moral universe: simple, honorable, real, symmetrical.

Basing morality on average numbers of good or bad actions, though, seems to be a damning signal. Nathan, crazy bellwether that he is, sees it. Numbers serve as the basis for the Farben enterprises administered by Durrfeld through Hoss, the gloss that Stingo hopes will explain Auschwitz.

Durrfeld is introduced very late in the narrative, chapter 13. Sophie's father sycophantically shows him around the industrial and cultural sites at Cracow even as the Farben boss and family man makes veiled glances at the young and pretty Sophie. The next time Sophie and Durrfeld meet she is an inmate of Auschwitz, so wasted that he does not recognize her. But she knows him by his voice. The scene has the thin feel of "Great Coincidents in History," but Styron's quest for the unlocking insight into Auschwitz carries him over the thin narrative ice before it breaks.

Sophie overhears some rather trumped up conversation in which both Hoss and Durrfeld discount "that mind doctor in Vienna" but go on to repress their direct complicity in mass murder: "'But when it comes to failure of production, do you think I can plead sickness--I mean schizo-phrenia--to my board of directors? Really!'" Durrfeld is already deeply schizophrenic; his usage of production for the actually correct destruction (for the inmates are systematically destroyed) is conclusive proof of the division of language and mind.

Later in the novel, in the climactic episode of Sophie's encounter with the SS doctor who forces her to choose between Jan and Eva, Stingo brings up I.G. Farben once again. In trying to assess the personality of this anyone-no one doctor, Stingo attributes an unspecified segment of his motivation to the military-industrial complex: "Besides, he was at bottom a vassal of I.G. Farben."

How much evil can be explained by this route of reasoning? Is the military-industrial complex or something like it, truly at the bottom? Durrfeld and the Farben connection do not carry enough weight to answer these questions. Within the pattern of language usage and corruption, the Farben excursus seems to work. Industrial man has been forced to adopt a new grammar. The privilege of the word in naming the world has been revoked. Hence Hoss himself gropes for "circumlocution" to deflect the actuality of murder and to give a false resonance to his claim to be a person, not a monster. Durrfeld calls the extermination of human beings by the name of "production" and justifies slave labor by a half-jocular allusion to the board of directors. "It would be pleasant," says the character of a Polish resistance fighter Styron uses late in the novel, "to speak a language other than that of an oppressor." That grace is not vouchsafed our new community, for Auschwitz signifies the accomplish-ment of a technologically efficient industrial order that has abolished the human world. The central sign is the separation of speech from the body. Stingo tries manfully to reinstate the erotic joy of speaking and hearing, but his success is incomplete.

Still, we must acknowledge Styron's huge gamble in flinging himself at the monolithic and inscrutable sign of the time, Auschwitz, with good faith, sincere emotion, and the English language. We must also acknowledge his considerable subtlety in diagnosing the malady in our tongue. He imagines a redemption for Hoss. Staring at Harlekin, the Polish Arabian that gambols in a corral at Auschwitz as the soot of thousands of human beings settles softly to the earth, Hoss nearly completes a passage that leaves Sophie speechless as she tells it and Stingo as he listens. Sophie cannot say what Hoss might have meant, but she can repeat his exact words: "'To escape the body of man yet still dwell in nature. To be that horse, to live within that beast. That would be freedom.'" "What?" Stingo implores when Sophie cannot say what these words mean. Is this a way out, or the route into the death camps? Is it a wish for release into the transcendent realm beloved of Western mystics from Augustine on? Or is it a self-contradicting and ultimately perverting dream of pseudo-life without the flesh--a dream falsely accorded the status of the real and then used in the "monstrous," unspeakable foundation of the crematoria at Birkenau? Here is yet another of Sophie's choices.

*From Southern Review 20 (1984): 546-61. Reprinted by permission.

THE ROOT OF ALL EVIL: THE THEMATIC UNITY OF WILLIAM STYRON'S FICTION*

John Kenny Crane

The Solitary

If irony is properly defined as a set of circumstances which is the direct opposite of what was expected or considered appropriate, Sophie's Choice is a book which presses irony to an extreme. Even the title, which refers to the fact that--on the platform at Auschwitz--Sophie was singled out because she was "not a yid," made special and alone above her fellow man on the train, is loaded with irony. Where the others are to be sent to the crematoriums or the work camp by totalitarian directive, Sophie, the Solitary and special, is given a choice. She can choose which of her children will be exterminated, which will live in bondage. This is the irony and ambiguity in the sense of specialness each of us cultivates for himself or herself from birth.

When the novel opens we view young Stingo, basking in the glorious sunshine of unwritten novels, monomaniacally carving his way through the manuscripts of lesser mortals at McGraw-Hill. He is simply different from anyone else, not bound in letter nor spirit to the expectations of his employers, whether they be ridiculous ones such as the proper hat to wear and newspaper to be seen reading or more reasonable ones such as performing his remunerated task rather than floating glue balloons out the window. When he is fired for this, he takes himself out for a "solitary banquet"(1) to celebrate this backhanded recognition that he is different and special. After finding residence in Yetta Zimmerman's Pink Palace, he tries for a time to create a solitude in which this specialness will remain unsullied by the outside world. He shrieks at the ceiling to demand that Sophie and Nathan cease their sexual olympics. When they attempt to initiate friendship by taking him with them to the seashore, he orders them out of his room. Even when he begins to yield to their irresistible attraction, he can still remark to the reader that he is being foolhardy. "I felt this not only because I was afraid of getting sucked toward the epicenter of such a volatile, destructive relationship, but because I had to confront the hard fact that I, Stingo, had other fish to fry . . . 'to write my guts out'" (SC, 62).

And yet the irony. For all the inclination people have to isolate themselves so that they may realize the future that has been promised them (or in Stingo's case, more appropriately, that he has promised himself), for all their propensity to be alone at the counting table when Fortune dispenses her favors, Styron demonstrates throughout the novel mankind's essential fear of being singled out, its basic disinclination to labor alone and apart from other mortals. Stingo is so drawn to Sophie and Nathan that he often allows his novel to simmer on the back burner while he suns with them on Jones Beach, that he devotes himself to Sophie's anguished stories of the War without any real hope of the sexual consummation he yearns for, that he makes it up with Nathan in an instant despite the most soul-shattering insults and accusations. Later Stingo confesses himself "smitten by the same horror of solitude that causes human beings to get married or join the Rotarians" (SC 112). When it seems as if Sophie will move out of the Pink Palace after her penultimate break-up with Nathan, Stingo feels "crippled, hamstrung" (305) by the potential loss.

This need to be both alone and not alone is manifest in Sophie herself. Free, physically at least, of the terrors of the concentration camps, she arrives in New York terribly alone simply by sheer uprooting. Her first inclination is "to spend the rest of her life avoiding people en masse" (92). She creates for herself a world of few contacts until finally her solitariness and defenselessness lead her into the humiliation from which Nathan saves her. From then on she is entirely vulnerable to Nathan, not only to his love but also to his atrocious maltreatment of her, not only to his sanity but also to his madness. Along the Merritt Parkway in Connecticut she will yield to his demand that she prostrate herself on the ground and allow him to urinate in her mouth, at which point even Nathan fiendishly remarks that she has "'absolutely no ego at all'" (340). As she later explains to Stingo, "'without Nathan I would be . . . nothing'" (344). This is spoken by the same lady who had earlier tried in every possible way to separate herself from all those around her by refusing to work for the Polish resistance, by claiming to be the lone anti-Semite incarcerated at Auschwitz, and by attempting to seduce Rudolf Hoss so that she can obtain favors that would be beyond the comprehension of most of her peers.

Now surely the difference between Stingo and Sophie on this point is that of innocence and experience. Sophie knows things now about life that this man ten years her junior does not. If Sophie discards her solitary identity to perverted extents in this novel--ultimately to a suicide pact which will protect her final union with Nathan--Stingo continues to try to regain his isolation any time his conscious mind considers the matter. He must write, become famous, critically admired, perhaps wealthy. He continually rationalizes, often in terms couched in anti-feminism and anti-Semitism, reasons why he would be better done with Nathan and Sophie and, at other times, with people in general.

It is in the character of Rudolf Hoss, and perhaps in his daughter Emmi, that Styron most clearly portrays the dangers of such a specialized view of oneself. "'I am very conscious,'" Hoss once told Sophie, "'that in many ways I am like most men of my calling--of men brought up in a military environment. I was never one of the fellows. I have always been aloof. Solitary'" (281). A man of discrimination and fine taste, a lover of beauty, he is also both a major theorist behind the "final solution" and the director of a camp where it is carried out. He has lost any sense of relationship or responsibility to his fellow man--even his wife is merely a vessel into which to deposit his seed and Sophie inspires in him much the same reaction. Likewise his daughter, Emmi, surely the only happy little girl in the surrounding several square miles, becomes as a result equally prejudiced and egocentric. Even in so harmless an activity as looking through a photo album, she is incapable of pointing out anyone in those pictures except "me," despite the fact that the pictures are mostly of her swimming "team." Bored as she listens, Sophie begins to notice, "ineluctable as a smotherer's hand, the odor of burning human beings" (399). But Emmi does not--"'Das bin ich . . . me, me, me'"(398).

Hoss is special in his own mind, Emmi in hers, Stingo in his, and, as we shall see, everyone in his or her own. In this sense of solitariness, we have the planting of seeds of human evil in all Styron's novels.

Fortune

In speaking of Fortune I choose the word over the alternative "Fate" because it connotes something more of <u>good</u> luck, of making one's fortune, of being blessed by Fortune than its more ominous substitute does. Good fortune is something the Solitary has either been taught or has imagined she will, somewhere, find; and so his or her life becomes a pursuit of it. Styron is suggesting that human beings, first, feel entitled to it and, second, that they will, even if deprived of their expectations, find some way to convince themselves (and others) that they have succeeded nonetheless.

Yet philosophers through the ages have continually insisted that, for any number of reasons, Fortune is fickle; and Styron insists upon this as well. Select virtually any historical metaphor for Fortune and her workings, and the same conclusion must be drawn. The Boethian Wheel of Fortune, for example, is a constantly rotating process in which the person currently blessed would do well to recall that what he or she has is transient and will shortly evaporate. The fellow down on his luck, at the bottom of the wheel so to speak, need only wait till his turn for possessing a measure of luck will spin his way. In addition, the Wheel of Fortune motif suggests that for one person to have <u>good</u> fortune, another must have an equal measure of <u>bad</u>. There is simply not enough to supply all men at all times. Thus, a tendency might easily set in to try to stop the Wheel, to keep the other down and oneself up.

Sophie's Choice abounds in examples of this. Sophie and the other Poles on her train arrive at Auschwitz at virtually the same moment that Hitler issues the order that the extermination facilities are henceforth to be used for Jews alone--hence, even in their pitiable state, the Poles are at the top of the Wheel so long as the supply of Jews to fill the crematoriums does not run dry. And there is the lesbian Wilhelmine who can lure the favors of other women because she has access to a supply of silk underpants stolen from slaughtered Jewesses. One's bad fortune is another's good fortune. Or, back home, Mr. Lapidus has invented "the Worm," a shell-detonating device, which has made him rich--had he not had the good fortune to have invented it at a time when American had to resist the destruction of European civilization, he would not have attained the wealth to amass the art treasures which he bought away from those smashed countries.

Another concept of Fortune prevalent, especially in post-Darwinian times, is that of Blind Chance. Styron has incorporated much of this as well. Take, for example, the poor swan Tadeusz, "a small male considerable less agile and scruffier than the others" (135) whom Sophie feeds on her outings to Prospect Park. This is Darwinian natural selection on one level, blind chance, though it is also blind chance that the poor creature has the likes of Sophie come along who will direct her offerings in his direction to make sure "that he got more than his share of the garbage" (136). Another example is Dr. Blackstock, Sophie's benevolent employer, who, Stingo says, "was one of God's blessed whose destiny had led him from the stony poverty of a <u>shtetl</u> in Russian Poland to the most sublime satisfaction that American materialistic success could offer" (96). Equally guided by blind chance is unexpected bad fortune, such as . . . Blackstock's loss of his beloved wife, decapitated in a boozy car wreck on the Triborough Bridge. His mainstay gone, Blackstock is suddenly no longer one of God's blessed and is on the verge of suicide before Sophie and others manage pull him through.

Fortune is portrayed through a number of other traditional metaphors as well, but I would like to cite just one. There is that curious undirected interlocking of human wills which Robert Penn Warren called "the Great Twitch," and which another of Styron's influences, William Faulkner, likened, via Judith Sutpen, to "five or six people all trying to weave a rug on the same loom,"(2) each to his or her own design. Philosophically this has often gone under the label of the Schopenhauerian "Will-Web" where each of us, no matter how virtuous, simply manages to get in the way of, and so impede and perhaps destroy, innocently but thoroughly, the designs of others. In the book's most memorable scene, if Stingo's interpretation is correct, Dr. von Niemand simply had had enough of blind slaughter which had failed to cause him the twitch of a moral eyelash. And so, in a supreme effort to make himself feel guilt once again by doing the most horrendous thing his liquor-soaked mind could conceive of, he forced Sophie to make the choice of which of her two young children she will send to the extermination chamber. His new design has therewith saddled Sophie with a guilt she will never fully shed. Or there is Feldshon, the Jewish underground leader who depends upon Sophie's friend Lotte to supply him with firearms, who feels betrayed by the designs of others when she can produce only three pistols--"'We are being left to drown by our countrymen!'" (472). Likewise, however, the will-web can occasionally bring someone else good fortune, such as Bronek who catches Hoss's fancy perhaps only by "the language he spoke, the droll garbled German of an uneducated Pole from Pomerania" (258) and so is moved into the protection of the Commandant's house.

Styron demonstrates, then, the irony of expecting to regulate Fortune when, whatever the metaphor, it is so essentially beyond anyone's control. Yet, man's self-respect and the admiration of others seems to stem entirely from at least appearing to control events and circumstances, and pecking orders are instantly established in all societies in order to evaluate one's ability--even in concentration camps. Sophie, for example, is given "a more favored position that many of the other prisoners" (145) because of her knowledge of German and Russian. Because she is the right age and in good health she is sent to Auschwitz to work instead of into the crematoriums to die. Given the limitations of her situation, she is high on Fortune's pecking order, one of the "chosen."

The novel is scattered with such blindly ironic estimations of one's own rank on Fortune's scale. The librarian who causes Sophie's collapse outranks her simply because he knows that there is no American poet named Dickens and Sophie does not. Stingo, having failed miserably in his attempts to seduce loose-mouthed, tightly-corseted Leslie Lapidus, actually moves himself up his own pecking order: ". . . in compensation, I reasoned, I had more exalted goals. After all, I was a writer, an artist, and it was a platitude by now that much of the world's great art had been achieved by dedicated men who, husbanding their energies, had not allowed some misplaced notion of the primacy of the groin to subvert grander aims of beauty and truth" (179). In a parallel situation at Auschwitz, two middle-aged Jewish sisters, dressmakers, are spared the collective fate of their race because of "their energetic yet delicate artistry with the needle and thread," all day long refurbishing for Hoss's women "much of the fancier clothing taken from Jews who had gone to the gas chambers" (254).

And so, in a world in which Fortune haphazardly doles out her expected rewards, Stingo, Sophie, and Nathan clamber blindly for their share. Because of the ill-treatment of the slave Artiste in the last century, Stingo suddenly receives a $500 legacy which will allow him to remain jobless all summer. (Until, that is, Fortune turns on him, and he has it stolen from his band-aid box.) The sad news of the suicide of his adolescent sex goddess, Maria Hunt, can be turned with the stroke of a pen, into the subject of Stingo's first novel, one which brought him fame and, trite though it sounds, fortune. Farrell's son was killed on Okinawa and Jack Brown lost part of a leg on Iwo Jima while Stingo, by lucky accident of birth, failed to get to the Pacific before the war ended. "Fortune's darling" (24) he labels himself early on.

Less fortunate is Sophie, who found her idyllic childhood erased by the horrors of the Holocaust. If her safety at Auschwitz was assured by the abundant supply of Jews to die in her place, most of the rest of Fortune's doles are horrid indeed. The simple act of stealing a ham for her tubercular mother lands her at Auschwitz, a fate she might otherwise have avoided. Moreover, it is such foul use at the hands of Fortune which drives Nathan to madness. A Jew blessed to live in the United States at the time his people were being indiscriminately destroyed, he cannot accept the fact that he was so cleanly spared. He tries to make amends, ironic in itself, by caring for Sophie, by lending Stingo money when his is lost to a Brooklyn catburglar, by imagining himself curing cancer for all mankind. But ultimately he goes mad, blaming Sophie for her sheer failure to die with the others and dragging her with him, as a consequence, into suicide.

That Nathan is Sophie's "savior . . . but her destroyer as well" (136), that Sophie and Wanda meet the same fate despite the fact that Sophie had stayed entirely clear of Wanda's subversive activities, that Senator Bilbo dies of tongue cancer after having used that organ to consolidate his political base through "promiscuous public use of words like 'nigger,' 'coon,' 'jigaboo,' (189)--all these are the ironies of uncontrolled and uncontrollable Fortune. Evil will result, however, when the individual, unable to tolerate these ironies, will not admit that they exist and so continues to try to shape Fortune to his or her own conception of how it should behave.

· · ·

Guilt

As the ironies of Fortune are exposed and misunderstood, as promises are not realized, as attempts to give Fortune a push or a kick prove useless, the human heart becomes hardened. It begins to isolate itself in a tacit belief that only oneself has been so treated, and the ability to feel guilt for one's actions is diminished. To my mind the root of all evil in Styron's universe is the inability to feel guilt for one's actions. For Styron, . . . modernity is getting ever worse, hence more evil, in this matter. Leslie Lapidus and her avant-garde group on the beach who speak so broadly of their psychoanalyses are all about the process of "shedding" guilt. For Styron it would be more appropriate to begin restoring much of what we have lost.

Styron underscores this point at his own cost from the book's earliest pages. There we see young Stingo, twenty-two, aspiring writer reading the hard-if-not-well-wrought work of others "with the magisterial, abstract loathing of an ape plucking vermin from his pelt" (5). Since I believe Stingo to be the central character of <u>Sophie's Choice</u> and not Sophie, I believe the novel's main thematic thrust to be Stingo's progressive learning of both guilt and the correspondent inability to commit or allow the sort of evil which left his sickly mother in an unheated room in his boyhood, and perhaps races of people--Jews, Negroes, Irishmen, or whoever might get in his way--the victim of his pen in his middle age.

Once again Styron places Stingo in a world in which such lack of guilt is the norm rather than the exception. The calumnies of the aptly named Morris Fink cause all sorts of difficulty early in the book for the jealous Nathan and the defenseless Sophie. An unknown hand on a darkened subway car seizes the opportunity to explore Sophie's vagina. Even the inmates at Auschwitz serve the sole function of keeping the crematoriums at Birkenau in operation. Over and over Styron gives us portraits of people--real and fictional--who cause great evil due to their inability to feel remorse or sympathy toward their victims. The cultured, disciplined, in other ways humane Rudolf Hoss cannot only operate the crematoriums but also forbid his children to mention it in the house so no reflection need be done on the matter.

Now Stingo, to this point in his young life, has not been victimized by this attitude in others, but surely Sophie has. Yet she still is able--not only before Auschwitz but during and after it as well--to repeatedly demonstrate this same, for Styron cataclysmic, shortcoming in herself. In the years before the Nazi horror touched her and her own family, Sophie, if not patently anti-Semitic, was able to type her father's fascist pamphlets and distribute them on command. Since her feeling for the Jews he was attempting to victimize was at best "indifference," his bestowal upon her of "small rewards . . . caused Sophie to accept without any conscious resentment his complete domination of her life" (241). . . .

Even after her good Fortune has long since ceased, the inability to feel the sort of guilt Styron suggests might be the best cure for evil persists unabated. She absolutely refuses to work for the Polish underground, even when she alone among them can command the German language. Although she can cite her maternal instincts as being the cause of her reluctance to participate in the salvation of her countrymen, she is able to believe for a long period of time that "the mere presence of the Jews, and the preoccupation the Nazis had with their extermination, would somehow benefit her own security. And the safety of Jan and Eva" (478).

Once "softly" placed above her fellows in Hoss's house, she is able to harden her heart against the well-being of others to secure her own continued safety. Even worse than what she had done for her father, she is able not just to type for Hoss but also to articulate his phrases better than he can and so become his "accomplice" (219). In order not to upset things for herself (and perhaps for Jan, about whose fate she is always in doubt), she is able to place herself "beyond repulsion" (263) and allow the brutish Wilhelmine to lingually rape her. In virtually every category, words and deeds that would have appalled her when she was more blessed by Fortune become "fleeting commonplaces" (226) in an environment in which Fortune has shortchanged her and so must be manipulated--forced-- no matter what the expense to others, themselves equally misused.

Even afterward, safe now in Brooklyn, she is able to utter anti-Semitic remarks about Nathan and random other Jews as if she had not been rescued by three of them--Nathan, Blackstock, and Larry Landau--and as if she had not for many months faced the same dreadful fate as they did for the same abstracted reasons. If Sophie is a valid case in point, no matter how blessed nor how defiled man is, always he is able to place himself first in the search for rewards and favors which, if the theories of Fortune I have discussed are accurate, must ultimately be gotten at the expense of someone else. The individual is always able to convince himself or herself that what he or she has is not enough, that he or she alone has been shortchanged, and that no guilt need be felt as a consequence of anything he or she will do to correct that. Hence, individual men and women manufacture Evil.

Nathan, though on the surface a different sort, is actually much the same. It is true that he does feel an enormous amount of guilt at having evaded the Holocaust, and this guilt takes positive shape in his favors for Sophie and his broadening concern for victimized minorities such as Southern Negroes. But, in being overblessed by Fortune, Nathan can also turn on himself and others whom he perceives to have been equally favored--whether they be rich chiropractors, Southern whites, or even a Polish Catholic girl who had the good luck to get out of the concentration camps alive. Nathan demands that all such make amends. In a certain sense this is not much different from the behavior of Stingo, Sophie, and others that I have been discussing: he has a mental vision of how Fortune should have behaved, will not now attempt to force it into shape, and so can leave hotelkeepers' dinners to burn, an aspiring writer's manuscript figuratively in shreds, and his beloved continually anticipating a cyanide capsule.

No theme in Sophie's Choice is, I think, pressed harder than this one, for Styron virtually litters his pages with cameos of people who possess this same fatal human failing. There is the cabbie who insults Stingo's father's dignity over the matter of a tip. Princess Czartoryska who visits Sophie's father to manufacture hatred against Jews while they listen to Lieder. The sycophantic Polish contractor who bewails his inability to transport gravel to the creatoriums fast enough. Even the Jews "posed as the only people worthy of salvation" (275), and thus, according to Sophie, are getting what they deserve. A Nazi guard strips the clothes off a nun and has his dog attack her. And there are Bilbo and von Niemand.

This inability to feel guilt, whether it be on monumental levels or on lesser ones, all reflects some dimension of what Stingo attributes the ability of the Nazis to build extermination camps to: "the simple but absolute expendability of human life" (235).

Yet not everyone succumbs to this instinct, and ultimately that will be the factor to which Styron will turn to seek a reversal of this destructive process and the answer to the question Sophie herself asks, midway through the novel: "'Why this man would allow himself to become a vicious Kapo, who would be cruel to his fellow prisoners and cause many of them to die. Or why this other man or woman would do this or that brave thing, sometime lose their lives that another could live'" (286).

God

Before turning to Styron's answers to that question, I would like to examine two further factors in the chain of reasoning I have been following. The first is Styron's consideration, on the surface all too standard, of the role of God in what might be termed more a "divine mistake" than a Divine Plan.

Many of the usual outcries of modern agnosticism are present in the book. Perhaps the first note sounded is the "inhumanity" of a God who would take Farrell's on in the bud of his youth. Then of course will follow the oft-asked questions about God's role in allowing the extermination camps to exist in the first place and permitting Evil to run loose in the universe even before that. The name of God and the name of Hitler will be invoked together on the same sampler in Emmi Hoss's room, and the middle-aged Stingo will go so far late in the novel as to say "I hate the Judeo-Christian God" (379). While listening to Sophie's final revelation about von Niemand, young Stingo invokes the name of God over and over, though for him it is little more than frustrated cussing, "that [was] whispered again and again [and was] as empty as any idiot's dream of God, or the idea that here could be such a Thing" (466). The "believers" he portrays as bombastic or happily unquestioning--the Reverend DeWitt, say, who delivers the homily at Sophie's and Nathan's funeral or the black woman on the bus up from Washington who fondles her bible even as the desperate Stingo does his own.

Yet the very fact that Styron has placed the religious experience at the penultimate point in his novel, much as he does in <u>Lie Down in Darkness,</u> should provide at least a small clue that he is not willing to travel the easy road on the subject that, say, post-War cant might have him do. Rather the novel seems to suggest that, in man's frustration at not having the promise realized, he is willing finally to turn on God and demand that He never existed in the first place. There is need for a scapegoat for all this, and God--at least for Stingo and Sophie--does quite nicely.

If my contention can be accepted that Sophie, for all the liking we usually have and the sympathy we always feel for her, is as flawed a human being as virtually anyone else in the tale, then it is unlikely that Styron would allow her to articulate his story's position on the subject of God. When she chases off mendicant nuns because they are God's earthly representatives, when she nearly commits suicide in a Swedish church to teach Him a lesson, when she imagines having sex with Durrfeld on an altar, when she tells Hoss--for gain, once again--that she "'abandoned that pathetic faith [Catholicism]'" (275), she is quite clearly trying to pay back what she feels she has unfairly received. She cannot even listen to Handel, and she buys a diaphragm to symbolize her final rejection of God and Catholicism.

But she has doubts as well, and it is these that Styron prefers to explore. "'I don't know any more, about <u>when</u> God leave me. Or I left Him'" (232). This confusion, expressed to Stingo in the earlier stages of their relationship, is meaningful. The latter sentence suggests Sophie in control, abandoning the deity in disgust. The former suggests exactly the reverse, that God in disgust abandoned her--and mankind. Though Styron does not develop this theme as thoroughly as might be expected, it does seem to me that he makes his position on who abandoned whom rather clear by the end of the book. If "Fuck God" is the last we hear from Sophie on the subject (500), it is not the last from Stingo. Walking on Coney Island beach after the funeral, he reflects on the familiar query "'at Auschwitz, tell me, where was God?'" and imagines the answer "'Where was man?'"(513).

This is precisely the point. Man was off in pursuit of the realization of the promises of Fortune, proceeding now to use others to attain what he has so far been deprived of. Auschwitz was simply the most extreme manifestation of the most banal of human weaknesses. The fault here is not God's--unless we wish to suggest that He should have done something about the peculiar workings of the Wheel of Fortune in the first place. The fault is man's.

But, as I would now like to demonstrate, man has yet one more way to exacerbate the horror of the life that he has made for himself.

Lying

". . . Sophie told me a number of lies that summer. Perhaps I should say she indulged in certain evasions which at the time were necessary in order for her to retain her composure"(97).

So says Stingo, openly, but I think Styron is demonstrating throughout Sophie's Choice that, given the collapse of one's promises and the failure of Fortune, lying to oneself and to others becomes the last resort in at least pretending that life did in fact finally take shape. But, as Stingo writes at another moment, lies serve a secondary function as well:

> . . . Sophie was not quite straightforward in her recital of past
> events. . . . in the long run there may have been multiple
> reasons, but the word "guilt," I discovered that summer, was
> often dominant in her vocabulary, and it is not clear to me
> that a hideous sense of guilt always chiefly governed the
> reassessments she was forced to make of her past. (146-47)

Lies, in other words, temper or eliminate the sense of guilt one might still have lingering for the actions he or she has taken to wrest Fortune's prize from her recalcitrant grip. Styron again shows character after character lying in countless different ways either to fool themselves or others or to eliminate torturous guilt. In the long run, however, Stingo-Styron seems rather to prefer the refusal to lie that Andre Gide demonstrates in his journals:

> I won't dwell on this passage here, except to note my admira-
> tion therein not only for the terrible humiliations Gide had
> been able to absorb, but the brave honesty with which he
> seemed always determined to record them: the more catastrophic
> the humiliation or the disappointment, I noted, the more cleansing
> and luminous became Gide's accounts in his Journals--a catharsis
> in which the reader, too, could participate. (172-73)

The lies perpetrated by various characters in this novel are so inventive that they ultimately defy classification, but they appear to fall into three broad categories. First, there are those which are simply fundamental conscious attempts to make facts seem other than they are. Among these would be simple untruths, such as Sophie's claim that Nathan is the only man other than her husband she ever made love to; her omission that she had two children, not one, at Auschwitz; or her attempt to justify Nathan's drugged speeding to a Connecticut policeman by saying that his mother was dying in Boston. Another of this sort might be called "purposeful ignorance," the refusal to learn the truth when it is readily available. Morris Fink, for example, never answers telephones for fear of what he will hear. Sophie retires to Hoss's basement so she will not have to view the newsreels of war-torn Europe. Another sort of lying that falls into this category is, I think, active denial of a truth another holds when it does not suit one's purposes. Nathan is perhaps the most adept at this in his constant refusal, at the height of his rages, to accept that Sophie is not sleeping with Katz, Blackstock, or Stingo and that she did not have sex with Hoss and every other Nazi at Auschwitz to gain favors. Last in this group is "simple self-delusion," such as believing oneself headed for better things because transported to the crematoriums in a tourist car rather than a boxcar, Sophie's uncle claiming that the Polish troops can defeat the invading Germans because they know the terrain, or Stingo's euphoria about returning to the South which makes him forget "blowflies, . . . underpaid darkies, . . . [and] pig shit" (462) in the Tidewater.

The second category of lies is those which dull the mind so that truth cannot be felt or comprehended. Sophie is virtually an alcoholic by the time of her death. Nathan is a drug addict. The triumvirate goes to Coney Island to experience "visceral glee" on the leftover World's Fair rides. Hoss busies himself with a manual on septic tanks which allows him to repress his camp's other business. Stingo tells Sophie Southern jokes to make. her forget her troubles as they fell from Nathan. If no such methods work, there is always "sleep [which] allowed the only sure escape from ever-abiding torment" (254). Despite their apparent dissimilarity, all of these activities are ways in which the mind can be deadened to the reception of truth.

I think sex fits this second category as well, especially as indulged in by Sophie and Nathan. While Stingo . . . presumes this is simple animal lust, he later, with Sophie in bed with him, revises his opinion, understanding now that sex, for her, "was a frantic and orgiastic attempt to beat back death" (496). Even Hoss, in his refusal to yield to Sophie's advances, admits that he would like to have intercourse with her because it "'would allow me to lose myself, I might find forgetfulness'" (282).

The third category of lying incorporates all those activities that attempt to rewrite reality in a different form, as opposed to denying it (the first category) or blinding oneself to it (the second). Prevalent in this group are dreams which various of the characters have. Stingo, after his failure with Leslie Lapidus, falls into a compensatory dream that he did in fact ultimately fondle one breast, "soggy ball of dough" (178) though it was. In prison camp Sophie dreams of an "averted veil, of safety, of answered prayer and jubilant resurrection" (256). Stingo even brings Maria Hunt back to life in a dream, totally changed, "standing before me, with the abandon of a strumpet stripping dow to the flesh--she who had never removed in my presence so much as her bobbysocks" (45). Although a number of dreams have the reverse effect--such as Sophie's frightening vision of Czartoryska or Stingo's final nightmare on the Coney Island beach, "a compendium of all the tales of Edgar Allan Poe" (515)--dreams are denials of reality as it is.

So are fantasies. Horny young Stingo fantasizes on the "real" life of the Winston Hunnicutts next door. Sophie and Durrfeld fantasize about the happy times they might have together in Bayreuth. Perhaps some of the saddest fantasies are those Stingo has late in the novel about his future life as a husband, father, writer, and Southern gentleman with Sophie by his side.

Other sorts of lies which seem to fit this category are such things as Stingo and Sophie assuming the identities of the Reverend and Mrs. Entwhistle to register in the Hotel Congress; Nathan's and Sophie's fancy dress costumes which allow them to pretend they live in another place and another time; and even Farrell's plan to live out his dream to be an author vicariously through his son.

If religion has failed as a way to demand that God repay us for our good behavior and redirect the course of time, history, and--especially--Fortune in our favor, the lie, in whatever category, pretends that it has been done nonetheless. It allows us to deny reality and remain atop the Wheel of Fortune even at the moment that same wheel is actually making grist of us. Sophie and Nathan die in an eternal embrace which is as pathetic in the symbolic value they had attached to it as it is actuality of two ruined lives.

Transfer

What then do we do? Better still, according to Styron, what should man have been doing all along to lessen the horror of the existence his novel portrays?

We come then finally to what I will refer to as Styron's theory of Transfer. Quoting Hannah Arendt, Styron-Stingo focuses on the problem of lack of guilt I discussed earlier, the passage itself setting up the possibility for what I call "Transfer." Writing of those who actually operated the extermination chambers, Arendt says:

"The problem was not so much how to overcome their conscience as the animal pity by which all normal men are affected in the presence of physical suffering. The trick used . . . was very simple and probably very effective; it consisted in turning those instincts around, as it were, in directing them toward the self. So that instead of saying: What horrible things I did to people!, the murderers would be able to say: What horrible things I had to watch in the pursuance of my duties, how heavily the task weighed upon my shoulders!" (153)

The "turning around" that Arendt speaks of is a pivot in the wrong direction, away from "Transfer" rather than toward it. Transfer, rather, is better represented in this quotation Stingo takes, at another point in the story, from George Steiner dealing with what Steiner calls "time relation." Discussing the deaths of two Jews at Treblinka, Steiner writes:

"Precisely at the same hour in which Mehring and Langner were being done to death, the overwhelming plurality of human beings, two miles away on the Polish farms, five thousand miles away in New York, were sleeping or eating or going to a film or making love or worrying about the dentist. This is where my imagination balks." (216)

For Styron it is where all imaginations should balk. Stingo reflects back on the day Sophie arrived at Auschwitz, April 1, 1943, asks himself what he was doing that day, and realizes he was gorging himself on bananas trying to make himself heavy enough for the Marines. The subtle humor of skinny Stingo's "plight," wherein he incurs a snotty remark from an old recruiting sergeant, forms an ironic contrast to the horror of Sophie, though we do not know it at this point in the novel, selecting which of her children is to be exterminated at virtually the same moment. Immediately thereafter he shifts to another date--October 3, 1943. On that date he was writing a letter to his father concerning the fact that the Rose Bowl game might again be played at Duke University. For Sophie it was the anniversary of the date of her marriage to Casmir Zawistowska. But, for 2,100 Greek Jews at Auschwitz-Birkenau it is the day of their incineration. Such thinking as this is Transfer in its most fundamental form, the reverse pivot on what Arendt suggested Nazi officials and soldiers were doing. Instead of saying what horrors I have been put through in pursuance of my duties (and so removing guilt by shifting the object of pain and suffering), rather ask "what would it be like if I, and not they, were the ones enduring the pain and suffering I am dispensing or is being dispensed by someone else?" This, Styron would say, is Transfer, inserting oneself in the place of those at whose expense one's own personal Fortune quest is able to be pursued.

Such transference unites man with his brother and reduces his position as what I have called "The Solitary"; it reminds him of the shifting nature of Fortune; it suggests that, however failed his own promises are in realizing themselves, they are better than those of his brothers; he understands that Fortune-forcing can only make his brother's condition yet worse; he feels guilt; in feeling guilt he ceases the evil he is producing and, perhaps, begins to rediscover God; he has no reason to lie. Stated simply, Transfer is man's ability to imagine himself in the position of the evil his own lack of guilt enables him to produce, tolerate, or ignore.

Just as Sophie called her father the source of all evil, Stingo's father seems to be the antithetic symbol of good, of Transfer. Where his own personal politics, for example, suggest that he should castigate and disassociate himself from the right-wing racist Frank Hobbs, he still sees him first of all as a human being. Though his politics are "ten miles to the right of Mussolini" (107), Hobbs, for Stingo's father, is still a "'good ole boy,' [yet] . . . a tragic man, lonely, a widower, and still mourning the death of his only child . . ." (107-08). Hobbs, in return, can equally transcend the apparent division between them and will his friendly adversary his peanut farm. And Stingo's father, having no need for such nor for the money it might fetch at auction, offers it to Stingo, whom he knows, though over twenty-one, is not financially ready to be so. Contrary to Sophie's father, who sees her as a typist and pamphlet hawker, Stingo's father maintains steady contact with his son, despite his choice to live in the North, and midway through the novel yields to his own need "to re-establish, face to face, eyeball to eyeball, our mutual love and kinship" (188).

On his trip to New York the old gentleman instructs his son in several matters after he manages to get into an altercation with an insensitive cabbie. In each episode, Styron again reveals his highly-developed ability to Transfer. He reminds Stingo, for instance, that the North is just as prejudiced as the South is--a typical piece of southern defensiveness, one might say--except that Stingo is quick to say as well that his father "had never been given to shifting unreasonably the various racial evils of the South onto the shoulders of the North," that he was a "lifelong Southern liberal" (289). In 1947 this last phrase would have been a contradiction in terms for most people, but not for Stingo's father. It is a prime example of his ability to Transfer, to escape the approach to life which would be most comfortable for him (and perhaps most uncomfortable for many others) and view human existence from the other side. Contrast this to Arendt's statements about the Nazi functionaries who could actually shift the sympathy of Jewish pain onto themselves.

What of the confrontation with the cabbie? Again I think, however ludicrous the event ultimately became, the right rests with Stingo's father. When the cabbie calls him a "fucking asshole" for a nickel tip, the older man's sense of duty to his fellow man has been shaken. He is appalled by the attitude and reacts against it, quite unlike those in, say, Poland at the time of Auschwitz who, if not incarcerated, can understand the camp as an asset to the local economy or, if an inmate, can slog through the shifting sands or Fortune in search of a foothold for themselves alone. "'Detestable scum that you are, you are no more civilized than a sewer rat! In any decent place in the United States a person like you disgorging your disgusting filth would be taken out in a public square and horse-whipped!" (193). If such a statement at first seems simply divisive, one need only reflect that it is a reminder to the cabbie of his own self-lowered place on the Chain of Being, as well as a reminder that other human beings have rights and dignity and perhaps need for a nickel as well. It is a demand, in short, that both the cabbie and the passenger be accorded an equal place on the human scale. It is the instructive dimension of Transfer.

Nor is it the only scene in which we see the elder man provide such instruction. Consider the episode when, to have a ride in a friend's convertible, Stingo forgot to stoke the fire for his sickly mother, only to return later to find her suffering from a severe chill. Stingo's punishment? "The blood-congealing cold and darkness of the woodshed where he marched me and where he made me stay until long after darkness fell over the village and frigid moonlight seeped in through the cracks of my cell. . . . I was only aware that I was suffering exactly in the same way that my mother had and that my deserts could scarcely be more fitting" . . . (297). This is transfer.

Generally, however, Styron does not seem to suggest that Transfer is something which must be learned. It seems rather a natural human instinct which the solitary pursuit of Fortune has repressed in men and nations. Emmi Hoss suddenly responds to Sophie, after she collapses, as a human rather than as a "Polack." Larry Landau worries about his brother's dementia rather than see him as a disgrace to a respectable and otherwise Fortune-blessed family. Blackstock sees to virtually every need Sophie has before she meets Nathan, and she supports him emotionally--at severe cost to herself--when his wife is killed. Nathan freely gives Stingo money as a gift when his band-aid box is pilfered. Even Morris Fink, full of ethnic slurs and tales out of school, can respond with human determination when he smells the final trouble developing with Sophie and Nathan. And, on the novel's final page, a group of otherwise rowdy young boys has taken the trouble to cover the drunken Stingo with sand to keep him warm until he awakens on Coney Island Beach. They could have picked his pocket.

Several characters stand out as people who, like Stingo's father, live by the principle of Transfer continuously rather than occasionally. Yetta Zimmerman imposes as few rules as possible upon her tenants--"'What I like to see is my tenants enjoy life'" (34). Never in thirty years has she evicted anybody, except of course the "weird oysvorf" she caught in 1938 "'dressed up in girls' panties'" (161). Another such person is Wanda, who tries relentlessly to break down the barriers which prevent human beings from such Transfer. As Sophie realizes in retrospect, Wanda and her brother, Jozef, were "two selfless, courageous people whose allegiance to humanity and their fellow Poles and concern for the hunted Jews were a repudiation of all that her father had stood for" (372). Nor will Wanda turn on Sophie despite her refusal to aid in the cause of resistance and despite the death of Jozef while fighting for it. She can still be tender and consoling when Sophie, at Auschwitz, is desperate over Jan's welfare.

Perhaps all the themes I have been discussing come to a head in the character Stingo names Dr. Fritz Jemand von Niemand, who provides Sophie with her titular "Choice." Alone on the platform at Auschwitz, he is Fortune's darling. He is rich, he is a doctor, he decides who shall live and who shall die, he controls Fortune. Thousands of other people are at his mercy. He is free of guilt and seems to have no reason to curse God nor to lie about his failures. He is as close to playing the role of God as an earthly man can get. But he is drunk, and his soul is ravaged. He is so isolated at the top that he is no longer a human. He cannot feel the guilt which will allow him to re-establish contact with his fellow man and with the real God, if there is one. If Stingo's interpretation is the correct one-- and surely in thematic terms it must be--in giving Sophie her choice he is simply trying to commit the greatest atrocity against mankind that he can think of, against one suffering being instead of against the faceless masses whom he turns into smoke, and thereby experience guilt for the first time in many monotonous years and so become human again.

In the final analysis, however, von Niemand is seeking what young Stingo himself searches for throughout Sophie's Choice: the ability to turn himself away from the lonely quest for Fortune's rewards and toward a brotherhood with his fellow man in a racial endurance against the atrocities Fortune offers instead. Perhaps, without human assistance-- without inhuman cabbies and librarians, without each man trying to better himself at the cost of another, without Southern bigotry and Polish anti-Semitism and the Nazi Holocaust--perhaps Fortune might reveal herself to deal more favorably and more equitably than the history of the world has yet allowed man to believe she has or can or will.

Notes

(1) Sophie's Choice (New York: Random House, 1979). All page references are to this edition. An objection to this novel has frequently been that it is disunified in subject and theme. For example, John W. Aldridge, reviewing for Harper's, remarks about such matters as the Leslie Lapidus episodes by saying "while there is a certain dismal comedy in all this, just what it has to do with the central story of Sophie is never made clear, evidently because Styron does not know" ("Styron's Heavy Freight," Harper's, Sept. 1979, p. 97). I am attempting here to respond to such criticisms as well as interpret the various the various dimensions of the novel's themes.

(2) William Faulkner, Absalom! Absalom! (New York: The Modern Library, 1936), p. 127.

*From The Root of All Evil: The Thematic Unity of William Styron's Fiction: 9-39.

WILLIAM STYRON'S SOPHIE'S CHOICE: THE STRUCTURE OF OPPRESSION

Carolyn A. Durham

In the face of repeated objections to the assertion in What is Literature (1948) that a "good" anti-Semitic or racist novel would be a contradiction in terms, Jean-Paul Sartre maintained that whatever the theoretical value of his analysis, no one had yet taken up the practical challenge: "show me a single good novel whose deliberate intention was to serve oppression, a single one written against Jews, Blacks, workers, colonized peoples."(1) If we judge his most recent novel, William Styron seems to believe that his own work may represent for some readers an attempt to satisfy Sartre. Sophie's Choice incorporates frequent and barely disguised references to the negative critical reception of Styron's earlier novels, which frequently include charges of racism. Such reminders have served as strong evidence for the many reviewers of Sophie's Choice who are insistent on identifying its fictional narrator Stingo with William Styron himself.

Thus Nathan Landau notes signs of "ingrained" and "unregenerate" racism in Stingo's first novel,(2) highly reminiscent of Styron's own Lie Down in Darkness; and the mature Stingo comments on similar reactions to what is clearly a version of The Confessions of Nat Turner: "as accusations from black people became more cranky and insistent that as a writer--a lying writer at that--I had turned to my own profit and advantage the miseries of slavery, I succumbed to a kind of masochistic resignation . . ." (p. 37). Moreover, Stingo's and Styron's current Sophie's Choice, for Stingo is writing the novel we are reading, has aroused general critical acknowledgment that its treatment of Jewish experience invites charges of anti-Semitism, even if none has materialized to date.

The textual connections Styron chooses to establish in Sophie's Choice among his various fictions do have both aesthetic and ideological significance, not unrelated to Sartre's identification of bad literature with a politics of prejudice. The emphasis this structure places on Styron's literary output as oeuvre, as a body of work dealing with the concept and nature of oppression through the successive examination of particular oppressive systems, can point us toward a rich reading of Styron in general and, in the case at hand, of Sophie's Choice. For Styron's work serves of course as an illustration not of Sartre's ironic challenge to skeptics but rather of his original thesis. Styron's novels--and the distinction is important--are not oppressive but about oppression, not racist but about racism, not anti-Semitic but about anti-Semitism, and, I shall argue, not sexist although, in the instance of Sophie's Choice especially, are persistently about sexism.

Readers primarily interested in ideology have tended to dismiss formalism as an invalid critical method, choosing to value or to criticize commitment to a cause without concern for the literary means used to convey it. They thus ignore Sartre's fundamental hypothesis that an essential relationship exists between world view and form: "a novelistic technique always reflects the metaphysics of the novelist."(3) Ironically, in this case, early critics of Sophie's Choice may be paying both too much and not enough attention to form or, at least, to the nature of its connection to content in Styron's novel. For all of their insistence on equating Stingo and Styron, few reviewers appreciate the structural consequences they subsequently attribute to this intermingling of fiction and autobiography. Sophie's Choice has been criticized particularly severely for its organizational weakness: the supposedly chaotic combination of Stingo's sex life with Sophie and Nathan's destructive love; the unjustified comparison of anti-Semitic to a racist American South; the confused linking of Stingo's experience as writer to Nathan's drug-induced madness; and, most importantly, the juxtaposition of all the above themes to the horrors of the Nazi concentration camps.(4) Those reviewers most sensitive to Styron's novel do glimpse in the multiple riches of Sophie's Choice a common pattern, but these critics tend also to see the subject of the novel as too general--Evil--or too specific--the evils of Nazi Germany.(5) That Sophie's Choice should be criticized for a lack of structural coherence or for an excess of structural exuberance seems highly ironic; for it is in fact a novel whose very meaning lies embedded in its structure and, even more specifically, in the very concept of structure itself.

Styron attempts to alert us immediately to this important theme by opening the novel with the single chapter he himself has characterized in interviews as autobiographical, and which we may therefore expect to find potentially irrelevant to the story of Sophie Zawistowska. But, in fact, the analysis of the McGraw-Hill publishing house where Stingo begins both his writing career and his narrative provides in its apparent thematic gratuity a paradigm of structure itself and therefore the very foundation of theme in Styron's Sophie's Choice. McGraw-Hill represents what Styron understands as system: the organized oppression of a given group of people in the name of their deviation from an established norm. Because this original form of systematic or organized evil remains free of any specific ideological content, it sets up a structural pattern that prepares us to comprehend the other systems which form the complex fabric of Styron's novel. Although no doubt pro-Wasp, pro-male, and certainly pro-conservative, McGraw-Hill is neither specifically racist, anti-Semitic, nor sexist; it is merely fundamentally pro-uniformity. Moreover, its function--the publication of good literature--and its fact--the publication of bad--serve from the very beginning of the novel to link Styron's concept of system to his conception of fiction.

Styron subsequently constructs Sophie's Choice upon a carefully woven network of parallels and repetitions in which all of the novel's characters gradually prove to share a single common characteristic: the same paradoxical form of prejudice. Only a few years after Auschwitz, the Jewish Morris Fink declares his hate for boogies (p. 69). Stingo's father describes his friend Frank Hobbs as a "good solid man," although Hobbs is both an anti-Semite and a racist (p. 34). Only Stingo's obsession with Nat Turner and with the institution of slavery rivals his interest in the situation of Jews in prewar Poland and in Nazi Germany; yet even Stingo proves capable of brief lapses into both racism and anti-Semitism, and his experience with the Lapidus family amply illustrates the extent to which he harbors remarkably naive and stereotypical notions of Jewish domestic and religious life (pp. 196-98). Nathan deplores the historic suffering of his fellow Jews, but he does not hesitate to label all Southerners racist. Stingo's father proudly calls himself a liberal Democrat but considers Northerners an ignorant and vulgar caste. German hatred for Jews barely overshadows their horror of "Polacks," and Poles share the barracks of Nazi concentration camps with the Jews they despise. Wanda may best understand the endlessly replicable structure of prejudice and the need therefore to attack the form itself beyond any of its particular contents; she explains to the Jewish Feldshon: "once they finish you off they're going to come and get me" (p. 579).

Although Wanda speaks for herself and her "pretty blonde friend" Sophie only as unlikely victims, it is not insignificant that they are women. In much of his previous work, notably in Set This House on Fire, Styron has used the condition of women as a central metaphor for the general degradation of the self and others. In Sophie's Choice, sexism serves as a pervasive model of oppression, functioning as do the novel's formal analogies to invite us to see the structural equivalence of all systems of organized evil.(6) Thus sexism proves common not only to the apparently neutral structural shell of McGraw-Hill in which women serve as "mainly secretaries" (p. 19) but to racism and anti-Semitism as well. Stingo's carefully developed comparison between Poland and the

American South includes the traditionally double-edged exploitation of females: "domination over women (along with a sulky-sly lechery)" (p. 301). In fact, virtually every chapter of Sophie's Choice contains the same consistent structural elements: a system of organized oppression, a particular example of sexism, and a commentary on language or literature, thus creating a structural paradigm in which sexism illuminates both the systems that oppress society and the literature that can lead toward an understanding of how they function.

Two episodes in particular of Sophie's Choice can quickly and effectively illustrate the structural and thematic importance that Styron attaches to sexism. Stingo's discomfort at inheriting money from his grandfather's sale of the slave Artiste and his horror at the lynching of Bobby Weed are directly related to racism and, because of the parallels Nathan establishes, indirectly related to anti-Semitism. But more importantly, the two events also reveal a hostility to women which constitutes both their common element and an attitude shared by Stingo and Nathan. Artiste (by his very name an ally of Stingo) must be sold because "in the first lusty flush of adolescence" (a situation painfully familiar to Stingo), he has made an "improper advance" toward a young white woman who turns out after the sale to be "an hysteric" prone to such false accusations (pp. 35-36). By the time Bobby Weed is castrated, branded, and lynched years later for the identical and equally nebulous offense, it has become a commonplace: "His reputed crime, very much resembling that of Artiste, had been so classic as to take on the outlines of a grotesque cliche: he had ogled, or molested, or otherwise interfered with (actual offense never made clear, though falling short of rape) the simpleton daughter . . . of a crossroads shopkeeper . . ." (p. 86).

Such stories impose an absolute double bind--one must necessarily choose to be either racist or sexist: either to condemn blacks for an attitude defined as normal in all other men or to condone the treatment of women as sexual objects. Moreover, whether the women in question tell the truth or lie, whether they are believed or not, they are directly responsible as females for both violence against men and for divisiveness among men. Stingo's attitude clearly implies that women are liars, hysterical, simple-minded, and either obsessed with sex and their own desirability or man-haters afraid of "normal" sexual advances. It is scarcely surprising that in Stingo's later resentment at his own metaphorical castration he should invent for Leslie a comparable racist rape fantasy: "I finished my account with one or two Freudian furbelows, chief among them being one in which Leslie told me that she had been able to reach a climax only with large, muscular coal-black Negroes with colossal penises" (p. 222).

Among critical objections to the structure of Sophie's Choice, or to its absence, distress at the inclusion of Stingo's sexual obsessions, fantasies, and adventures ranks particularly high. Robert Alter's comments reflect a typical discomfort with episodes perceived as tasteless and trivial when combined with the horrors of Nazi concentration camps: "it is hard to see how such concentration on a writhing priapic Stingo helps us to grasp the novel's subject of absolute evil."(7) Ironically, one consequence of a growing awareness of feminist concerns may be to provoke an almost instinctive reaction of hostility to every situation that even hints at the sexual exploitation of women. Yet, as is the case here, specific examples of prejudice, however offensive in themselves, may well function in a larger context to expose and consequently to undermine oppression. To focus our attention on the contextual importance of Stingo's sexual experiences, an issue first raised by his encounter with Leslie Lapidus, Styron has Stingo himself worry about the structural coherence of his novel.

> In itself this saga, or episode, or fantasia has little direct
> bearing on Sophie and Nathan, and so I have hesitated to set it
> down, thinking it perhaps extraneous stuff best suited to another
> tale and time. But it is so bound up into the fabric and mood of
> that summer that to deprive this story of its reality would be
> like divesting a body of some member--not an essential mem-
> ber, but as important, say, as one of one's more consequential
> fingers. Besides, even as I set these reservations down, I sense
> an urgency, an elusive meaning in this experience and its
> desperate eroticism by which at least there may be significant
> things to be said about that sexually bedeviled era. (p. 143)

In defining himself as one of the sexual "survivors" of the fifties (p. 145), Stingo by his vocabulary establishes a clear parallel between himself and Sophie. Although such a comparison may seem to undermine the importance of Sophie's fight for her sanity and for life itself, it in fact serves to emphasize the centrality of sexual experience in both of their lives, for Nazi Germany and prewar America. Stingo's sexual fantasies thus relate directly to Styron's attack on the evil of sexism; those critics who denounce the former as gratuitous or trivial may well regard the latter in the same light.

For Stingo, "Little Miss Cock Tease" (p. 145) epitomizes the era of the fifties and, in general, he adheres to the standard male dualistic view of women. Yet, Stingo's division of the female sex into "cock teasers" or "cock suckers" differs sufficiently from the classic angel/whore dichotomy to reveal usefully the true hostility the latter conceals. The apparent idealization of women as pure and virginal reflects in fact a belief that such women are teases, frigid and inhuman. Thus Stingo's system corresponds to an absolute degradation of women; indeed, as he informs us, he has "not idealized 'femininity' in the silly fashion of the time" (p. 147).

Stingo illustrates this view of women through the repetition of a paradigmatic pattern into which his experience with Sophie eventually fits. The original model provided by Mavis Hunnicutt in the structurally rich opening chapter of Sophie's Choice makes it clear that nonsexual relationships with women are inconceivable for Stingo. The "loneliness" on which he insists throughout this period translates unambiguously as sexual frustration: "she could not know what she did to the loneliest junior editor in New York. My lust was incredible . . ." (p. 15). Through Mavis and her subsequent incarnations in Leslie and Mary Alice, Stingo fantasizes the women as cock sucker and cock teaser in turn, unfortunately in that inverted order. Stingo idealizes the female as sexual initiator or, in any case, as always responsive to male advances; thus, women are allowed volition to want what men do. Invariably, however, women who appear appropriately welcoming ultimately reject Stingo with increasingly dire consequences for him. Merely chagrined at Mavis' imaginary dismissal of him, Stingo falls ill after his failure with Leslie; and Mary Alice--"worse than a Cock Tease, a Whack-off artist" (p. 527)--drives him from his "lifelong efforts at good, wholesome, heterosexual screwing" (p. 534) toward homosexual relations. Stingo claims a distinction between the women he desires and the women he loves for which, in fact, the novel provides no evidence. Stingo's expression of chaste adoration for Maria Hunt produces a "ferociously erotic" (p. 52) dream in which Maria behaves, to Stingo's delight, with "the abandon of a strumpet" (p. 53). Similarly, although Stingo professes a "poetic and idealistic" (p. 145) passion for Sophie, she too supports the fixed model of sexual identity already established. Stingo's initial encounter with Sophie occurs as Nathan defines her as "cunt" and "whore" (p. 55); Stingo's attention focuses immediately on her body and her sexuality; his desire "to win the affection" of Sophie marks at best a necessary step toward his real goal: "to share the bed" abandoned by Nathan (p. 63). Moreover, so that any lingering idealization of the female may be rigorously exorcised, Stingo finds Sophie most arousing when she is least erotic; her most tender, affectionate and vulnerable moments become an invitation to seduction. When Sophie collapses, shattered by the loss of Nathan and her revelation just moments before of the existence of her son Jan, only Stingo's fatigue persuades him to forgo a sexual pass: "Lying there, she seemed terribly vulnerable, but my outburst had tired me, leaving me somehow shaken and empty of desire" (p. 376). During the desperate and exhausting flight South to escape Nathan, the sight of Sophie asleep produces in Stingo a similar "seize of pure lust" (p. 558). Thus, Stingo's synthetic dream in which he makes love to Leslie, transformed in quick succession into Maria and Sophie (pp. 363-64), has particular significance; it both confirms that love is inseparable from lust for Stingo and draws the inevitable conclusion: all women are equivalent and therefore interchangeable.

Yet Sophie does stand apart from other women as an ideal; she is the perfect woman as defined and perceived in a male world. Originally a cock teaser--"a young woman brought up with puritanical repressions and sexual taboos as adamantine as those of any Alabama Baptist maiden" (p. 117)--Sophie has been transformed literally into a cock sucker, "the world's most elegant" (p. 602) according to Nathan, thereby proving the male maxim that women, however much they may initially resist, really welcome sexual advances.(8) Moreover, Sophie's behavior perpetuates the particularly vicious myth that women respond to physical and mental violence as pleasurable. In the midst of an orgy of abuse, Sophie blissfully sucks Nathan's cock (pp. 413-14); and after hours of torture involving physical beating, verbal abuse, and psychological assault, she welcomes immediately and without hesitation Nathan's invitation "to fuck" (p. 422).

Nathan misdirects his jealousy of Sophie, since its justification lies not in her attraction to other men but in their obsessive interest in her; for every man she encounters, however briefly or infrequently, Sophie becomes an object of desire, a seducible prize. But in the sexist world that Styron portrays, once Sophie has allowed herself to be seduced, she must be degraded as the whore she has become. Her very submission to Nathan confirms the justice and accuracy of his accusations, and marriage logically becomes the prize that Nathan proffers or withdraws on the basis of his current beliefs about Sophie's sexual fidelity. Stingo, tormented for months by his desire for Sophie, nonetheless characterizes her seduction of him on the beach as "forthrightly lewd" (p. 436), and the episode illustrates with particular clarity the incredible double standard to which women are subjected, the inescapable vicious circle in which they are trapped. When Sophie initiates lovemaking, immediately after her latest revelations about her past, Stingo implicitly condemns her for frivolity, capriciousness, an inability to feel deeply: "The shift in mood--the grisly chronicle of Warsaw, followed in a flash by this wanton playfulness. What in hell did it mean?" (p. 437). But when Sophie returns to her story after Stingo's premature ejaculation, his renewed horror is heightened. Sophie's failure to be appropriately affected by their recent intimacy, to live this sexual adventure as "cataclysmic" and "soul-stirring," offers evidence of an insensitivity far greater than any Stingo had yet imagined and leads him to one of the novel's relatively rare generalizations about "women": "Could women, then, so instantaneously turn off their lust like a light switch?" (p. 440).

Styron's careful construction of a globally sexist world provides a context in which the events of Sophie's arrival at Auschwitz cannot possibly be dismissed as an aberration. However great our shock and our horror, the "choice" that Doctor Jemand von Niemand imposes on Sophie marks the logical extension of all male behavior toward women recorded in Sophie's Choice up to that point. Despite Stingo's elaborate attempts to "understand" the Doctor's action, to offer an explanation that inevitably becomes a defense, Jemand von Niemand fits into a clearly established pattern. He makes Sophie the same proposition that virtually every other man in the novel, implicitly or explicitly, has made her--"I'd like to get you into bed with me" (p. 586)--and when she fails to respond, he destroys her. For with tragic irony the perfectly pliant Sophie, who has always understood the necessity of female submission in a male world, fails to react quickly enough at the single moment when the metaphorical survival of the female becomes literal. Yet, the greatest horror recounted in Sophie's Choice may be less the cruelty of the Nazi doctor than its perpetuation in Stingo. For Stingo's reaction to the story of Eva's death is virtually indistinguishable from Jemand von Niemand's behavior during the actual event: Stingo too wants to go to bed with Sophie. The fact that she clearly initiates their night of inexhaustible sex changes nothing in a world in which women are required to be both prey and predator, except perhaps to confirm once and for all how well Sophie learned her lesson at Auschwitz.

The role of sexual oppressor that links all men and the use of sexism as paradigm to connect Nazi Germany to postwar America extend to the reader as well. One of the most remarkable successes of Styron's attack on sexism comes from his ability to implicate the reader himself in the system that victimizes Sophie; the male pronoun is for once authentically generic since all readers, male or female, will be forced to view Sophie from a masculine perspective. Our limited, popular, and generally sensationalist knowledge of history prepares us to suspect Sophie's involvement in sexual crimes or experiments at Auschwitz, and the mysterious secret announced in the novel's title encourages us to believe she participated more as collaborator than as victim. Moreover, Nathan serves as our representative in the text. He gradually plants the idea that Sophie's survival at Auschwitz is linked to her sexual behavior; this insidious process, reinforced by Sophie's evident obsession with her own guilt, culminates in his identification of Sophie with Irma Griese: "hey Irma how many SS pricks did you suck to get out of there, how much master race come swallowed for Freiheit?" (p. 411). Styron's technique effectively exposes the reader as participant in the same system of sexism the novel as a whole reflects; for at the moment we learn the true nature of Sophie's "choice" or "crime," we are forced to confront the discrepancy between the truth and our assumptions.

Women can ultimately be reduced to interchangeable sex objects, because sexist society denies them a personal identity, a sense of self. Styron's novel, consistent with much feminist theory, locates the origin and the model of female oppression in the father dominance of the traditional family. In general, Sophie's father reduces her to "virtually menial submission" (p. 293), but the most significant assault is aimed at Sophie's love of music, the representation throughout the novel of her identity, her individuality. As a significant prelude to her account of her arrival at Auschwitz, Sophie relates a dream in which she explicitly identifies her father's will to deny her access to music with the death of the self:

> "So in the dream that has returned to me over and over I see Princess Czartoryska in her handsome gown go to the phonograph and she turns and always says, as if she were talking to me, 'Would you like to hear the Brahms <u>Lieder</u>?' And I always try to say yes. But just before I can say anything my father interrupts. He is standing next to the Princess and he is looking directly at me, and he says, 'Please don't play that music for the child. She is much too stupid to understand.' And then I woke up with this pain. . . . Only this time it was even worse, Stingo. Because in the dream I had just now he seemed to be talking to the Princess not about the music but about . . ."
> Sophie hesitated, then murmured, "About my death. He wanted me to die, I think." (p. 506)

On at least three occasions in the novel, Sophie repeats the most fundamental of her lies and the one most puzzling to Stingo: she makes of her father a decent, brave, and loving man. Because Sophie has no sense of self--because her identity is entirely relational, alienated in that of the men who control and protect her--her only opportunity to experience self-esteem, however vicarious and reflected, is to belong to men of whom she and others can think well. Logically, when her hated father and the husband who is his mirror image are murdered, Sophie grieves not for their death but for her own: "Her entire sense of self--of her identity--was unfastened" (p. 416). Nathan offers Sophie an exact replica of her relationship with her father: she receives protection and identity at the price of "childlike dependence" (p. 388), a total self-alienation that Nathan correctly identifies: "My darling, I think you have absolutely no ego at all" (p. 416). In this context, the story of Blackstock and his wife Sylvia, structurally gratuitous if the unity of Styron's novel is situated elsewhere than in the institution of sexism, serves a central metaphorical function. Blackstock's adoration for Sylvia turns her into a pet, a doll, a pampered child whose total irresponsibility is not merely tolerated but encouraged; and Sylvia destroys herself in an automobile accident, the head she has never had occasion to use severed from her body and lost.

Styron continually places Sophie in impossible situations which have particular metaphoric significance for women: if they prove appropriately selfless, they participate in their own alienation and destruction, but any claim they make for the right to self instantly backfires by proclaiming them to be selfish. Not only does Stingo openly condemn Sophie: she traps herself in her own narrative. For example, Sophie justifies her attempt to seduce Hoss as the disinterested and courageous effort of a mother to save her son, but until all hope is clearly lost, we hear Sophie ask Hoss only for her <u>own</u> freedom; we are in fact still unaware that she has a child (pp. 330-45). Sophie demands what she desperately needs and deserves--the right to exist--but she does so in a morally ambivalent context in which we are led to condemn female selflessness: motherhood. But Sophie cannot win, for when she acts as the good mother, she is also condemned for the same female sin of selfishness. Both Sophie's refusal to help the Home Army in Warsaw, out of fear for her children's safety, and her inability to steal Emmi's radio, lest she lose her last chance to save Jan, demonstrate the selfless other-orientation traditionally required of women. But through our identification with Wanda and the Resistance movement, we come to regard Sophie as not only morally weak and irresponsible but indeed as selfish for her inability to put the plight of the Jewish people before her own, suspecting as well that she uses her children as an excuse to hide her own cowardice. Condemned for her maternal role, whether she fulfills it adequately or not, Sophie immediately must act as the quintessentially bad mother: she becomes a Medea, morally guilty of infanticide. Not only has she implicitly preferred one child to another in a society in which maternal love is by definition unconditional and all-encompassing, but she whose value as woman is based upon her ability to give life has sent one of her children to death.

Although Styron uses the concept of a slave world, common to the Nazi concentration camps and to the history of the American South, to examine the condition of women as well, slavery serves him as contrast as much as comparison. For Styron understands the limits of the analogy even if in his existential world it may in some terrible sense be preferable to remain an absolute slave. The ultimate horror of the situation of women rests precisely on the two factors that distinguish them from the Negro slaves and from the Jewish inmates of Auschwitz: choice, however limited, and collaboration, however enforced. Sophie may have been prepared to act in a particular way at Auschwitz because of her gender identity: "she had been a victim, yes, but both victim and accomplice, accessory" (p. 266). Certainly, Sophie's understanding of her "complicity" (p. 296), not only in her own oppression but in a world in which systematic oppression is possible, long predates the war. The typing and distribution of her father's murderous tract force her to acknowledge her tragic possibility: a volition too strong to allow her the comforting status of victim but too weak to permit her to revolt:

> "And this terrible emptiness came over me when I realized just
> then there was nothing I could do about it, now way of saying
> no, no way possible to say, 'Papa, I'm not going to help you
> spread this thing.' . . . And I was a grown woman and I wanted
> to play Bach, and at that moment I just thought I must die--I
> mean, to die not so much for what he was making me do but
> because I had no way of saying no." (p. 300)

Certainly Sophie's enforced choice between her children represents the ultimate tragic dilemma, for she is made to choose in a situation in which no meaningful choice is possible: any decision will produce morally and emotionally identical results. And yet Dr. Jemand von Niemand is not totally wrong to call Sophie's right to choose "a privilege" (p. 589); for as Sophie herself understands, without choice as possibility or concept, women would remain helpless victims, unable to institute change. Ultimately, Sophie can choose for herself only on choosing suicide, but the importance of that decision should not be underestimated. Not only, as Phyllis Chesler has pointed out, does physical action--including suicide--remain extraordinarily difficult for women(9), but Sophie selects death over a new loss of identity in the marriage and motherhood that Stingo offers. Throughout Sophie's Choice, all questions of sex and sexism are linked to language and literature: to Stingo's vocation as writer, to the construction of the novel we are reading, to the creation of the story of Sophie. For Stingo, writing and sex are inseparable, indeed indistinguishable. In the key first chapter of Sophie's Choice, Stingo professes "an affinity for the written word--almost any written word--that was so excitable that it verged on the erotic" (p. 12). The urge to masturbate invariably accompanies Stingo's one creative task of the moment, the composition of jacket blurbs (p. 14); and the fantasy garden parties he imagines from his window are not only dominated by his lust for Mavis but people with famous authors: "In these demented fantasies I was prevented from immediate copulation on the Abercrombie & Fitch hammock only by the sudden arrival in the garden of Thornton Wilder. Or e.e. cummings. Or Katherine Anne Porter. Or John Hersey. Or Malcolm Cowley. Or John P. Marquand" (pp. 15-16). To Stingo as hero, the equivalence of language and sex becomes a source of almost unbearable frustration. He consistently finds himself a sexual eavesdropper, a sort of oral voyeur, for whom knowledge of the act of love is limited to the words other people pronounce during sex (pp. 91, 362). With comic irony, the woman Stingo selects as his sexual initiator has a totally lingual sex life: Leslie only kisses and talks about sex, and the single concrete result Stingo gleans from the adventure is an inflamed tongue.

But to Stingo as writer, sex is language in the most positive of senses: both the source and the subject of art. Susan Gubar and Sandra Gilbert in The Madwoman in the Attic postulate that the pen acts as "a metaphorical penis";(10) and Stingo illustrates particularly well their thesis that male sexuality is the essence of literary power. The opening chapter of Sophie's Choice sets up a paradigmatic model of male bonding through art: an older male, denied a writing career, devotes himself instead to the support and encouragement of a younger and more gifted "son" or "brother."

Farrell's intention to write is transformed into the nurturing of his talented son, subsequently replaced by Stingo: "Son, write your guts out" (p. 28). Nathan, a gifted mime and storyteller, has also wanted to write and becomes instead a "supportive brother-figure" for Stingo and the only reader and critic of his novel. Even the narrative technique of Sophie's

Choice contributes. The dialogue between the old and the young Stingo provides an affectionate father/son tone which guarantees a constant framework of male bonding in the joint pursuit of the ultimate male task of artistic creation:

"How I now cherish the image of myself in the earlier time . . .
supremely content in the knowledge that the fruit of this happy
labor, whatever its deficiencies, would be the most awesome
and important of man's imaginative endeavors--the Novel. The
blessed Novel. The sacred Novel. The Almighty Novel." (p. 133)

On the other hand, the relationship of women to language in Sophie's Choice reflects their negative status with equal accuracy. Women are not only degraded by the sexist language men use to reduce them to their sexual anatomy--for example, "a piece of ass" (p. 144)--but women are obliged to degrade themselves through their own use of language. Leslie's uninhibited sexual language is her greatest "turn-on," since "this concubine's speech" (p. 153) serves to assure Stingo that the Jewish princess is in reality only a whore. The degradation of Sophie, whose linguistic ability far surpasses that of any male in the novel, illustrates particularly well the obstinate determination of sexist society to deny women any authentic use of language. Fluent in German, Polish, French, and Russian, Sophie finds herself in a situation where she must speak English, the single language in which Stingo and Nathan retain total superiority. Indeed at our first encounter with Sophie, Nathan is berating her for the parallel female sins of sexual and linguistic infidelity: "I can't be a cunt, you dumb fucking Polack. When are you going to learn to speak the language?" (p. 55). Stingo periodically quotes Sophie's speech verbatim so that we may observe for ourselves that it is indeed "fetchingly erratic" (p. 106), that is, riddled with lexical and syntactical errors. Moreover, Sophie essentially parrots Nathan: "All at once I became aware of the way in which Sophie echoed so much of Nathan's diction" (p. 78). The one linguistic skill for which we hear Sophie consistently praised is her perfect command of German, an ambivalent accomplishment at best given the historical setting of the novel; the writer Stingo, on the other hand, commands the "gorgeous" English tongue (p. 133).

If Nathan in his roles as knowledgeable reader, critic, and literary historian predicts the coming of Jewish Writing to replace Southern Writing, certainly neither he nor Stingo ever foresees a tradition of Women's Writing. By the time Sophie expresses the astonishing desire to write a novel about her own experiences, her linguistic incompetence has been sufficiently proven to make her project seem not only improbable but almost comic; should any doubt remain, we are treated immediately to the single sample of her writing included in the novel: "it was testimony indeed to the imperfect command of written English of which Sophie had so recently lamented to me . . ." (p. 606). Since Sophie nonetheless retains a terrible obsession with her personal history, she must delegate her history to a man.

Although Stingo apparently accepts the passive role of listener, comparable both to the religious confessor and to the analyst (p. 177), for Sophie there is ultimately neither redemption nor cure. The story she believes she is assigning to Stingo's pen is in the process stolen from her. As Gilbert and Gubar point out, not only does a writer "father" his text in Western literary tradition but "the chief creature man has generated is woman" (p. 12). Stingo, who places himself in the category of writers who exploit the tragedies of "others" (p. 132), that is, of women, continually generates the same female story of self-destruction: in every important sense, Maria Hunt is already Sophie Zawistowska. Moreover, the female story ultimately turns out to be in the service of and subservient to that of the male. Stingo sees in Sophie the experience of love and death he must have to mature into a writer (p. 28) as he reads <u>Sophie's Choice</u> as his own picaresque novel.

The peculiar interplay of the narrative voices in <u>Sophie's Choice</u> illustrates particularly well the respective roles of men and women in a sexist literature and society. Not only is Sophie's narrative punctuated with reminders of Stingo's presence, but in most cases Stingo and not Sophie actually recounts her past. As "herstory" becomes "History," a clear narrative pattern emerges to distinguish the female from the male narrator. Sophie tells her own story only when she is lying or confessing previous lies. Thus, Sophie's major interventions involve her creation of a false childhood in Cracow (pp. 93-104), a misleading portrait of Nathan as a supportive and loving "Prince Charming" (pp. 188-93), and so on. Not only is unreliability thus attributed to the female, but the male voice becomes in contrast the voice of Truth. Indeed, the male narrator is consistently obliged to identify the female as liar: "But now it again becomes necessary to mention that Sophie was not quite straightforward in her recital of past events . . ." (p. 176).

At other times, Stingo uses the opposite but functionally identical technique of the insistent assurance that Sophie tells the truth, or rather-- and the distinction is important--that Stingo believes her (see pp. 294, 296, 306). Not only are Stingo's reassurances suspiciously overdone, not only do they imply that Stingo did not believe her at other times and thus remind us that Sophie lies, but they make it clear that truth is male-defined and that to merit belief, Sophie's story must receive male validation.

Moreover, Sophie's lack of credibility is directly and significantly linked to her alleged lack of fidelity: women are whores and liars. We should carefully note the context in which the issue of Sophie's credibility is first raised:

> Blackstock was a truly happy man. He adored Sylvia more that
> life itself. Only the fact that he was childless, he once told

Sophie, kept him from being <u>absolutely</u> the happiest man on earth.

. . .

As will be seen in due course (and the fact is important to this narrative), Sophie told me a number of lies that summer. (p. 116) By juxtaposing the first mention of Sophie's lying to the protestations of Blackstock that he is a truly happy man who adores his wife, Stingo at least suggests by association that Sophie's "lies" may include her denial of sexual involvement with Blackstock. In any case, Sophie's initial lie to Stingo falsely represents her sexual fidelity: "I note that Sophie told me a lie within moments after we first set eyes on each other. This was when, after the ghastly fight with Nathan, she leveled upon me her look of desperation and declared that Nathan was 'the only man I have ever made love to beside my husband'" (p. 116). The possibility that Sophie may be lying about her fidelity is further reinforced by Nathan's accusations, and this extraordinary promotion of Nathan to a figure of authority permits Styron to expose the irrational bias of systematic sexism. For insane or not, pathological liar or not, Nathan is established as credible, given the insistence elsewhere on his prescience, his insight, his power to predict correctly, and by his general association with the representation of the male as the possessor of knowledge.

While Sophie remains obsessed with her personal life and story, Stingo seeks to place the former in its historical and theoretical context. The female lies; the male provides statistics, information, facts. Styron portrays the male in general as the learned, objective, neutral scholar; for the liar Nathan, who inexhaustibly researches Nazi anti-Semitism and the Civil War, fulfills this vision as much as Stingo. Ironically, of course, Sophie's lies essentially concern men. She accepts her female role as their promoter and protector, perpetuating to the best of her ability one of the central myths of a world in which men dominate, namely, that men are <u>good</u>: Sophie's father risked his life to save Jews; Casimir was a generous, loving, intelligent husband; Nathan is a gentle and tender savior, Stingo a devoted friend. And yet, or so a system founded on sexism would have it, Sophie is a liar, and Stingo and Nathan, who perpetuate harmful and degrading misrepresentations of women, are not only imaginative and creative but factual and reliable.

Although Styron has been repeatedly accused of exploiting the experience of others for his own personal and literary benefit, no one seems yet to have questioned his right as male to usurp a female life. Stingo himself expresses some concern that he may have "intruded" on Sophie's privacy, but his scruples involve Sophie not as woman but as survivor of a concentration camp (p. 265). In fact, Styron demonstrates that the experience of women can be a particularly effective means of understanding an experience of oppression otherwise foreign. In part, Sophie's life attracts Stingo as the possibility for a story because of certain similarities between the two of them: both are non-Jews isolated in a Jewish community; the war leaves both to suffer from some degree of survival guilt; both feel shame for the racial or religious prejudice of their compatriots; and so on. Such parallels serve not to trivialize Sophie's experience, as many critics have suggested, but to insist on the important generic sense Styron means ultimately to attach to her life. Mary Daly has no doubt correctly identified the technique of "universalization" as one means used to deny the reality of the specific oppression of women. Styron uses the opposite method of particularization: the situation of women becomes the basic model through which a general concept of systematic oppression can be illustrated. In seeking a confrontation with the reality of twentieth-century dehumanization, Styron has understood the usefulness of women whose intermediate position between victim and collaborator permits him to illustrate the necessity of choice and responsibility for the liberation of the self. Thus does Stingo appropriately feel rage and sorrow at the end of Sophie's Choice not just for Sophie but for all "the beaten and butchered and betrayed and martyred children of the earth" (p. 625) who have peopled his fictional world.

Notes

(1) Jean-Paul Sartre, Qu'est que la litterature (Paris: Gallimard, 1948), p. 85, n. 3. [Durham's] translation.

(2) William Styron, Sophie's Choice (New York: Bantam Books, 1980), p. 253. Future references appear parenthetically in the text.

(3) Sartre, Situations I (Paris: Gallimard, 1947), p. 86. [Durham's] translation.

(4) James Atlas (New York Times Book Review, 27 May 1979, p. 18), for example, finds the canvas of the book "crowded with incidents that bear no relation to the book's theme"; Robert Towers (New York Review of Books, 9 July 1979, p. 12) notes the "tenuous" and "less than convincing" connection between Poland and the American South; John W. Aldridge (Harper's Magazine, Sept. 1979, p. 97) sees in Stingo "a character seemingly without thematic relevance to the main action"; and Julian Symons (Times Literary Supplement, 30 Nov. 1979, p. 77) discerns in Sophie's Choice two separate novels, one Jewish and one Southern, whose linking he perceives as arbitrary and artificial.

(5) See, for example, Philip W. Leon, Virginia Quarterly Review, 55 (1979), 740-47; Jack Beatty, New Republic, 30 June 1979, pp. 38-40; Edith Milton The Yale Review, Autumn 1979, pp. 89-103; and John Gardner, New York Times Book Review, 27 May 1979, pp. 1, 16-17.

(6) Styron potentially offers support for the position of Mary Daly and other contemporary feminists that sexism is "the basic model and source of oppression," that exploitation as concept can be eradicated only with the termination of the universal exploitation of women. See Daly, Beyond

God the Father (Boston: Beacon Press, 1973), p. 190; Shulamith Fire-stone, The Dialectic of Sex (New York: Bantam Books, 1970), pp. 105-25; and Dorothy Dinnerstein, The Mermaid and the Minotaur (New York: Harper, 1976), p. 102.

(7) Robert Alter, Saturday Review, 7 July 1979, p. 43; see also reviews by Beatty, Aldridge, and Towers.

(8) Significantly, the first time Sophie appears in sexy clothes (selected and paid for by Nathan), she is made to confuse "seersucker" with "cocksucker" (p. 233).

(9) Phyllis Chesler, Women and Madness (Garden City, N.Y.: Doubleday, 1972), p. 49.

(10) Sandra Gilbert and Susan Gubar, The Madwoman in the Attic (New Haven: Yale Univ. Press, 1979), p. 3.

*From Twentieth-Century Literature 30 (1984): 448-64.   Reprinted by permission.

THE REACH OF FICTION: NARRATIVE TECHNIQUE IN STYRON'S <u>SOPHIE'S CHOICE</u>*

Richard G. Law

In <u>Sophie's Choice,</u> the telling of the tale is contrived to display the capacity of fiction to illuminate a subject that baffles ordinary inquiry and to test the claims of art against perhaps the extreme form of knowledge: the meaning of Auschwitz. The novel also makes imperious demands on the reader, who is lured into constructing a text of the Holocaust--a process which, while productive of insights that are perhaps available in no other way, comes at the cost of a painful imaginative involvement. An essential part of the "argument" of <u>Sophie's Choice</u>--and of the implied claims for fiction which are embodied in it--is that the direct and unmediated encounter with the heart of darkness is not only dangerous, but may, by its very nature, prevent comprehension.(1) Given a subject which cannot be confronted without danger of engulfing the viewer, the controlled distancing of art may be a necessary component of understanding.

Accordingly, the novel alternates between intense glimpses of its subject and moments of great psychological distance and abstraction, drawing the reader into a rhythm of confrontation and evasion. One of the primary means by which the reader's encounter with Auschwitz is controlled and manipulated is through the alternation of complementary but quite different narrative perspectives. Stingo's point of view provides a direct though naive experience, approaching Auschwitz more or less accidentally and unwillingly. Through Stingo, the reader has a direct glimpse not of Auschwitz, but of the delayed <u>effects</u> of Auschwitz on another. Stingo's experience is supplemented by the point of view of the mature authorial voice of the narrator, who offers a retrospective, frequently satirical reconstruction of his younger self's encounter with

Sophie and her past. This retrospective view is informed by a broad scholarly rumination on the records of and commentary about the Holocaust, including extensive quotations from both victims and Nazi officials. In this way the book gives expression to many voices (no one of which can presume to capture "Auschwitz") even as it assimilates them to its own ends.

I

The subject of the Holocaust represents a test case for exploring the limits of what we conventionally call knowledge. It is hard to "know" Auschwitz. The experience of the camps exists so far outside normal human frames of references that the very facts of the case are, in a sense, unimaginable.(2) As Styron himself has asserted, "Auschwitz can be compared to nothing"(3); "Auschwitz must remain the place on earth most unyielding to meaning or definition."(4) Moreover, the mind has defenses against such horror which are not easily overcome. It is no small task, then, to attempt to link the incommensurate with the familiar, to bring what lies at such an extremity within range of our ordinary powers of vision. What can be known of the phenomenon of industrialized mass murder is also complicated by the different senses by which we understand the word "knowledge." One kind of knowledge is the historian's, which is abstract and retrospective--its value deriving in part from its very distance from the events themselves and from the extent to which the events can be processed (interpreted) for general use. Quite another kind of knowledge is, of course, to have been there: "Only survivors of Auschwitz know what it meant to be in Auschwitz."(5) Such knowledge is untranslatable and incommunicable; it not only transcends interpretation but defies attempts to make sense of it.

Between the former kind of knowledge and the latter, of course, lies an enormous distance which the novel invites us to contemplate. As Styron was aware, formidable commentators like Elie Wiesel have advised that fiction writers not even try to deal with the subject--that to make it a subject of fiction is somehow a desecration of the memory of the victims. Similarly, George Steiner has asserted that the only proper response is silence.(6) Styron's novel, however, is directed squarely at the Steiner-Wiesel position that art can only trivialize an experience like the Holocaust. The "ultimately transcendental and important thing about art," Styron has claimed, "is its ability to do anything--that's the definition of art. It can deal with any experience--past, present, or future. . . ."(7) In dramatizing the position that silence will not do as an answer to the camps, the novel has as much to say about the nature and capabilities of art as about Auschwitz. It is as if the novel accepts its subject as a challenge: if Sophie's Choice can provide a medium in which Auschwitz can, in some meaningful sense, become known, then literature can treat anything; no subjects are off-limits; no veils may be drawn across any area of human experience.

II

If <u>Sophie's Choice</u> is as preoccupied with the problem of knowledge as <u>All the King's Men</u> or <u>As I Lay Dying</u>, it also attempts to overcome the obstacles to knowledge with techniques familiar from those precedents: It explores minutely a particular instance (Sophie's season in Hell) as a synecdoche of the Holocaust. The text draws a familiar distinction between abstract and concrete knowledge, the historian's knowledge vs. the victim's, and it relies heavily on the power of imagery to combine both, to fuse concepts and emotions, the general and the particular, in complex, highly charged dramatic actions. Like Faulkner's <u>The Sound and the Fury</u>, Styron's novel is constructed around a powerful germinal scene which the rest of the work may be said to gloss. Styron has referred to the genesis of the novel as a waking dream which imposed itself on him and became the controlling metaphor for the whole work.(8) The image which troubled Styron involved a young woman on the platform at Auschwitz being forced to choose between her children. That image focused and contained several decades of his pondering on the meaning of the death camps: "I suddenly realized that this had to be the metaphor for the most horrible, tyrannical despotism in history, that this was a new form of evil . . . ."(9) This single scene defines the world the Nazis made; it explains the secret wellspring of Sophie's mystifying behavior and the source of the irrational guilt which destroys her. It also dramatizes--by a process this essay will explore--as much of the heart of the darkness as is possible to dramatize.

It is critical to note that the reader encounters the core scene of Sophie with her children on the platform at Auschwitz on page 484 of a 515-page text, by which point the narrative, through the powerful spectacle of her suffering, has converted the reader's initial gossipy interest in Sophie into a profound sense of empathy. Knowledge of her "choice" is withheld until the reader is prepared for it, subtly, by sensing in her attempts to start a new life in New York the consequences of some unknown event--the shadow of some unspeakable experience in her past--which has left Sophie obscurely crippled. In the meantime, by becoming gradually acquainted with Sophie and her story, the reader has descended, step by step, through layer after layer of her psychic pain, each layer worse than the last--and each, in a sense, unimaginable, unevocable, except by the process and in the context of the tale in which we have become immersed.

Because of its literally almost unspeakable subject, the manner of the unfolding of the tale is an exercise in overcoming, or putting to sleep, reader resistance. To keep the reader's imagination from evading the nature of Sophie's experience, Styron employs a variety of stratagems, some simple and others Byzantine in their elaborateness. The unfolding of the narrative, then, is a kind of trick which simultaneously carries us toward and hides its destination. The whole narrative is skillfully crafted to get us in a frame of mind where we cannot evade, or fail to imagine, the experience of genocide from the point of view of one of its victims.

Given the gruesome opportunities of the subject matter, there are very few actual scenes of Auschwitz, and few of them are particularly sensationalized or physically brutal. Although his portrayal of the camp is carefully based on surviving documents, Styron resists, for the most part, direct representation of its most sensational features. A careful reader of Emily Dickinson, Styron evidently holds with her that because of its power to blind, "the Truth must dazzle gradually." Accordingly, most of the brutal realities of the camps are realized by suggestion, by brief direct glimpses, and by analogy. We acquire a sense of the degree to which Sophie has been brutalized in the camp from the way her father, an ardent fascist, treats her before the war and from the way her lover, Nathan Landau, treats her afterwards; we sense something of the camp's limitless oppression and dehumanizing impersonality from the anonymous digital rape of Sophie in the subway in New York. Similarly, from Stingo's haunted conscience about failing his cancer-stricken mother, we acquire the barest inklings of Sophie's sense of guilt--just the faintest sense of that open oven door of memory she encounters when she thinks of her children.

Such reserve and indirection are characteristic of the narrative stratagems generally in Sophie's Choice. The experience of direct, scalding pain is, of course, not the object of the narrative, but rather a sympathetic intuition of the dimensions of Sophie's agony. Styron uses very shrewdly his art form's ability to move toward insight by the "stairway of surprise." By careful preparation and frequent deception, the narrative takes us up to one threshold of revelation after another and then stops, the narrator seeming always just about to show us things or tell us things.(10) By such means it manages to take us places we would refuse to go if we sensed the destination. The components of the victim's experience of Auschwitz are vividly suggested in the narrative, but the task of assembling and understanding them belongs to the reader.

Sophie's Choice is presented in the form of a Bildungsroman in which the organizing axis of the narrative is Stingo's quest for knowledge. All of the elaborate excursions and digressions contribute to that developing line. Stingo is presented as a characterization of Styron himself at 22: a lonely ex-Marine with both literary and amorous ambitions, seeking his fortune in the city. Stingo's is a familiar tale of initiation in which a callow, superficial sense of self and world is demolished by his "education." Stingo's attainment of a more mature and adequate perspective is not dramatized, although his having arrived at it is implied in the presence of the mature authorial voice, who has somehow survived and come to terms with the knowledge that Sophie represents. In reminiscing about the summer of 1947, the mature narrator speaks to us out of a successful career as a writer--a success which has, by some means difficult to fathom, been engendered by the experience that overwhelms his younger self. In mediating between the reader and the traumatic experience which constitutes Stingo's education, the mature narrator plays an unobtrusive but significant role in assembling the tale and controlling reader responses. Using the guise of confessional autobiography, the mature narrator dramatizes his younger self's failure to comprehend and assimilate his education while simultaneously taking the reader on a tortuous journey almost to the center of the experience.

The narrative he constructs of his early shortcomings is self-consciously intertextual; it casts Stingo as a twentieth-century version of Melville's Ishmael, setting out in Brooklyn on a "voyage of discovery": "my spirit had remained landlocked, unacquainted with love and all but a stranger to death" (24-25). In a technique also reminiscent of Moby-Dick, the narrative has a double story line with dual protagonists and dual centers of interest, so that Stingo's own story emerges out of his telling us the story of the second figure, Sophie, whose name means "wisdom." The narrative is structured so that for Stingo to discover the answers to the riddle of Sophie, to know Sophie, as it were, would amount to a resolution of his quest. What Stingo acquires by way of an education is an experience of "evil," which is also the subject of the mature narrator's brooding enquiry.

Styron gives Stingo's initiation story important twists: his education involves gaining a perspective adequate for his ambition to become a writer. The narrative therefore recounts Stingo's discovery of both a subject and the resources within himself to treat it--the knowledge, presumably, to interpret it. Organized in this way, the fictive world which emerges in the narrative has a bearing on and provides a partial definition of the writer's craft and calling. However, Stingo's education consists largely of discoveries--in scenes such as the revelation of Nathan's madness--of the invalidity or unreliability of knowledge.

Learning of Sophie's past and observing her eventual death constitute the chief means through which Stingo acquires an experience of evil. The two mysteries, Sophie and Auschwitz, are telescoped together, with Sophie serving as the focal point through which the mystery of Auschwitz can be glimpsed: "I have thought that it might be possible to make a stab at understanding Auschwitz by trying to understand Sophie . . ." (219). However, the youthful Stingo is too stunned to assimilate, even vicariously, Sophie's experience of evil. A product of a safe, white, middle class, protestant Tidewater Virginia upbringing, Stingo appears an unlikely candidate for either mature understanding or Parnassus. He suffers from a peculiarly American innocence, epitomized by his "virginity," which not even a hitch in the Marine Corps in World War II could alter. Naive, frequently obtuse, and sexually obsessed, he is, for much of the narrative, essentially a comic figure, providing a kind of bizarre (but often welcome) relief from the unfolding horrors of Sophie's past. But it is important to note that the mature narrator, even in his retrospective account, is not readily able to follow the track of Sophie's experience to her nightmare encounter on the platform either. One index to the difficulty the narrator has in assimilating the knowledge that Sophie represents is the manner of the telling of Sophie's tale, which is as circuitous in its own way as the telling of <u>Absalom! Absalom!</u> To an extent, the narrative technique dramatizes not just Stingo's repeated failures to comprehend, but the older narrator's cautious approach toward the death camps. Aspects of her past, or aspects of what is known of Auschwitz, are worried at length, as if no context could be large enough to encompass and no background sufficient to explain the impending revelation. Typically, key information is offered up piecemeal, in fragments which have to be assembled by the reader, or as generalization separate from context or details. Events and information come jumbled together in baffling counterpoint, sometimes juxtaposed as if to comment on one another, and at other times seemingly to retard the action, as if to postpone the platform encounter.

The gradual unfolding of Sophie's past is structured around a number of moments of revelation which require revisions of Stingo's previous estimates of her. These moments function as mileposts in the narrative's approach toward the secret of her life. The need for continual revision is partly a result of Sophie's reticence about things and partly of her active duplicity. She lies about her unhappy marriage and her relationship with her father, fabricating a parent who is a kindly paragon of virtue and learning, rather than a fanatical anti-Semite who had imagined and passionately advocated for others the kind of fate which overwhelms his daughter and grandchildren (237ff.). She suppresses her wartime experiences in Warsaw and the fact that she had a son at Auschwitz (345) and a daughter also (368). Last of all, the revelation that she was forced to choose between them (484-87) comes only slowly, after many evasions, so that each revelation forces Stingo to construct a new interpretation of her past and therefore of her "present" character and situation. Also absent from early accounts of her past is the "fact" that, in the moral quagmire that was Auschwitz, Sophie was not simply a victim of the Nazis, but, in a complex and extremely tenuous way, an accomplice.

But the need for revision is also partly a result of the strangeness and enormity of what is to be understood. Preoccupied by his own sexual enterprises and blinded by his infatuation with her, Stingo is obviously not very astute in his reading of Sophie. He is taken in by her evasions and fails to comprehend her real needs for assistance. For example, after his comically disastrous attempts with Leslie and Alice, Stingo has his longed-for sexual encounter with Sophie, but the act is a grim parody of intimacy, and it fails to effect the magical changes in himself that he had hoped for. In fact, the loss of his "virginity" is largely ancillary to his education, and it certainly does nothing for his powers of observation. Stingo fails to realize that, for Sophie, the experience is merely a brief anodyne for her pain, which is intense enough to make death desirable. Stingo, the aspiring novelist, is not astute enough to recognize how little his offer of a Southern pastoral retreat, complete with matrimony and an on-looking Protestant community, could appeal to Sophie in these circumstances. He also fails utterly to grasp the dual roles Nathan has played in her life as healing savior and the pursuing demon of her conscience. By presenting himself in the role of yet another male savior, Stingo shows himself insensitive to the elements of her life of struggle for independence of male domination. Finally, he is oblivious to her dread of having more children. His catalog of missed signals is great enough to suggest that another, less tragic outcome might have been possible, had he truly known Sophie.

Stingo misunderstands Nathan as thoroughly as he does Sophie, oscillating until nearly the end between admiration and loathing of this older, mysterious figure. In one typical revelation, Sophie confides to Stingo that Nathan was addicted to drugs. "How blind I had been!" Stingo exclaims, in the throes of a complete reinterpretation of Nathan's past behavior (311-12). For a time, Nathan's demon acquires a specific shape and rationale in Stingo's mind, only to be expunged as an explanation by Larry Landau's further revelation of Nathan's madness a hundred pages later. But these failures of Stingo to comprehend critical issues throughout the narrative are not merely illustrative of his flaws of character.(11) They dramatize the elusiveness of the understanding he seeks. And because the mature narrator does not share with the reader the benefits of his own hindsight, but withholds information and silently encourages false or incomplete appraisals, the reader is left equally at sea--therefore sharing with Stingo multiple experiences of disquieting misapprehension, revision, and reinterpretation. This technique involves the reader intimately in Stingo's experiences, in Stingo's "voyage of discovery." By such means, as we shall see, the narrative encourages in the reader a sense of involved discovery which is closely akin emotionally to actual experience. Drawing the reader into constructing the text also has the function of bringing into consciousness the provisional nature of the kind of knowledge at issue: the "truth" is invariably grimmer and more complex than the reader's first estimates of it. At the same time, the center of attention in the novel is subtly shifted from the events themselves to the process of interpreting experience as text and to the writer's act of reconstituting experience in the text. Thus, the technique also illustrates the arbitrary nature of the discourse in which knowledge is ordinarily framed.

III

Larry Landau's disclosure, "the truth is that my brother's quite mad," is one of the most significant expectation-shattering revelations in the novel (424). Like the revelation of Darl's insanity in <u>As I Lay Dying</u>, it has the effect of dramatically overturning the reader's previous estimates and forcing a fundamentally different reconstruction of the narrative. The revelation about Nathan's clinical history of insanity demolishes the most fundamental interpretive paradigm of the narrative as the reader had been led to conceive it--the novel as essay on the nature of evil. Nathan's violent abuse of Sophie has had the function throughout most of the narrative of embodying the principle of evil that has deformed Sophie's life and prospects. As Sophie's torturer in the New World, Nathan is presented, seemingly, as a "mirror" or extension of Auschwitz.(12) By bringing atrocity on a mass industrial basis down to a recognizable human scale, Nathan had also served as one of the means by which the reader is empowered to imagine the larger "absolute evil" of the camps. Consequently, Dr. Landau's description of his brother Nathan's diagnosis-- "Paranoid schizophrenic, or so the diagnosis goes, although I'm not atall sure if those brain specialists really know what they're up to"--is a transforming event which wrenches the frame of reference onto an entirely different plane. The terms of explanation shift: "insanity" is suddenly substituted for "evil"; the language of morality is replaced by a discourse which is secular and scientific.

The discovery of the cause of Nathan's behavior--or rather, this definition of it--forces us to revise our understanding of the relationship between Sophie and Nathan and its role in Sophie's impending doom. Having been invited by the narrative to construct an indictment of Nathan as brute and torturer, the reader finds this indictment suddenly quashed. It is no longer clear, given this revelation, whether Nathan functions as a moral extension of the camps--or whether the camps, too, represent a manifestation of collective madness (an idea which is hinted at once, in a thought attributed to Nathan on page 323). The "fact" of Nathan's madness therefore leaves the reader unhooked from any certain set of terms or interpretive frame and unsure of how to judge what has happened. Schizophrenia, that mysterious and tragic ailment, is an acid capable of dissolving even complex moral judgments--thus denying us the moral judgment of Nathan which we had been permitted to make and robbing us of the precious sense of comprehension that condemnation of Nathan had provided.

The operative definition of evil--the version of it which presents itself as an issue in the text--is domination: evil consists of exalting either self or some abstract value into the supreme or sole value and reducing all else, including others, to instruments. In the autobiographical treatment of Commandant Hoss, for example, "real evil" appears as a kind of twisted piety, joined with an egotism which directs all natural pity away from one's victims and toward one's self (151-54). Simone Weil and Hannah Arendt are quoted on the "true nature of evil," which is allegedly "gloomy, monotonous, and boring" (148-49). Whether boring or flamboyant, evil appears to consist of one human being's ruthless use of another, with the Nazi concentration camps, with their total and utterly uninhibited domination of human beings, illustrating evil in its ultimate or "absolute" form (235-36). This definition allows the narrator to place American slavery, Professor Bieganski's treatment of Sophie, and Nathan's behavior as her lover in a moral continuum.

The paradigm of evil demands, as terms of discourse, some axiomatic concept of value (e.g., human life), a perversion or privation of that value, along with the concept of choice. The paradigm of mental illness, on the other hand, implies a determinative chain of causes and effects operating uniformly in a physiological system. In the latter kind of discourse, value and choice can scarcely enter into the operations of "indifferent nature"; thus, any supposed agency responsible for "evil" recedes into the recesses and obscure chemical transactions of Nathan's brain.

By a kind of Faulknerian irony, almost immediately after the revelation of Nathan's insanity, Nathan finally succeeds in seducing Sophie into suicide. Or at least they both die. Like Cash Bundren witnessing his brother Darl trussed up and carted off to Jackson, the reader is forced to confront the tenuousness of the connections between our language and the world which it organizes for us--particularly the arbitrariness of our collective definitions of "sane" and "insane," and of the terms of discourse which they evoke. Denied the explanation of evil, the reader must grope for some alternative interpretive map, for a language past the "sanity and insanity" of human doings but adequate to our "horror and astonishment" at both.(13) Thus, this "epiphany" does not so much enlighten us as bring us up short against the limitations of our perceptual templates and the poverty of our explanations. This encounter with a paradigm-shattering event is especially significant in a narrative which identifies Auschwitz as a kind of ultimate object of knowledge, because it appears to problematize the narrator's meditations on the nature of the "evil" which Auschwitz represents in so ghastly a form.

IV

By these means, the question, what can be known of Auschwitz? is transformed by the novel into a kind of megaquestion: what is the form of such knowledge? What can be said about Auschwitz as an object of knowledge which is uniquely the province of fiction? And what does conventional discourse about evil tell us about how we make sense and meaning out of experience? These highly abstract issues are set loose by the narrative precisely at the point that the reader is most baffled about the immediate, tangible, and quite unabstract issue of Nathan's role in Sophie's fate.

As we have seen, one part of Styron's strategy of conveying the incredibly ugly reality of Auschwitz as it "really" was(14) is to set before us the excruciating experience of a survivor, realized dramatically through her memories and through the effects of that experience on her subsequent life. Another strategy involves a thorough appropriation of the abstract, scholarly overviews of what happened, to show what Auschwitz means by exploring the sense others have made of it. In the service of that aim, the narrator summons up an impressive array of the scholarship, commentary, and eye-witness accounts of the Holocaust, including Bruno Bettelheim, Elie Wiesel, and George Steiner. The works of Simone Weil and Hannah Arendt are consulted on the nature of totalitarian societies, the banality of evil, and the psychology of mass murderers. The autobiographical statements of Auschwitz Commandant Hoss are even quoted at length. The most curious and unexpected source of ideas in the book is probably Wilhelm Reich, whose theories about the relation between sexual and political repression pervade the narrative and provide an intellectual framework linking Sophie's childhood under the sway of her tyrannical Polish Catholic father, her experience at Auschwitz, and her suffering under the domination of her periodically insane lover.(15)

This material is employed in tension-breaking digressions and speculative meditations by the mature narrator as he closes in, slowly and reluctantly, on the sources of Sophie's pain. At one level, this assembled erudition is highly satisfying; it speaks to what we usually mean by understanding. As Philip W. Leon has pointed out, Styron's narratives convey ideas.(16) And it is obvious that the narrative of Sophie's Choice presents, in its smallest as well as largest details, a carefully worked out and complex view of the nature and meaning of Auschwitz. Sophie's Choice dramatizes not just the historically established verities about Auschwitz, but the threat it poses for the future by incorporating the conclusions of one of the most searching of recent scholarly meditations on the meaning of the Holocaust--Richard Rubenstein's The Cunning of History: The Holocaust and the American Future.(17) Both Styron and Rubenstein reject an eschatological reading of the camps and place them in an essentially secular context, as an example of genocide rather than as a holocaust (in the primary meaning of the word, a burnt offering, and hence, by extension, a pagan sacrifice and therefore an event in an ongoing sacred history). To view the camps in terms of human rather than Divine history means that the horrifying events enacted in them touch upon the mystery of human nature rather than the mystery of God's will. One of the paradoxes of a theocentric view of the camps is that the calculated destruction of the Jews is, in a sense, a ratification of the Jews' special status as the Chosen People,(18) just as it ratifies the status of the Gentiles as people appropriately left outside the covenant. It is that sense of moral vindication through persecution which presumably renders such a heritage of suffering "precious" (a view explicitly rejected in the novel on page 473). Even while acknowledging that the Jews were the chief targets of this instance of "genocidal fury," Styron and Rubenstein see the Holocaust as a general conflagration, the flames of which continue to threaten humankind in general. "Anti-Semitism," Styron has asserted, "is not the sole touchstone" by which to examine the phenomenon of the death camps; rather, in their ultimate depravity, they were anti-human. Anti-life."(19)

Furthermore, according to Rubenstein, the death camps were neither a unique event--a claim implicit in some theocentric views--nor were they contrary to or a denial of the essential features of the Judeo-Christian tradition. These horrors were, rather, a full flowering and expression of central tendencies in that tradition and civilization: "we are more likely to understand the Holocaust if we regard it as the expression of some of the most profound tendencies in Western civilization in the twentieth century" (21). Auschwitz, in this view, represented not just a place of execution but a "new form of human society," a "society of total domination," and an ultimate form of slavery uninhibited by taboos about the value of human life (46). Rubenstein extends the observations of Max Weber earlier in the century concerning the tendency of modern Western culture to "rationalize" more and more of its experience, to remove more and more areas of activity from the inhibitions of custom, taboo or religious scruple, while at the same time developing both the techniques and an impersonal, rational, and amoral ethos of bureaucracy. By the Second World War, this "all-conquering rationality" had acquired an enormous momentum in precisely the most "civilized" of the Western nations. Rubenstein argues (again drawing on Weber's insights), this outcome is itself the legacy of Judeo-Christian civilization. The Nazis' program of industrialized slaughter, he concludes, is therefore an extreme, but probably repeatable, expression of that cultural legacy. The camps were thus far more of a "permanent threat to the human future than they would have been had they functioned solely as an exercise in mass killing" (79).

These views find expression in the narrative of Sophie's Choice in ways too obvious to require much illustration: in the choice of Sophie as protagonist, in the narrator's comparison of the camps with American slavery and with sexism, and through such minor characters as Sophie's friend Wanda and the I.G. Farben executive, Walter Durrfeld. Through these means, Sophie's experience at Auschwitz dramatizes a generalized threat of dehumanization and destruction which is aimed, potentially at least, at the reader. But this reading of the past also involves the reader as potential perpetrator as well as victim. Such an indictment is implicit in Rubenstein's disturbing assertion that the camps were manifestations of the basic religious traditions of the West, not departures from them. The Nazi ideology of a master race, he suggests, is a caricature of the Biblical concept of the Chosen People and also represents a recurring tendency in Western culture--what he calls that "night side" of the Judeo-Christian religious heritage. "What makes the problem so serious is that there is no escape from [this] . . . ethos of exclusivism and intolerance . . . as long as our fundamental culture is derived from a religious tradition that insists upon the dichotomous division of mankind into the elect and the reprobate" (93). To divide mankind with its infinite shades of gray into sharp categories of black and white is, to Rubenstein, a basic feature of "the illness we call Judeo-Christian civilization." It follows, then, that the forms of perception common in our culture--particularly our assumptions about the nature of good and evil--are critical to understanding the historical and moral significance of genocide and the lethal potential in Western culture to repeat it.

Rubenstein's book, then, profoundly affects the manner of the telling of Sophie's Choice as well as its content.(20)   While Styron has been attacked in some quarters for emphasizing the humanity of the mass killers, it is, following this de-mythologizing and non-demonized view of the Holocaust, precisely in the human qualities of the organizers of geno- cide that the mystery of Auschwitz lies. Moreover, rather than presenting the "absolute evil" of Auschwitz in rigidly dichotomous terms, the narrative continually presses (to borrow the language of one of the novel's epigraphs, from Malraux) toward "that essential region of the soul where absolute evil confronts brotherhood." It is a feature of the narrative to suggest, paradoxically, by means of the language in which it is constitut- ed, the original, undifferentiated, seamless flow of experience prior to conceptualization in language. Similarly, the narrative approaches the subject of Auschwitz through a consideration of the nature of evil, but at the same time subjects that very consideration to an acid bath of irony. One of the points Rubenstein makes about apparent extremes actually residing and coexisting within a complex whole may offer a clue to Styron's narrative technique: "It is an error to imagine that civilization and savage cruelty are antitheses. On the contrary, in every organic process, the antitheses always reflect a unified totality, and civilization is an organic process" (92). To dramatize the whole, to express the unified totality of any complex situation or concept, the writer must present the extremes, the antitheses--"Die Schizophrenie," if you will--which are in fact encompassed within it. Antitheses, apparent incompatibles, are, in a sense, a projection of the observation; they emerge almost as by-products of meaning-endowing acts of interpretation.

It follows, then, that "schizophrenia" is not merely the unsettling diagnosis of Nathan Landau, but a motif implanted in the narrative, like a jarring fragment of discord in a musical composition or a recurring pattern of shadow in a painting. Stingo puzzles over the "centuries-long, all-encompassing nightmare spells of schizophrenia" in the histories of both Poland and the South, where the "abiding presence of race has created at the same instant cruelty and compassion, bigotry and understanding, enmity and fellowship, exploitation and sacrifice, searing hatred and hopeless love" (247). We observe Sophie struggling with a "schizoid conscience" a page later (248); we learn that Hans Frank, governor-general of occupied Poland and a key figure in the destruction of Poland's Jews, was himself a Jew (249); we overhear Commandant Hoss and Walter Durrfeld, the I.G. Farben executive in charge of slave labor, discussing the inconsistencies in Nazi policy concerning the use or disposal of undesirables. One ministry desires them for slave labor; another snatches them away for "special action":

> "The result is a split--completely down the middle.
> A split--You know . . . what is the word I mean? That
> strange word, that psychological expression meaning--"
> "Die Schizophrenie."
> "Yes, that's the word," Hoss replied. "That mind
> doctor in Vienna, his name escapes." (406)

Throughout the book, we see a pattern of schizophrenic doubleness and contradiction: Nathan's worst psychotic depressions flow out of exuberant "highs"; his insane accusations of Sophie proceed out of quite sane questions; Sophie's vitality is nearly always juxtaposed against premonitions of her death. Extremes meet, perversely, everywhere, in the narrative. In fact, the whole of Nathan's and Sophie's relationship exemplifies this kind of split or doubleness, in its simultaneous fusion of devotion and cruelty, healing and rending, eros and thanatos. Nearly everything in the narrative presents itself in terms of a contradictory or paradoxical doubleness; Sophie, we recall, is both victim and accomplice, Nathan both savior and golem; Hoss, who as commandant at Auschwitz, retains, even there, some absurd fragments of bureaucratic scruple: "Do you think," he asks Sophie, "[that] I am some kind of monster?" (287). The blasphemy contained in Sophie's suicide note (499-500) is a revelation not just of the vehemence with which she has rejected her childhood faith, but evidence of how much of it she has retained.

Even Stingo's vocation as a writer is subjected to this corrosive irony: the disparity between Stingo's ideal of authorship as a high calling and his "ghoulish opportunism" is apparent from the beginning. His early acquaintance with Sophie coincides with his discovery of the subject of his youthful novel, the suicide of Maria Hunt. His developing friendship with Sophie and Nathan stimulates him to pursue a subject that involves a number of parallels with Sophie's situation, including a tangle of "unresolved guilt and hatred" (44) and the tragic death of a beautiful young woman. Sophie, who possesses a "distant but real resemblance to Maria Hunt," provides not only a "lovely simulacrum of the dead girl" but an image of the "despair . . . worn as Maria surely must have worn it, along with the premonitory, grieving shadows of someone hurtling headlong toward death" (46). To Stingo, Maria's death seems "perfectly marvelous, a gift from the sky," while Sophie's pain provides a convenient gloss on Maria's: "<u>scratch scratch</u> went the virginal Venus Velvet" (110).

> "Consider, Sophie love," Nathan says at another point, consider
> how intimately life and death are intertwined in Nature, which
> contains everywhere the seeds of our beatitude and our
> dissolution. This, for instance, HCN, is spread throughout
> Mother Nature in smothering abundance in the form of
> glycosides, which is to say, combined with sugars. Sweet,
> sweet sugar. In bitter almonds, in certain species of these
> autumn leaves, in the common pear, the arbutus. Imagine,
> then, when those perfect white porcelain teeth of yours bite
> down upon the delectable macaroon the taste you experience
> is only a molecule's organic distance removed from that of
> this [cyanide capsule]. . . . (332)

In this world spun cunningly out of the novelist's language, opposites intermingle, surprise lurks in the nature of things, death in the midst of life, like the "choking core of a sweet apple."

One such moment of extreme paradox occurs in the scene of Sophie's choice on the platform at Auschwitz. The scene as presented is a fiction within a fiction, the narrator's extension of what his younger self had heard and been unable to comprehend. Upon Sophie's account, upon the "facts" of the case, the narrator has constructed a wholly conjectural account of the motives and state of mind of the Nazi doctor(21). The narrator gives the man a name--Dr. Fritz Jemand von Niemand--and endows him with a past and aspirations for the ministry which were frustrated by a domineering father. Serving the Nazis, he "had to replace God with a sense of the omnipotence" of the business and the state for which he worked. But the caprice (or schizophrenia) of Nazi policy, which periodically forced him out on the platform to make "selections," or alternately spared him this "duty," had begun to destroy him:

> The renewed horror scraped like steel files at the doctor's
> soul, threatened to shred his reason. He began to drink, to
> acquire sloppy eating habits, and to miss God. <u>Wo, wo ist her
> lebende Gott</u>? Where is the God of my fathers? (486)

At some point, the hypothetical Dr. Jemand von Niemand realizes that the absence of a sense of sin about what he is doing is connected with his sense of the absence of God in his life:

> No sin! He had suffered boredom and anxiety, and even
> revulsion, but no sense of sin from the bestial crimes he had
> been party to, nor had he felt that in sending thousands of
> the wretched innocent to oblivion had he transgressed against
> divine law. All had been unutterable monotony. All of his
> depravity had been enacted in a vacuum of sinless and
> businesslike godlessness, while his soul thirsted for beatitude.
> Was it not supremely simple, then, to restore his belief in

God, and at the same time to affirm his human capacity for
evil, by committing the most intolerable sin that he was
able to conceive? Goodness could come later. But first a
great sin. (486-87)

This fictional extension of Sophie's account of what happened to her
not only gives the epitome of "absolute evil" a human face, but joins the
motif of "die Schizophrenie" to the novel's consideration of evil. "I have
always assumed," the narrator tells us, that when he encountered Sophie,
Dr. Jemand von Niemand was undergoing the crisis of his life: cracking
apart like bamboo, disintegrating at the very moment that he was reaching
out for spiritual salvation" (485; emphasis added). The doctor's atrocity,
then, is inextricably bound up with his conception of good, and his act of
ultimate evil is presented as born of an impulse toward the good. In its
very doubleness, this definition of the encounter on the platform connects
"ultimate evil" with the other, smaller acts of evil in the book; it joins it
to the familiar without making it less mysterious--or less repugnant.
Moreover, it displaces the mystery of evil from Auschwitz to the reader,
who could be "anyone from anywhere."

The motif of schizophrenia, then, is a way of dramatizing tendencies in
the way we perceive the nature of things. We organize our experience, the
novel suggests, in "dichotomous divisions"; we convert the spectrum of
actual experience into extremes of black and white; we write our personal
histories and we dress our historical experience in the clumsy, ill-fitting
garments of morality plays. We slaughter each other in the name of our
highest moral values. In a sense, the values create the slaughter, but
without ceasing to be values.

Consequently, the novel's definition of evil, like the young Dr. Jemand
von Niemand, disintegrates precisely at the moment it finds absolute
expression. Evil appears most elusive, most baffling in nature, in the very
language which sets it before us in its most palpable form. Furthermore,
the mystery of evil is inextricably linked in the narrative with the even
murkier issue of guilt. The novel dramatizes, most notably with Sophie,
the pitiless tenacity with which individuals hold themselves accountable--
even knowing, as Sophie does, that her guilt is a consequence of how she
was treated at Auschwitz, not of what she has done: "This guilt is
something I cannot get rid of. . . . And because I never get rid of it,
maybe that's the worst thing the Germans left me with" (286). Styron
quotes Simone Weil's astute observation about the effects of great
suffering: "Affliction stamps the soul to its very depth with the scorn, the
disgust and even the self-hatred and sense of guilt that crime logically
should produce but actually never does" (147).

To the mystery of iniquity and the phenomenon of guilt, often
irrationally founded, Styron adds the concept of "collective guilt."
Together the three issues--evil, guilt, collective guilt--form links in an
endless circular argument that mocks the usual sense we make of things.

The concept of collective guilt is succinctly expressed in George Steiner's assertion: "Treblinka is both because some men have built it and almost all other men let it be" (quoted on 216). By this familiar formulation, "almost all the men" share the responsibility for the genocidal acts of the Nazis Sophie overhears a friend of Nathan's express a logical extension of the concept: "It is the German people who should themselves be executed--they who allowed these men to rule them and kill Jews" (328). The Poles, in his view, are hardly less guilty--a charge that the daughter of Professor Bieganski feels incapable of refuting. Nathan shares the extreme view of collective guilt and, in moments of paranoia, holds Sophie responsible for the crimes of the Holocaust. Unfortunately for Sophie, Nathan's raging accusations objectify her own unrelenting inner voice, which torments her beyond the capacities of her most sadistic oppressors--thus making her again, though in a sense that defies analysis, an "accomplice" of the Nazis. However, perhaps to prevent us from absolving her completely from guilt, we learn in the account of Sophie's past not only of the anti-Semitic cultural environment in which she was raised but of her own insensitivity to Jews and to the climate growing around them: "They simply did not concern her" (341). While she does not share her father's extreme views, her indifference could be construed, following Steiner's formula, as consent. The problem with such an argument is that it engages in a crude group stereotyping which is little different from the anti-Semitism of the Nazis.

Nathan also periodically charges Stingo, as a white Southerner, with complicity in the racial oppression in the South, holding him responsible for the grotesque death of Bobby Weed and the political career of Mississippi's Senator Bilbo. In spite of the ludicrousness of the specific charges, the comparisons drawn between the two environments of racial hostility, Poland and America, are uncomfortably apt. If we are to believe Stingo (who is being supported in Brooklyn on the proceeds of the sale of a family slave named Artiste), history--or mere distance in time-- effectively absolves one of complicity in evil. If we are to believe Sophie, however, one is absolved by nothing.

What saving knowledge, then, can be wrested from experience in such a world? The Stingo who emerges from his grave of sand on the beach that morning after the funeral of Nathan and Sophie is chastened and subdued at the same time he is cleansed and exalted. By some strange compensatory economy in the nature of things, his loss is a gain, somehow energizing his career as a writer. If the deaths of Sophie and Nathan and his own symbolic death constitute Stingo's rite of passage, the cost would seem incommensurate with any imaginable gain. But by a logic now familiar in the novel, the triumph of life would necessarily be intimately conjoined to death, as joy is to pain. Such success is doubly ironic in that one of the chief pieces of knowledge that Stingo has acquired is an awareness of evil in himself--including his monumental self-centeredness and his capacity to use others as instruments. Ultimately, then, rather than providing a definition of the most spectacular historical manifestation of evil, the narrative demonstrates what Styron has called the "ecumenical nature" of evil(22) and its omnipresence in human experience. In effect, rather than resolving the mystery of the veil which Auschwitz represents, the narrative displaces the mystery from its form as monstrous other to the familiar and near, and from external world to self.

In spite of the book's implicit claims advanced early in the narrative, Sophie's Choice has not, by the ending, truly "dealt" with Auschwitz. On the other hand, by not dealing with it (in the sense of resolving or putting to rest the issues it presents), the narrative has forced the reader to encounter Auschwitz imaginatively on many levels--even to consider in self-reflective ways the manner by which we conceptualize Auschwitz. Sophie's encounter--and the mature narrator's re-encounter--with the seamlessness of experience, with the nature of things beyond our language for it, paradoxically affirms the need for speech, for coherence and meaning, and therefore for art, at the same time that it demarks their limitations and acknowledges their frailty. The subtle changes dramatized in the mature narrator represent a recognition of those limits. Early in the book, the authorial voice had ventured to assert: "I have thought that it might be possible to make a stab at understanding Auschwitz by trying to understand Sophie" (219). The humbler speaker at the end of the book has abandoned such ambitions: "Someday I will understand Auschwitz. That was a brave statement but innocently absurd. No one will ever understand Auschwitz. What I might have said with more accuracy would have been: Someday I will write about Sophie's life and death, and thereby demonstrate how absolute evil is never extinguished from the world. Auschwitz itself remains inexplicable" (513).

Notes

(1) George Steiner warns those who would study the Holocaust that it is not clear "that those who were not themselves fully involved should touch upon those agonies unscathed." Quoted on p. 218, Sophie's Choice (New York: Random House, 1979). (Subsequent references to Styron's novel will be indicated by page number in the body of the text.) George Steiner also quotes Elie Wiesel's admission, "I who was there still do not understand."--in "Postscript," Language and Silence: Essays on Language, Literature, and the Inhuman (New York: Athenaum, 1967), p. 167.

(2) Steiner, pp. 156-57.

(3) William Styron, in "Why I Wrote Sophie's Choice," interview with Michel Braudeau (1981); rpt. in Conversations with William Styron, ed. James L.W. West, III (Jackson and London: University Press of Mississippi, 1985), p. 252.

(4) William Styron, "The Message of Auschwitz," rpt. in <u>Critical Essays on William Styron</u>, ed. Arthur D. Casciato and James L.W. West, III (Boston: G.K. Hall, 1982), p. 285.

(5) Elie Wiesel, "Does the Holocaust Lie Beyond the Reach of Art?" <u>New York Times</u>, 17 April 1983.

(6) Steiner's and Wiesel's remarks are quoted at length in the novel; see especially pp. 215-18.

(7) "William Styron: The Confessions of a Southern Writer," interview with Georgiann Eubanks (1984), rpt. in <u>Conversations</u>, p. 275.

(8) See, for example, "Why I Wrote <u>Sophie's Choice</u>," in <u>Conversations</u>, p. 246.

(9) Interview with Stephen Lewis (1983), rpt. in <u>Conversations</u>, p. 258.

(10) See Styron's comments about the narrative technique in "Creators on Creating: William Styron"--an interview with Hilary Mills (1980); rpt. in <u>Conversations</u>, p. 236.

(11) As Benjamin DeMott has perceptively remarked, the "portrait of Stingo . . . shows the lameness of our own incomprehension." In "Styron's Survivor: An Honest Witness," rpt. in <u>Critical Essays on William Styron</u>, p. 261.

(12) See Styron's comments in "William Styron," an interview with Stephen Lewis (1983); rpt. in <u>Conversations</u>, p. 263.

(13) According to Benjamin DeMott, one of Styron's insights as a novelist of the Holocaust "is that the task of searching for a language not wholly incommensurate to the [genocidal] slaughter . . . can never be finished." In "Styron's Survivor," p. 261.

(14) See Styron's comments on the novel's ability to deal with historical reality in "The Uses of History in Fiction" (1968) [with] Ralph Ellison, William Styron, Robert Penn Warren, and C. Vann Woodward, rpt. in <u>Conversations</u>, p. 132.

(15) Styron appears to have made serious use of Wilhelm Reich's exploration of the relation of sexuality and power or sexuality and political oppression, as well as satiric use of his reputation for quackery.

(16) "Styron's Fiction: Narrative as Idea," in <u>The Achievement of William Styron</u>, pp. 124-46.

(17) Richard Rubenstein, <u>The Cunning of History: The Holocaust and the American Future</u> (New York: Harper and Row, 1975). Subsequent references to Rubenstein appear in the body of the text.

(18) See, for example, George Steiner's reading of God's will in the events of the Holocaust in "A Kind of Survivor," in <u>Language and Silence</u>, p. 142.

(19) Styron, "The Message of Auschwitz," pp. 285-86.

(20) G.A.M. Janssens has noted that Rubenstein's book stands in the same relation to <u>Sophie's Choice</u> as Stanley Elkins' <u>Slavery</u> does to <u>The Confessions of Nat Turner</u>." In "Styron's Case and Sophie's Choice"

(1980), rpt. in <u>Critical Essays,</u> p. 277. See also Styron's introduction to the 1978 edition of Rubenstein's <u>The Cunning of History,</u> p. vii.

(21) Richard Pearce has commented that "it is important to realized that Jemand von Niemand is Stingo's creation and fulfills Stingo's needs." In "Sophie's Choices," <u>Achievement,</u> p. 294.

(22) See William Styron, "The Message of Auschwitz," p. 286.

*From <u>Southern Literary Journal</u> 23 (1990): 45-64.   Reprinted by permission.

DARKNESS VISIBLE: A MEMOIR OF MADNESS

SURMOUNTING THE INTOLERABLE: RECONSTRUCTING LOSS IN SOPHIE'S CHOICE, "A TIDEWATER MORNING," AND DARKNESS VISIBLE*

Thornton F. Jordan

From Lie Down in Darkness to Darkness Visible Styron's writing has borne the "steady, honest grace" he so admired in James Jones ("James Jones" 270). No wonder that Styron's lucid, courageous reflections on the murky terrain of depression have been so well-received. For the surprising number of readers who have suffered prolonged depression, Styron has clarified their experience; for those who have not, he has persuaded them to regard depression in a more sympathetic light.

But writing for Styron is more than an achievement in honesty and grace. As we can see once again from Darkness Visible, writing is, and has been, a form of behavior which stands between Styron and despair. Writing well is Styron's very act of mental health.

Even as he prepared for suicide, he "felt obsessed with a necessity to compose . . . the most difficult task of writing [he] had ever tackled"--his suicide note (Darkness Visible 65). In spite of his dangerous, numbed detachment from all his other actions, characteristically his critical standards as a writer were intact as he "wished to infuse his testament with at least some dignity and eloquence" (65), which he fortunately found himself unable to achieve. Instead, he judged his intended last words as offensively pompous. I say fortunately because, in part, not being able to write a satisfactory suicide note saved Styron's life. According to the logic of his account, suicide would have followed from having written his last words well. What he did write was not an ending he could accept. Instead, it was "an exhausted stutter of inadequate apologies and self-serving explanations" (65).

Having failed to write his own ending with dignity and eloquence, he resolved to go out in silence. But as Michael Kreyling observes in "Speakable and Unspeakable in Styron's Sophie's Choice," Styron's commitment in his works all along has been to "deny the unspeakable any ground" (548), to invade silence as a blight on the human community. In effect, in Styron's larger ethos, silence is suicide. Fortunately, at some instinctive level, even on the brink of self-annihilation, Styron had more to say.

Many of Styron's works, of course, have brought forward a story long embedded either in the silence of history, like Nat Turner's, or in one's private life, like Peyton Loftis's, or Sophie's, or Paul Whitehurst's, or Styron's itself. The issue of wresting from silence a character's story or an episode from the writer's life is complicated by the long intervals during which the story is borne by Styron's narrators. Not only is the story wrested from silence, but once it is inherited, or imagined, or suffered, Styron's narrators characteristically carry the stories themselves for long years in silence and retrospection before finally feeling compelled to tell them. Stingo bears Sophie's story for 25 years, for instance. In "A Tidewater Morning," the 13-year-old narrator, Paul Whitehurst, reconstructs the story of his feelings over the death of his mother only after 30 years have passed. And only near the very end of Darkness Visible does the 64-year-old Styron cite his unresolved grief, anger, and guilt over the death of his mother 51 years earlier when he was 13 as the most probable root of his long-suffered depression.

At the end of Darkness Visible, Styron speculates that self-destructive conduct may be "a strategy through which the person involved comes to grips with his guilt and rage, and triumphs over self-willed death. Such reconciliation may be entwined with the quest for immortality"--for a writer, "to vanquish death through work honored by posterity" (80-81). Beyond the unacceptable suicide note, and beyond the unacceptable choice of going out in silence was, of course, Darkness Visible, surely a work to be honored by posterity. In time, out of the experience of depression which almost overwhelmed him and rendered him inarticulate Styron rose to write about depression, which he has now so clearly and eloquently illuminated for a nation of readers. Returning from silence to language, through his gifted style he has reconstructed his experience, universalized it, and regained perspective in terms suitable to his own critical standards.

It is this issue of perspective that draws my attention to Sophie's Choice (1979), "A Tidewater Morning" (1987), and Darkness Visible (1990). In Darkness Visible, beyond genetic predisposition for depression and his struggles with Halcion and alcohol, Styron concludes that an "even more significant factor was the death of my mother when I was thirteen; this disorder and early sorrow" (79), and that in his self-destructive behavior he was "subconsciously dealing with the immense loss while trying to surmount all the effects of the devastation" (81). Though Styron cites this loss as significant only near the end of <u>Darkness Visible</u>, he had previously reconstructed the story twice before in his fiction, though with differing content and to different ends.

To say that such differences merely amount to different perspectives on a single, historical event, though, would be inaccurate. Samuel Novey, in <u>The Second Look: A Reconstruction of Personal History in Psychiatry and Psychoanalysis,</u> argues that all personal history is a combination of actual events and a reconstruction of past events to serve present needs. "What is commonly described as an historical event is composed of the actual happening and assumptions about the meaning of the happening" (42). As a person recreates his historical episodes, in "describing significant persons in his life, he is describing not only them but also attitudes toward himself and projections of his own inner life as well" (6). Since present experiences modify our reconstructions of the past, one can regard such reconstructions as symbolic. Novey cites Carl Becker: "It is dangerous to say . . . that it is true or false. The safest thing to say about a symbol is that it is more or less appropriate" (23). To judge appropriateness, one needs to consider the content, manner, occasion, and ends of the reconstruction.

In <u>Sophie's Choice</u> Stingo's memory of the death of his mother is filled with self-recrimination followed by a resentful dismissal of guilt. As she was dying of cancer, restricted to the house by feebleness and a metal leg brace, his job was to hurry home from school each day to stoke the fire. But one winter afternoon, invited to ride in a friend's new Packard, he was "lured away . . . mad for that car, . . . drunk with its vulgar elegance" and filled with "idiot vainglory." Suddenly, "sick with alarm," he felt: "I abandoned her" (296). Stingo rushed home two hours late to attend to his mother, whom his father had found shivering helplessly, "her lips bitter and livid." The room was filled with smoke where she had tried to shove wood into the fireplace with her cane.

As he recreates the scene in memory, Stingo escalates his guilt: "God knows what Eskimo ice-floe visions had engulfed her when she sank back amid her best sellers . . . with which she had tried to barricade herself against death" (297). He remembers that when he burst into the room, she looked at him then turned away swiftly, and he judges that it was "the swiftness of that turning away which would thereafter define my guilt." His guilt, even ten years later, is "ineffaceable" (296). In fact, he has been tormented by a recurrent dream of his mother in her garden in an open coffin, "her rain-damp ravaged face gazing at me in agony" (462). But guilt here is not merely self-recrimination for selfishness and neglect. It is anger deflected inward, since "I realized with horror how much I resented her burdensome affliction." At the end of the scene, both Stingo and his mother wept, "but separately, and we listened to each other's weeping as if across a wide and desolate lake" (297).

Even though his father punished him by leaving him a cold woodshed for several hours--a punishment Stingo found entirely appropriate--he still feels that "[his] crime was beyond expiation" (297). Seven months later, in a sweltering July, "she died a disgusting death, in a transport of pain, . . . while all the night before, I pondered over and over those feeble embers in the cold smoky room and speculated with dread on the notion that my abandonment that day had sent her into the long decline from which she never recovered. Guilt. Hateful guilt. Guilt, corrosive as brine. . . .[G]rief drove like a spear of ice through my chest when I recaptured the fright in my mother's eyes, wondered once again if that ordeal had not somehow hastened her dying, wondered if she ever forgave me. Fuck it, I thought" (297-298).

Stingo's memory of this scene ten years after the event is part fact, part second-hand information, part a double reconstruction. His mother's "bitter lips" Stingo did not hear from first-hand in the scene; they were only so characterized to him by his father. The reconstruction by Stingo in his 20s, ten years after the event involves resentment, projection, aggressiveness, and guilt--characteristic ways that he is attempting to integrate his feelings about his adolescent place in the family dynamics in the service of the current context of his relation to his father, Nathan, Sophie, and his work (Ross, passim). Beyond that first level of reconstruction, the 47-year-old narrator of Sophie's Choice is reconstructing his memory of how in his 20's he had reconstructed his memory of the event which had occurred when he was 13.

The emotion at the core of this reconstruction seems to me resentment, with guilt as a means of managing resentment. Resentment for his mother's debility would explain why he allowed himself to be lured away from his duty. It would explain the veiled criticism in his remark about the Eskimo ice-floe visions which might have engulfed her as she fell back against her best sellers. After all, Stingo, who is currently ambitious to produce a work the caliber of Faulkner's, remarks that while his mother read Wolfe, she also read plenty of junk fiction whose clichés were obviously inadequate to "barricade herself against death" (297). Resentment would explain, too, the "wide and desolate lake" between Stingo and his mother as they wept in each other's presence, but without any forgiving touch. In fact, lacking any images of tender connection to his mother, Stingo's literal loss of his mother would seem to explain his deep loneliness less adequately than years of habitual distance between them might. Whatever the case, he offers no image of reconciliation. Instead, he closes his memory left to wonder whether his mother forgave him. Unable to know, he dismisses the question with a resentful expletive.

The guilt which manages resentment serves two needs. For one thing, it serves a moral compunction by inverting his unacceptable resentment towards his mother and turning it back towards himself instead. For another, as Dan Ross shows, reconstructing his own past in terms of guilt binds his story to Sophie's. In Stingo's relation to Sophie, and in Sophie's relation to Nathan, both attempt to reconstruct past family dynamics. Sophie dooms herself to please Nathan, the sadistic surrogate father, and Stingo fails to rescue Sophie, a mother-surrogate, but inherits a haunting responsibility for her death and a need to tell her story (Ross passim).

The immediate occasion for Stingo to recall the episode of his mother's death is the presence of his father, who is sleeping in an adjacent hotel bed. His father has obtruded into Stingo's adult life in Brooklyn, where he is pursuing both a career as a writer and Sophie, to try to lure him back to Virginia. Reminded of his conflicting allegiance to his career and to home, Stingo entangles his current erotic interest in Sophie (whom he senses is doomed) and the memory of his mother's death. Unable to sleep because of his father's snoring and the sounds of a couple making love in the next room, Stingo lies awake and his thoughts drift first from guilt over his mother's death, to erotic excitement over Sophie, and "finally to a wrenching, sweet, nearly intolerable memory of the South" (295). That last memory is of wanting to make love to the girl who had first awakened his erotic fantasies, Maria Hunt. Her recent suicide in Brooklyn inspired his first novel and foreshadows the suicide of Sophie, the subject of his future novel. His fantasy over Maria yields to a wet dream of Sophie, and he moans out Sophie's name loud enough during orgasm to awaken his father. Stingo's memory of the South, quickened by his father's presence, inextricably fuses erotic arousal for Sophie with Maria with his mother's and Maria's death. Stingo attempts to resolve his conflicting resentment and guilt over the death of his mother by confession, by dismissal, and by transference to Sophie. But even though he satisfies his youthful fantasies by having sex with Sophie, as Ross shows, he fails to rescue her from her doomed relationship with Nathan. As he constructs perspective years after her death, he comes to believe that both Sophie and he were bound to larger historical contexts, hers involving Nazism and his slavery. In telling her story 25 years later, he insists "on the necessity of speaking the unspeakable in order to remind his listeners that there is a chance of redeeming the world even after Auschwitz, while drawing countless analogies between his and Sophie's lives, in an effort to expiate his guilt for having failed her" (Ross 145). That is, his reconstruction of guilt in his own memory finds a larger moral analogue and empowers Stingo as a writer.

In terms of form, Stingo's reconstruction involves a doubling of perspective. Throughout the novel, the 47-year-old Stingo recounts the Brooklyn experience of the 22-year-old Stingo, "whom [he] once inhabited" (513), with self-deprecating hyperbole, especially his sexual frustrations and fantasies. In recapturing Stingo's youth from a more mature perspective, the narrator both indulges and stands apart from his former self. In the later chapters of the novel, when he devotes more and more time to Sophie's reconstruction of her Auschwitz experience, the narrator periodically slides out of the first-person narratives of Stingo and Sophie and appropriates more and more of Sophie's story to a third-person omniscient point of view in a noticeably more mature prose. In appropriating Sophie's story in this way, not only does he fuse Stingo's and Sophie's story, but he casts her story in a more morally sober language than the 22-year-old Stingo might have been able to command. The doubling of perspective both indulges and stands apart from Stingo's tangled erotic and moral interests in Sophie with self-deprecating irony. In effect, it provides historical perspective on two levels--on Stingo's personal life and on human history--and it holds both up to standards of critical judgment.

Though he would carry Sophie's story for thirty years before he would wrest it from silence, the emotional seal to Stingo's commitment to tell it came on the night of Sophie's funeral in a flood of tears and "a letting go of rage and sorrow for the many others who during these past months had battered at [his] mind and now demanded [his] mourning" (515). The list of those who demanded his mourning included Sophie and Nathan; Sophie's children; Eddie Farrell, the cynical McGraw-Hill editor who had lost his talented son in the war and who had advised Stingo to "write his guts out"; Bobby Weed, the 16-year-old black lynched in Virginia; Artiste, the slave boy whose sale indirectly had underwritten Stingo's time in Brooklyn; Maria Hunt, his first love, who had committed suicide in Brooklyn; Nat Turner, "whose ghost had seared [his] imagination throughout [his] boyhood and youth"; and Wanda Muck-Horch von Kretschmann, Sophie's friend in the Polish resistance. If the list is long, it is short by the conspicuous absence of one other whose death had battered at his mind in the past months--his mother. It is that pointed and unresolved personal loss, not the loss of figures from history, to which Styron returns twice in his subsequent work, in "A Tidewater Morning" and Darkness Visible.

Eight years after Sophie's Choice, Styron published in Esquire a piece he offered as the introductory section of a new novel he was working on. "A Tidewater Morning" is his second fictionalized reconstruction of the death of his mother. The double perspective is the similar to that in Sophie's Choice. The narrator, an adult Paul Whitehurst, is recalling events from thirty years earlier, during the Depression, when he was 13 and his bedridden mother was dying of cancer she had contracted when he was 5. Paul's feelings about her dying are interwoven with other confused feelings about isolation and intimacy, sexual awakening, ambivalence about assertiveness, and guilt. Styron's means of dealing with these conflicts in both fictions anticipate many of the resources Styron would experience later in coping with his depression in Darkness Visible--doubling of perspective, dissociation, aggression, guilt, moral sensitivity, and reconstruction of loss.

The physical geography of "A Tidewater Morning" centers on the mother's sickroom. All the other spaces take on significance in relation to it: Paul's bedroom, his father's scholarly cubbyhole, his mother's music room, the bedroom of their servant, Florence, and the outdoors. In relation to this geography, the emotional lives of Paul, his father, and his mother are mutually isolated. In Paul's memory, his parents "never much touched each other in a loving way" (90). Towards the end of his mother's life, Paul is forbidden to go into her sickroom. Because of her intense pain, he is forbidden to touch her at all.

On the night before her death, Paul is lying in bed with no pajama bottom on in sweltering July heat, inhaling the odor of late-blooming clematis, and listening to his mother suffering. He is helpless to comfort her, as is his father, who keeps insisting without effect that the nurse give her more morphine. As he tries to shut out the scream, he thinks of his mother's nurse, Miss Slocum, massaging her. As an only child, out of touch with his mother himself, he feels profoundly lonely. Because he feels isolated, he envies the large families in his village, "a place and an era of busy procreation" (87). He envies especially one family whose daughter had been killed in a horse-riding accident, because he imagines that in solacing each other, it was "as if their grief were lessened by simple contact with their common origin of flesh. And for some nights they slept sprawled together in one bed, holding on to one another, preventing even sleep from separating them in their mourning. In my room I felt as if I were in a dungeon" (87).

He puts on his pajama bottom and slips downstairs to the refrigerator and with a twitch of guilt gulps directly from the water jar. He recalls that his mother had admonished him once before, so his "guilt was intensified by everything that was going on upstairs" (87). Such an act of forbidden contact and others like it are pointedly against his mother, since he judges that even in a pre-penicillin world, his mother was "overly zealous" (87). In crossing a boundary of her caution in a passive-aggressive way he makes contact with her but suffers anxiety. In a free association, he remembers a man who scratched his nose and died of an infected pimple, so that infection means vulnerability to death. Although the instance is milder in Paul's episode, both Paul and Stingo are haunted by the idea that their selfishness might have hastened their mothers' deaths.

On the way back to his bedroom, he passes the small alcove of the family servant, Florence, who had thrown over him "the cloak of surrogate motherhood" (88). She is, in fact, the only significant toucher in his life. In contrast to his mother's sickroom, Florence's room is a place where Paul can hold this caring mother's hand, share honest grief, and listen with her to gospel music on her radio, music which gave him "a charge that began to encircle my bottom and then moved straight up my spine to my skull, where it climaxed in a mini-electrocution" (88). Hers is the one room in the house where both sincere affection, touching, and his sexual resonance find safe expression.

His mother's music room is more unsettling. Music, especially German lieder, was her one passion in life. But the images of her youthful passion are slightly repugnant. Her alcove, her "little sanctum," is surrounded by busts and photos, including one of her as a bosomy 16-year-old young woman in Vienna in 1904, infatuated, smiling, and leaning against the paunch of "a whiskered old satyr," her voice teacher who had introduced her to Mahler (91). Not only is her music more intellectual and distant than Florence's, but it is comes from an exotic past associated for him with ambivalent erotic fantasy.

These mixed feelings over attraction and repugnance affect other associations with touch in the story as well. The body of the girl killed while horse riding, whose family touching Paul so envied, was found a day and a night later, "part of her face . . . eaten away by vermin, preventing the open-coffin viewing" (87). The nurse hired to bathe and massage Paul's mother, Miss Slocum, was a buxom 30-year-old woman with an extra vestigial thumb on each hand, and his mother "had a professed abhorrence at the idea of twelve digits stroking her flesh" (87). A department store in a nearby town displayed a bronze portrait plaque of the former owner who had died four days after scratching a pimple on his nose, and Paul's eye is "drawn inevitably to the tip of the burnished nose and its pathetic inevitability" (87). When his boss's wife, a foul-mouthed slattern, raises her rayon shift to show off her thigh tattooed with flowers, Paul feels torn between "shock and enchantment" (86).

His most aggressive initiative is the handwritten note left to be found in his room by his mother, "I want to fuck Lilly Fletcher." Her response we know only through a scene which obtrudes into the first-person narrative and is reported in italics, with no indication that Paul ever overheard it or witnessed it. As far as we know, it is the reconstruction in Paul's imagination of what might have been, or should have been, said. The mother, who cannot say the "f" word even to her husband, finds the note "dangerous" for a 12-year-old. The father, emboldened by the episode, defends his son and charges the mother with being "as usual boringly puritanical," then presses on: "It is pronounced incidentally fuck and I should have liked many times, in the old days, to have spoken it to you, saying fuck me fuck me and hearing you joyfully say the same! But I couldn't ever--" (93). Retreating, he quickly apologizes and asks forgiveness, deferring to her propriety. She clarifies that "It's not just the sex thing" but Paul's "retreat into solitariness" that distresses her. She fears "him losing touch with reality," though more probably her fear is a double projection, since she is slipping towards death herself, and she senses that her son's sexual blooming and solitary withdrawal indicate he is moving beyond the sphere of her control (93). Since the authority for this scene is Paul's imagination alone, the mother's concern is, in effect,

Paul's negative projection, which ineffectually polices his desires. By judging her propriety as restrictive, he sanctions his sexual awakening and his aggressive language. His father, Paul's positive projection, finds Paul's sexual excitability very much in touch with reality and uses his son's initiative to voice his own, at least until he folds apologetically.

Paul's usual defense is to remove himself from the house dominated by his mother's untouchable presence and her smothering scruples. Emerging from his bedroom's "lonely cocoon," he seeks out his pier, his "salvation." There, lounging in the sun on the dock on the James River, he reads Freeman's R.E. Lee, a book that would have been dear to his Virginia father, not to his Pennsylvania mother. But more importantly, he swims nude, in water he later realizes contains floating condoms, fully in touch with his senses and beyond his mother's overzealous fear of contact. There "the health worries of the period ceased at the waterside; everyone swam in the dirty James and so did I" (94).

Such initiatives as these shut out his mother's influence. In fact, shutting out her influence and her painful dying runs like a leitmotif throughout the story. The father retreats to his cubby-hole to read Nietzsche. Paul retreats to his solitary room and tries "to think of anything but [her] scream" (87). He frequently returns to his last memory of her singing in her garden before she became bedridden: "I wanted to shut out all impressions of her illness" (90). In his boss's store, unable to keep her dying at bay, he deliberately counts the objects in a glass case "freeing myself of my mother's image" (92). He tries to focus on news of pending world war to "distract . . . me from the gloom that encompassed me" (85).

Although the mother's lingering death is the central occasion which Paul tries to shut out of his mind in a variety of ways, two other episodes about self-assertiveness result in the most emotionally intense dissociations in the story. The first involves Paul's quitting his job. In one scene, in frustration against his stingy, mean-spirited boss, Paul throws his newspapers into the river. The narrative point of view in this scene shifts suddenly, as if the viewfinder of a movie camera is "drawn back" and Paul watches himself "unshouldering that ubiquitous bag," heaving the newspapers into the James, then standing on the shore, "a boy shaking with rage and exhaustion" (94). Much as the doublings in Sophie's Choice and Darkness Visible, this shift of point of view at once enlarges perspective and dissociates the observing self from the acting self.

The second, more intense, episode of dissociation involves his father's quitting God, when Paul makes the import of this kind of shift clear. His father, drinking and bitter over his wife's long suffering, explodes the shell of his gentility in an overt atheistic attack against the minister and his wife who had come to offer conventional consolation. " . . . I execrate God, if he exists. . . . Cursed be the name of the Lord!" (95). Paul flees from the front porch where he has overheard his father's bitter outburst. Not only has Paul lost his mother, but, more profoundly, his father, whom he fears might go whirling off in space. When he returns, his father is still drinking and playing his dead wife's favorite Brahms on the record player. He asks Paul to kneel with him and repeat with him a fierce vow of self-assertion: "Although earth's foundations crumble and the mountains be shaken into the midst of the seas, yet alone shall I prevail!" Dreading, shrinking, and cowed by his father's insistence, Paul once again removes himself from the scene by two means. As a counter-text to his father's binding oath of radical self-sufficiency, Paul's "mind composed such other words as would distract me from the moment's anguish. My name is Paul Whitehurst, it is the eleventh of September 1938, when Prague Awaits Hitler Ultimatum. Thus lulled by history, I let myself be elevated slowly up and up through the room's hot, dense shadows. And there, floating abreast of the immortal musicians, I was able to gaze down impassively on the grieving father and the boy pinioned in his arms" (96). That is, from his detached perspective, he is at once bound to and free of the scene. It is an act of deliberate dissociation, his "means of escape from the intolerable" (96). At the same time, he ties to ground himself in a larger human community beyond his immediate terrors of family loss and isolation.

To understand "the intolerable" here is to realize how Styron's reconstruction of loss differs in "A Tidewater Morning" and Sophie's Choice. Stingo and Paul share anxiety over self-centered behavior. Stingo held himself directly accountable for hastening his mother's death and suffered ineffaceable guilt. Paul's accountability for his mother's death is less overt. While Stingo felt he had abandoned his mother by a selfish act, Paul's guilt would have arisen only because he drank out of the water jar or because of his offensive language in the explicit note he left for his mother to find. That note merely emboldened his father to be direct to his wife about his desires, or at worst allowed Paul to imagine voicing aggressively his own desires through his father in a scene Paul reconstructed in his own imagination. Thus, the ravaged face which stared at Stingo from his mother's coffin is, in Paul's case, displaced onto the vermin-eaten face of the neighbor girl simply killed in an accident. In Stingo's reconstruction, history serves as an analogue to his own unresolved guilt and a selfless opportunity to serve others by giving their stories voice. In Paul's, history serves as a distraction from the pain of loss and the fear of isolation, a field of human connections in which Paul wishes to stay grounded. The core terror of Paul's story is of losing touch--not merely with his distant mother, but through his apostatic father, with God and humanity, a terror of the unbounded self lost to desperate moral isolation. Perhaps a similar terror accounts, for Stingo's peculiar insistence that even the behavior of the Nazi doctor who forced Sophie to choose between her children at the death camp could be explained as having a moral, if perverse, core.

In <u>Darkness Visible</u> Styron takes the terror of profound isolation to the edge. Just prior to his intended suicide, the same cinematic shift of perspective he used as a fictional device to surmount the intolerable in "A Tidewater Morning" he now reports as a felt experience. As if through a viewfinder, he witnesses himself acting out one of the dramas he intends to be final, of sealing his notebook in an old cereal box and burying it in the garbage can. The detached, witnessing self he calls "a wraithlike observer who, not sharing the dementia of his double, is able to watch with dispassionate curiosity as his companion struggles against the oncoming disaster, or decides to embrace it" (64). Once again, the observing self is dissociated from the feeling, acting self. Dissociation here betokens deep personal danger, for, in effect, the observing Styron stands apart, out of touch with the acting self who is irreversibly preparing for suicide. Yet even here, while his benumbed, acting self feels that his actions are irreversible, his observing self maintains the critical judgment of a writer in that he can judge the quality of the suicidal preparations of the acting self a "melodrama."

What stops Styron just this side of suicide? After he had decided to tear up the suicide note and "go out in silence," he is brought back from despair by a voice. In a film he is watching on video, an actress is moving down the hall of a conservatory and hears from unseen musicians beyond the walls disembodied voices singing <u>Alto Rhapsody</u>, Styron's mother's favorite piece of Brahms. In his two fictionalized reconstructions of the disorder and early sorrow over the death of mother figures, music had been an important bond. Just as music had bound Sophie to the memory of her mother, music had fixed in Paul Whitehurst's memory his favorite image of his mother before she became bedridden, "so that my mind for a moment at least, might be filled with the resonance of the voice and its awesome, rhapsodic praise" (90). Now, in an autobiographical crisis, a disembodied voice singing Brahms's <u>Alto Rhapsody</u> pierces Styron's heart and triggers a flood of sensual memories of his home--of children, love and work, sleep, voices and commotion, and family pets. Styron's "last gleam of sanity" is the moral awareness that his self-desecration would inflict pain on all those held in the web of his memories. What calls Styron back from despair to the present relationships he is about to lose is the voice that prompts him to reconstruct memory of past loss. Whatever the tenor of this unresolved sorrow as he had reconstructed it in his fiction and his autobiographical essay--whether grief, resentment, guilt, self-recrimination, desire, or terror--the memory of loss binds Styron's past, unresolved grief to his present moral responsibility. He awakens his wife, checks into a hospital the next day, and begins his recovery. Just as Stingo's and Paul's recreations of loss bound them to larger human experience, Styron's ongoing moral commitment as a writer is to surmount the intolerable, to turn back from silent despair to human responsibility, "to be the voice for a lot of people" (Glendinning 25).

Works Cited

Glendinning, Victoria. Rev. of Darkness Visible by William Styron. New York Times Book Review 19 August, 1990: 1 & 25.

Kreyling, Michael. "Speakable and Unspeakable in Styron's Sophie's Choice." Southern Review 20 (1984): 546-61.

Novey, Samuel, M.D. The Second Look: The Reconstruction of Personal History in Psychiatry and Psychoanalysis. Baltimore: Johns Hopkins UP, 1968.

Ross, Daniel W. "A Family Romance: Dreams and the Unified Narrative of Sophie's Choice." Mississippi Quarterly 42 (1989): 129-45.

Styron, William. Darkness Visible: A Memoir of Madness. New York: Random House, 1990.

___. "James Jones" (1977). Rpt. This Quiet Dust and Other Writings. New York: Random House, 1982. 267-70.

___. Sophie's Choice. New York: Bantam, 1979.

___. "A Tidewater Morning." Esquire (August 1987): 84-97.

*Written for this collection.

Bibliography of Criticism

EDITOR'S NOTE: Because of the availability of two fine bibliographies published in 1978 (one by Philip K. Leon, published by Greenwood Press, the other by Jackson Bryer, published by G.K. Hall), I have limited this list to works published since the appearance of those bibliographies.

Books

Casciato, Arthur D. and James L.W. West, III, ed. Critical Essays on William Styron. Boston: G.K. Hall, 1982

Coale, Samuel. William Styron Revisited. Boston: Twayne, 1991.

Crane, John Kenny. The Root of All Evil: The Thematic Unity of Styron's Fiction. Columbia: U of South Carolina P, 1984.

Morris, Robert K. and Irving Malin. The Achievement of William Styron. Rev. ed. Athens: U of Georgia P, 1981.

Ruderman, Judith. William Styron. New York: Ungar, 1987.

Sirlin, Rhoda. William Styron's "Sophie's Choice": Crime and Punishment. Ann Arbor: University Microfilms International Research Press, 1990.

West, James L.W., III, ed. and introd. Conversations with William Styron. Jackson: UP of Mississippi, 1985.

Dissertations

Cash, Jean, W. "Spiritual Alienation and Secular Redemption in the Works of William Styron." DAI 44 (1983): 1790A.

Chinn, Nancy. "William Styron's Sophie's Choice: A Study." DAI 43 (1982): 799A-800A.

Cologne-Brookes, Gavin. "From History to History: The Shifting Patterns of Discourse in the Novels of William Styron." DAI 51 (1990): 1611-1612A.

Garr, Donna Gladys. "The Southernness of William Styron." DAI 41 (1981): 4399A.

Palm, Elaine Amanda. "The Integrative Vision: Ritual Action in the Novels of William Styron." DAI (1979): 259A.

Sirlin, Rhoda A. "William Styron's Sophie's Choice: A Wisdom That is Woe, A Woe That is Madness." DAI (1989): 1306-1307A.

Sisney, Mary Frances. "Black Fiction, to Discriminate or Not to Discriminate: A Comparative and Rhetorical Study of Native Son, Invisible Man, The Man Who Cried I Am, Intruder in the Dust, and The Confessions of Nat Turner." DAI 40 (1979): 4045A.

Articles

Amis, Harry D. "History as Self-Serving Myth: Another Look at Styron's The Confessions of Nat Turner. College Language Association Journal 22 (1978): 134-46.

Arms, Valerie. "An Interview with William Styron." Contemporary Literature 20 (1979): 1-12.

___. "William Styron and the Spell of the South." Mississippi Quarterly 34 (1980-81): 25-36.

___. "William Styron in France." Critical Essays on William Styron. Ed. Arthur D. Casciato and James L.W. West, III: 306-15.

Askin, Denise T. "The Half-Loaf of Learning: A Theme in Styron's The Confessions of Nat Turner." Notes on Modern American Literature 3 (1978): Item 6.

Betts, Richard A. "The Confessions of Nat Turner and the Uses of Tragedy." College Language Association Journal 29 (1984): 419-35.

Burch, Beth. "The Image of the Garden in William Styron's Lie Down in Darkness." Ball State University Forum 23 (1982): 23-29.

Casciato, Arthur D. "His Editor's Hand: Hiram Haydn's Changes in Styron's Lie Down in Darkness." Studies in Bibliography 33 (1980): 263-76.

___. "Styron's False Start: The Discarded Opening for Set This House on Fire." Mississippi Quarterly 34 (1980-81): 37-50.

Casciato, Arthur D. and James L.W. West, III. "William Styron and the Southampton Insurrection." American Literature 52 (1981): 564-77.

Cash, Jean W. "Styron's Use of the Bible in The Confessions of Nat Turner." Resources in American Literary Study 12 (1982): 134-42.

Chametzky, Jules. "Styron's Sophie's Choice, Jews, and Other Marginals, and the Mainstream." Prospects 9 (1984): 433-40.

Christian, Henry A. "William Styron's Set This House on Fire: A Fulcrum and Forces." Acta Neophilologica 21 (1988): 53-61.

Coale, Samuel. "Styron's Choice: Hawthorne's Guilt in Poe's Palaces." Papers on Language and Literature 23 (1987): 514-22.

___. "Styron's Disguises: A Provisional Rebel in Christian Masquerade." Critique 26, no. 2 (1985): 57-66.

Cobbs, John L. "Baring the Unbearable: William Styron and the Problem of Pain." Mississippi Quarterly 34 (1980-81): 15-24.

Cologne-Brookes, Gavin. "Discord and Toward Harmony: Set This House on Fire and Peter's 'Part in the Matter.'" Papers on Language and Literature 23 (1987): 449-64.

Coltrane, Peter. "The Unity of This Quiet Dust." Papers on Language and Literature 23 (1987): 480-88.

Colville, Georgiana.   "Killing the Dead Mother: Women in Sophie's Choice." Delta Ecrivains du Sud aux Etats-Unis 23 (Oct. 1986): 111-35.

Crane, John Kenny.   "Laughing Backward: Comedy and Morality in Styron's Fiction." College Literature 14 (1987): 1-16.

___. "Looking Down the Barrel of Your Own Gun: William Styron and the Cessation of Warfare." Delta Ecrivains du Sud aux Etats-Unis 23 (Oct. 1986): 19-33.

Dickstein, Morris.   "The World in a Mirror: Problems of Distance in Recent American Fiction." Sewanee Review 89 (1981): 386-400.

Durham, Carolyn. "William Styron's Sophie's Choice: The Structures of Oppression." Twentieth-Century Literature 30 (1984): 448-64.

Faltacosh, Monty Lowe. "Wolfe and Sophie's Choice." Thomas Wolfe Newsletter 4, no. 1 (1980): 39-41.

Firestone, Bruce M.   "The Early Apprenticeship of William Styron." Studies in Short Fiction 18 (1981): 439-43.

Francoisi, Robert. "Perverse Medicine: Holocaust Doctoring in William Styron's Sophie's Choice." The Body and the Text: Comparative Essays in Literature and Medicine." Ed. Bruce Clarke and Wendell Aycock. Lubbock: Texas Tech UP, 1990: 195-205.

Friedman, Melvin J. "William Styron's Criticism: More French than American." Delta Ecrivains du Sud aux Etats-Unis 23 (Oct. 1986): 61-75.

___.   "William Styron's 'Fiction and Essays: A Franco-American Perspective.'" The Comparative Perspective on Literature: Approaches to Theory and Practice." Ed. Clayton Koelb and Susan Noakes. Ithaca: Cornell UP, 1988: 117-29.

Galloway, David D. "Holocaust as Metaphor: William Styron and Sophie's Choice." Anglistik & Englischunterricht (April 1981): 57-69.

Heath, William. "I, Stingo: The Problem of Egotism in Styron's Sophie's Choice." Southern Review 20 (1984): 528-40.

Huffman, James R. "A Psychological Redefinition of William Styron's The Confessions of Nat Turner." Literary Review 24 (1981): 279-307.

Kort, Wesley. "Styron's Corpus and Sophie's Choice." Christianity and Literature 30, no. 2 (1984): 64-70.

Kreyling, Michael. "Speakable and Unspeakable in Styron's Sophie's Choice." Southern Review 20 (1984): 546-61.

Lang, John. "The Alpha and Omega: Styron's The Confessions of Nat Turner." American Literature 53 (1981): 499-503.

___. "God's Averted Face: Styron's Sophie's Choice." American Literature 55 (1983): 215-32.

___. "In Quest of Redemption: The Religious Background of Peyton's Monologue in Lie Down in Darkness." Southern Humanities Review 17 (1983): 121-31.

Law, Richard G. "The Reach of Fiction: Narrative Technique in Styron's Sophie's Choice." Southern Literary Journal 23, no. 1 (1990): 45-65.

Lawson, Lewis. "William Styron." The History of Southern Literature. Introd. Louis D. Rubin, Jr. Ed. Blyden Jackson, Rayburn S. Moore, Lewis P. Simpson, Thomas Daniel Young. Baton Rouge: Louisiana State UP, 1985: 479-82.

Leon, Philip W. "Styron's Fiction: Narrative as Idea." The Achievement of William Styron. Ed. Robert K. Morris and Irving Malin: 124-46.

McGill, William J. "William Styron's Nat Turner and Religion." South Atlantic Quarterly 79 (1980): 75-81.

Mellard, James M. "This Unquiet Dust: The Problem of History in Styron's The Confessions of Nat Turner." Mississippi Quarterly 36 (1983): 525-43.

Morris, Robert K. "Interview with William Styron." The Achievement of William Styron. Ed. Robert K. Morris and Irving Malin: 29-62.

Motto, Anna Lydia and John R. Clark. "The Senselessness of an Ending: Comic Impression upon the 'High Seriousness.'" West Virginia University Philological Papers 29 (1983): 1-7.

Nagel, Gwen. "Illusion and Identity in Sophie's Choice." Papers on Language and Literature 23 (1987): 498-513.

Nolan, Richard. "Psychological Themes in Sophie's Choice." Delta Ecrivains du Sud aux Etats-Unis 23 (1986): 91-110.

Parrish, James A. "No Home to Go to: Suicide in Lie Down in Darkness." Youth Suicide Prevention: Lessons from Literature. Ed. Sara Munson Deats and Lagretta Tallent Lenker. New York: Plenum, 1989: 155-70.

Pearce, Richard. "Sophie's Choices." The Achievement of William Styron. Ed. Robert Morris and Irving Malin: 284-97.

Reitz, Bernhard. "'Fearful Ambiguities of Time and History': The Confessions of Nat Turner and the Delineation of the Past in Postmodern Historical Narrative." Papers on Language and Literature 23 (1987): 465-79.

Richardson, Thomas J. "Art and Angry Times: Apocalypse and Redemption in William Styron's The Confessions of Nat Turner." Mississippi Folklore Review 19 (1985): 147-56.

Rose, Lloyd. "Hearts of Darkness: Everything You Wanted to Know About Depression." Village Voice Supplement 90 (Nov. 1990): 12-14.

Rosenthal, Regine. "Defying Taboos: The Sense of Place in William Styron's Sophie's Choice." Dolphin 20 (1991): 76-88.

Ross, Daniel W. "A Family Romance: Dreams and the Unified Narrative of Sophie's Choice." Mississippi Quarterly 42 (1989): 129-45.

___. "'Things I Don't Want to Find Out About': The Primal Scene in The Confessions of Nat Turner." Twentieth-Century Literature 39 (1993): 79-98.

Rubenstein, Richard L. "The South Encounters the Holocaust: William Styron's Sophie's Choice." Michigan Quarterly Review 20 (1981): 425-42.

Ruderman, Judith. "Milton's Choices: Styron's Use of Robert Frost's Poetry in Lie Down in Darkness." College Language Association Journal 27 (1983): 141-51.

Scheick, William J. "'Discarded Watermelon Rinds': The Rainbow Aesthetic of Styron's Lie Down in Darkness." Modern Fiction Studies 24 (1978): 247-54.

Schultz, Lucille M. "Lie Down in Darkness: A Story of Two Processions." Southern Literary Journal 18, no. 2 (1986): 62-75.

Shepherd, Allen. "The Psychopath as Moral Agent in William Styron's Sophie's Choice." Modern Fiction Studies 28 (1982-83): 604-11.

Shore, Laurence. "William Styron's Nat Turner: The Monster and the Critic." Journal of Ethnic Studies 11, no. 4 (1984): 89-101.

Smith, Frederik N. "Bach vs. Brooklyn's Clamorous Yawp: Sound in Sophie's Choice." Papers on Language and Literature 23 (1987): 523-30.

Stern, Frederick C. "Styron's Choices." South Atlantic Quarterly 82 (1983): 19-27.

Strine, Mary S. "The Confessions of Nat Turner: Styron's Meditation on History as Rhetorical Act." Quarterly Journal of Speech 64 (1978): 246-66.

Telpaz, Gideon. "An Interview with William Styron." Partisan Review 52 (1985): 252-63.

Trouard, Dawn. "Styron's Historical Pre-Text: Nat Turner, Sophie, and the Beginnings of a Postmodern Career." Papers on Language and Literature 23 (1987): 489-97.

Tutt, Ralph. "Stingo's Complaint: Styron and the Politics of Self-Parody." Modern Fiction Studies 34 (1988): 575-86.

West, James L. W. III. "'Blankenship': An Introduction." Papers on Language and Literature 23 (1987): 425-48.

___. "Introduction." Inheritance of Night: Early Drafts of "Lie Down in Darkness." Durham: Duke UP, 1993: xi-xix.

___. "William Styron: A Biographical Account." Mississippi Quarterly 34 (1980-81): 3-14.

Index

About the Editor

DANIEL W. ROSS is Associate Professor of English at Columbus College in Columbus, Georgia, where he specializes in Southern literature. His articles have appeared in such journals as *Studies in English Literature*, *Modern Fiction Studies*, *Mississippi Quarterly*, and *Conradiana*.

ISBN 0-313-28000-2

9 780313 280009

90000>

EAN

HARDCOVER BAR CODE